INQUIÉTUDE

Thanks to Chris Oswald, Victor Chininin Buele,
Steven Opp, David Robertson, Travis Finley,
Albert Garlando, Mark French, and Chris Wooldridge
for proofreading and for their helpful contributions,
to Richard Bledsoe for his encouragement,
and especially to Jared Leonard,
whose eagle eyes went to-and-fro for many days
upon the face of a restless sea.

Mike Bull is a graphic designer who lives and works
in the Blue Mountains west of Sydney, Australia.
His passion is understanding and teaching the Bible.

Also by this author:

Totus Christus: A Biblical Theology of the Whole Christ

Bible Matrix: An Introduction to the DNA of the Scriptures

Bible Matrix II: The Covenant Key

God's Kitchen: Theology You Can Eat & Drink

Reading the Bible in 3D

The Shape of Galatians: A Covenant-Literary Analysis

Sweet Counsel: Essays to Brighten The Eyes

INQUIÉTUDE

ESSAYS FOR A PEOPLE WITHOUT EYES

BIBLE
MATRIX

M I C H A E L   B U L L

ISBN-13: 978-1516883530
ISBN-10: 1516883535

Designed and typeset by Michael Bull

Front cover image:
Paul Cézanne, *Pyramid of Skulls* (1898-1900)
Back cover image:
Paul Cézanne, *The Three Skulls* (1900)

For Richard Bledsoe,
whose great big heart
and great big mind
continue to inspire.

TRANSFORMATION

VINDICATION

REPRESENTATION

"You never change things by fighting the existing reality. To change something, build a new model that makes the existing model obsolete."
— Buckminster Fuller

INTRODUCTION
HOT FOR TRUTH
THE SECRET ARCHITECTURE

"With an apple I will astonish Paris." — Paul Cézanne

T he problem with bad theologians is that they do not think in pictures. The problem with good theologians is that they do not think in *moving* pictures.

Although the Bible is a book with no pictures, it is in fact a book of nothing but pictures, *pictures that move.* Visualizing while reading or hearing the Bible is the only way to comprehend all that is being said. The textual flow is motion designed to make an *impression,* and once this is made, the reader perceives similar types as they shape subsequent texts and events.[1]

For the Impressionists of the 19th Century, painting was not about reproducing what one saw, but about capturing (often very quickly) one's response to it. The brilliant hues and seductive glooms are all depictions

---

[1] The word "type" in biblical theology is derived from a Greek term *(tupos),* which occurs 16 times in the New Testament. It refers to a person, event or thing which represents or prefigures another. The type and its "antitype" are linked by their similarity in purpose, form, and/or position in the Covenant process.

1

of emotion, images captured in the rods and cones of both the eye and the heart. The most mundane object could thus be masterfully corrupted or glorified in order to communicate a mood. As Cézanne said, "The day is coming when a single carrot, freshly observed, will set off a revolution."

Unfortunately for the Impressionists, this revolution in art was slow in coming. After countless rejections by the jury of the official exhibition, the Paris Salon, the despondent—and diverse—group of artists mounted their own independent showing in 1874. Although the endeavor was not a success, it garnered a number of favorable reviews and put Impressionism on the map.

Cézanne's paintings were the most challenging of all in this new school, and even among the Impressionists he managed to upset the apple cart. Only after many years did his way of "seeing" catch on.

His style is unique, but many of his works intrigue because they are also extremely eccentric. A painting which lacks rhyme or reason is easily dismissed, but Cézanne in fact beckons the beholder to *discover* his reasons. The method behind his apparent madness is a craft so diligently honed, so carefully planned and executed, that it discloses the nature of the mind for whom truth and wisdom in painting made fame irrelevant. Robert Genn writes:

> I'm one of those painters who is forever fascinated with the work of Paul Cézanne. I've tracked down his locations around Mont Sainte-Victoire and peered

2

out at the village of Aix through the wavy glass of his studio windows. Looking closely at his paintings and trying to figure out what was going on in his head has been a major preoccupation of mine. So I paid attention when Dewain Boyce sent me his latest findings.

Dewain is making a case that Cézanne imbedded cones, ovals and other geometric motifs in his work. Dewain claims this is the basis of structural strength in the compositions. He leaves it to someone else to figure out whether this was conscious or unconscious. Why should we care about Dewain's well conducted research? It's just possible that Cézanne shows us a way to give weight, mass, volume, compositional integrity and harmony to our paintings.

Cézanne gave us lots of clues to the pictorial harmony he was seeking. He told Émile Bernard that one needs "an invisible scaffolding of spheres, cones and cylinders." Like the Classical tradition of *entasis* and other devices in Greek architecture, he had an understanding of hidden structure. "To paint is not to copy the object slavishly," he said, "it is to grasp a harmony among many relationships."[1]

Art critic Sheldon Cheney (1886-1980) wrote:

Beyond the three dimensions of length, breadth, and perspective depth, there is a rhythmic, voluminous movement, or a poised spatial relationship that speaks emotionally to the spectator. In a great many

---

[1]   Robert Genn, *Cézanne's Ghosts*, robertgenn.com

INQUIÉTUDE

of Cézanne's canvases one detects a fluctuation of the volumes and planes—a palpable feeling of emotional organization.

This "palpable" sense of emotional organization is present in the Bible. The architecture is not only breathtaking, its seamless integration is nothing short of impossible. In hindsight, with our opened eyes, we can see that from the very first page, the ending of the book is already clear in the mind of the divine Author. The sacred texts are a living architecture, a tree for fruit, a growing body, a city whose footprint enlarges due to its vibrant life. The Word is a single burgeoning household of inextricable relationships.

However, we moderns are not trained to read texts with detailed literary form in mind. We miss much, if not all, of the meaning conveyed in structural devices and visual associations. Truth is a place to be inhabited and explored, a gallery with walls, doors, and windows. Its objects possess their meaning only *in situ*. Persons depicted are proposition *in process*. The Word *moves,* and the eye is a lens for the heart. For Man, order and beauty are things to be grasped, but for God, order and beauty are the outcomes of holiness.

With the text as a window into the mind of the Author, we discover a meticulousness in the placement of every stroke, a playfulness in the degree to which something might be hidden or revealed, a tenderness in the relationship between every type and its antitype, and an almost pathological perfectionism in His quest

4

Above: Paul Cézanne, *The House of the Suicide* (1873).
Below: The painting with cones revealed by Dewain Boyce.

as a craftsman to achieve His vision. If there is to be any further progress in theology, there must be some kind of artistic revolution.

In the life of Cézanne, this last characteristic was symptomatic of his *inquiétude,* the restless anxiety of a dissonant personality seeking resolution. Picasso said:

> It is not what the artist does that counts, but what he is. Cézanne wouldn't be of the slightest interest to me if he had lived and thought like Jacques-Émile Blanche, even if the apple he painted had been ten times as beautiful. What is of interest to us is Cézanne's *inquiétude,* that is Cézanne's lesson... that is to say, the drama of the man. The rest is false.[2]

In his biography of Cézanne, Alex Danchev writes:

> Who first pinned *inquiétude* on him is difficult to establish with certainty, but by 1907 it was already received wisdom... *Inquiétude* was his lot, or the cross he bore: his fate, his plight, his tragedy. But it was also the mark of his moral stature. Chronic doubt made for epic struggle. That was the drama of the man: the hard-fought engagement on the battlefield of the interior."[3]

However, despite the gossip concerning the artist's instability and apparent madness, Danchev argues that Cézanne's *inquiétude* has been misrepresented, or at least misunderstood:

2 Christian Zervos, "Conversation avec Picasso" (1935), in Picasso, *Propos sur l'art* (Paris, Gallimard, 1998), 36.
3 Alex Danchev, *Cezanne: A Life,* 14.

In fact he was not so much anxious as restless, temperamentally and intellectually. Questing, perhaps would be a better way of capturing it, or normalizing it; for he was more normal and less pathological than the traffickers in *inquiétude* are wont to imply. The eccentricity has been overdone... Whatever the gossips might say, he was neither demented nor depressed. The salient thing about his condition was that he had purpose—moral purpose—he was *inquiet de vérité*, in Geffroy's phrase, hot for truth. "He is *inquiet*," wrote Charles Morice, who conducted the survey of artists, "but only to know if his values are true, and the humanity in his paintings rests on the value of a value"—a pun on moral values and color values... Painting was truth telling or it was nothing. That was his quest.[4]

Most of the "technicians" of modern Christian academia would no doubt write off any comparison between artistic truth and moral truth as vague and whimsical, an analogy which is as hard to pin down as art itself. But the truth is that the form in which the Word of God has been given to us is undeniably *les beaux arts,* "fine art." If we as Christians are indeed hot for truth, this is an aspect of the Scriptures which we can no longer ignore.

The spheres, cones, and cylinders drawn across the Bible's canvases in the following essays (and in my previous books) are my own attempt to understand the

4   Danchev, 317.

INQUIÉTUDE

strength and harmony in the images of our uncreated Master. They are the product of my own *inquiétude*, a desire for order and beauty in a world of dissonance. I am desperate to realize the glory of that first piece of fruit, and the drama of the Man.

At most, I hope for a theological revolution. At the least, the upsetting of some apple carts.

Michael Bull
Katoomba, July 2015

INITIATION

1
THE ART
OF WHY

"Stories are equipment for living."
— Kenneth Burke

As Christians, we are rightly taught that we must not question God's Word. The problem is that the Scriptures record many things which appear to have been given to us for the precise purpose of triggering questions. Even the provocative parables of Jesus are a breeze next to the arcane stipulations of the Torah. Those dark sayings were given to us as examples. They were not intended to be simple but they were intended to be understood.

We are to read the Bible faithfully, but our familiarity with the text often means that we fail to ask the right questions, the most important of which is simply "Why?" This is not the "Why?" of unbelief or rebellion, which delights in the Word's crude curiosities, brutish caprice and blatant contradictions because they can serve to justify its dismissal. It is the "Why?" which desires to know the mind of God, to get at the cause behind the effects. It is the "Why?" which diligently searches the Scriptures for clues concerning the things which God has veiled from us. The same God has given us delicious glimpses through that veil of what lies beyond to whet our appetites for more. Our problem is that we have grown so accustomed to the Bible that we have forgotten how astonishingly eccentric it is.

It is sad that many faithful Christians are not interested in discovering why the Bible is so strange. They trust in linguistic technicians who most often study without an ounce of the childlike imagination the Bible requires to be understood, and teachers who no longer ask "Why is it so?" For them, it is simply so, and must be accepted without question. The oddities are merely tricks of the text, or a reflection of the times of the original audience rather than a reflection of who God is and how He communicates with His people.

God deals in images, sequences and patterns, so the riches of the wisdom of the Scriptures remain unperceived. The Bible is allowed to challenge us morally, intellectually and even spiritually, but not visually, and definitely not "architecturally." It has the answers to all of the deepest questions of the modern world, yet they remain unanswered, skipping like tiny pebbles across the face of our God's wondrous literary fathoms. Until Christians learn to open their minds like children once again, they will remain unteachable.

Of course, modern Christians *do* open their minds

like children, but not to the Bible. This is why the best Bible teaching is always that which bridges the gap between popular culture and the ancient text. Like all the biblical prophets, our artists, musicians, novelists and poets not only understand the connection between the everyday and the sublime, they also know how to obscure it just enough to make it tantalizing. To become truly wise, the saints must be taught that the skills they gain from well-written books, television, and cinema should not be shelved when reading the Bible. The Bible is indeed a good book.

THE ART OF STORY

We all know when a book or a movie is missing something, even if we cannot put our finger on exactly what is wrong. But the best authors all know how to identify the problems and put them right. That list of best authors would include some screen writers, those who have to say everything the author of a novel says, but in less words. Robert McKee writes:

> From inspiration to last draft you may need as much time to write a screenplay as to write a novel. Screen and prose writers create the same density of world, character, and story, but because screenplay pages have so much white on them, we're often mislead into thinking that a screenplay is quicker and easier than a novel. But while scribomaniacs fill pages as fast as they can type, film writers cut and cut again, ruthless in their desire to express the absolute

maximum in the fewest possible words. Pascal once wrote a long, drawn-out letter to a friend, then apologized in the postscript that he didn't have time to write a short one. Like Pascal, screenwriters learn that economy is key, that brevity takes time, that excellence means perseverance.[1]

Aaron Sorkin, Academy and Emmy Award winning American screenwriter, producer, and playwright, says that what began his addiction to writing was watching a play and being fascinated by the "music" of the dialogue. Screenwriting teacher and "script doctor" John Truby says that plot is not something you make up as you go along, and that all the best stories use the element of surprise.

In every case, the musical flow, the wonder and surprise are what get people hooked and keep them reading or watching. The Bible was completed two millennia ago, yet it still manages to surprise us. The surprises are not new. They appear as our eyes continue to adjust to the "light" of the text. However, because we are not taught the internal logic of the Bible, we either see things which are not there, or we see nothing because we no longer expect to be surprised.

1   Robert McKee, *Story: Substance, Structure, Style and the Principles of Screenwriting*, 5.

SEED AND FRUIT

The Bible is much like a screenplay in the way it uses vivid images, clever plotting and careful structure to resonate with us, but it also uses a method very familiar to screen writers, and that is the technique of "plant and payoff." At the heart of every narrative surprise (the good ones, anyway), there is a clue which leads to a later revelation. A plant without a payoff is not a plant, but a denouement without some prior hint, some dark saying serving as a foundation, is unsatisfying and cheap. The author is sovereign, but we will only revel in his authority if it demonstrates his beguiling wisdom.

"Plant and payoff" is the basis of typology, the earthy type and its glorious antitype, Adam and Eve, Garden and City, so I would argue that this is an application of God's own Covenantal pattern of "forming and filling." The writer plants a single seed which seems utterly insignificant, if not irrelevant. It dies in the ground and is forgotten, but later produces a miraculous harvest.

The clues in the Bible are typically images and sequences of events, but sometimes they are technicalities which seem superfluous to the modern mind. As in every good story, there are no trivialities in Scripture. Every jot and tittle must earn its keep, awaiting the time when its potential will be fulfilled (Matthew 5:18). We must eye with suspicion every petty detail because, like its Author, it is self-effacing, that is, it points to the glory of something else. In the Bible, there are dark sayings, but there are no idle words, and no red herrings. (That is the opinion of Satan who leads men not to glory but to oblivion.) Even if its purpose is not immediately apparent, each strange word is a seed carefully planted for a payoff later on. The insignificant stone overlooked by the builders becomes the head of the corner.

FERTILE MINDS

Some teachers claim that the only true types in the Bible are those which are explicitly explained. This is why they cannot make much sense of either the Bible or the world around them, since these are written in the same language, the language of image. They have no excuse because we in this age not only have the complete Word of God, putting us in possession of all the seeds and all the payoffs, we also have the Spirit of Christ who reveals the relationships between them. Every payoff is paid forward by God, invested in an even greater harvest. As we study, the Spirit fills the deliberate gaps between the lines, the isolated textual neurons begin to glow and hum with electric life, and the synapses in the written Word of God are bridged in the fleshy hearts of regenerate men. We become part of the story as it is written within us, seed and fruit. We ourselves become the conduits for the connections, fertile ground. Biblical theology is an extension of the glory of the Word.

Good storytelling makes excellence possible in just

about any genre, and the best storytelling transforms the reader because it contains elements which must be chewed upon and digested. It engages and involves the reader through the use of mystery and symbol. Lewis and Tolkien understood that the best perspective on this world was from the vantage point of another one. All the visions of the Bible do this. They take place in the heavenly court, whose words and images are expounded in the subsequent events of history. What happens on the earth is glorious exposition of the compact types that issue from the mouth of God. Of course, this is still the case today. The power of the resurrection of Christ is paying a dividend in a billion stories that the world itself will not be able to contain.

> "Holy, Holy, Holy, is Jehovah of Hosts, The fullness of all the earth is His glory." (Isaiah 6:3, Young)

ASKING WHY

If we are not asking "Why?" the Lord cut into Adam, "Why?" Moses' hand became leprous, "Why?" David heard angels in the tops of the trees, or "Why?" the ax head floated in the Jordan, we are not sitting like children at our Father's feet. Instead of desiring to see the logic behind His idiosyncrasies, which are sometimes delightful but most often bizarre, we act like staff members too afraid to question our eccentric boss, yet willing enough to question his character. We look for wisdom elsewhere, as did Adam, and wind up listening to the slanderers of God. We must be bold enough to question God, as was Job, who stood against the accusers and discovered through faithful persever- ance that the answers were all around him, hidden in plain sight.

Biblical theology is the art of "Why?" By faith it understands that we have a God who hides things because He loves to be sought out, chewed out and found out by those who love Him. He never opens our eyes without also opening our hearts (John 16:25-33).

The original version of this chapter was written for
Theopolis Institute, published at www.theopolisinstitute.com

2
FORMING
WORDS

THE CONSTRAINT OF INSPIRATION

"Truly, truly, I say to you, (TRANSCENDENCE)
   the Son can do nothing of his own accord, (HIERARCHY)
   but only what he sees the Father doing. (ETHICS)
For whatever the Father does, (OATH/SANCTIONS)
that the Son does likewise." (SUCCESSION)
(John 5:19)

The premise that every part of the entire text of the Bible shares a common structure, one which operates at multiple levels, has numerous implications. Besides the fact that this is clearly a miracle, there is the question of why such a limitation would be placed by God upon His Words when the words of Man are not constrained in this way. It is certainly a testimony to the Bible's divine origin, but perhaps there is more to it than this.[1]

---

1   For an introduction to the fractal nature of the Bible,
      see Michael Bull, *Reading the Bible in 3D.*

INQUIÉTUDE

The answer may be found in the Covenant process of *Forming* and *Filling*, the "there-and-back-again" shape of every Bible story. Both *Forming* and *Filling* are found in every part of Scripture (and even in the point that Hebrew is written right to left, and Greek is written left to right: there-and-back-again). But what if we also consider the entire Bible itself as a single unit that comprises one great *Forming*, the historical and literary establishment of a foundation for the age of the Church? This relates to something I mentioned in *Bible Matrix II*:

> Everything the Lord does is like building a house. He forms it and then fills it. Man's domain has boundaries, or *external* walls, and every delegated subdomain is formed with *internal* walls. These are all spaces to fill. Reality, like the Bible, is a house of many Covenant rooms. And reality, like the Bible, has corners. It can be quite angular and sharp, because it is *formative*. It is not always pleasant, because it is a tool for the construction of something beyond our own experience and, indeed, our own ability. Yet, like the Bible, each room is *sacred*.[2]

Numerically, Israel is *Formed* in Genesis and *Filled* in Exodus. The Abrahamic promises are *Formed* in the books of Moses and *Fulfilled* after his death. The end of the Tabernacle and each Temple brought an end to a process of *Forming* (as did the cutting of Adam), and

---

2   Michael Bull, *Bible Matrix II: The Covenant Key*, 28.

Israel entered into a greater *Filling* (as did the construction of Eve, the multiplier). Just as the books of Moses
finish before the conquest of the Land, so the entire
Bible testimony was finished before the beginning of
the conquest of the World (AD70, which supports a
preterist view of the Revelation).

This meticulously executed "Covenant constraint"
upon the arrangement of every inspired Word, the
requirement that every line, stanza, list and story must
recapitulate the Creation-Covenant sequence, might
relate to the sacrificial process of binding and loosing.
Every mediator between heaven and earth is bound
that an abundant blessing might be poured out, or
"loosed."[3] This process works in ever-increasing
circles. The Day of Atonement prescribed the binding
of one goat and the loosing of another; both goats were
bound for service so that the members of the priesthood might be loosed from death; the priesthood itself
was bound (consecrated) so that Israel might be
loosed; Israel was bound by the Law of Moses so that
all nations might be loosed.

All the Words of the Bible are bound by Covenant,
and are thus "Covenant-shaped." Jesus spoke the
Words the Father gave Him, like all the prophets
before and the apostles after Him. This might explain
a strange turn of phrase in the commission of Ezekiel,
"the son of man."

---

3   See the chapter "Binding and Loosing" in Michael Bull,
     God's Kitchen: Theology You Can Eat & Drink.

INQUIÉTUDE

And he said to me, "Son of man, stand on your feet, and I will speak with you." And as he spoke to me, the Spirit entered into me and set me on my feet, and I heard him speaking to me. And he said to me, "Son of man, I send you to the people of Israel, to nations of rebels, who have rebelled against me. They and their fathers have transgressed against me to this very day." (Ezekiel 2:1-3)

Apparently, the phrase translated "I will speak to you" in Ezekiel 2:1 is a gloss. Literally, it says, *I will speak [you]*. The Lord gives Ezekiel a scroll to eat and sends him as a son of man *(ben-'adam)* against Jerusalem. For this purpose, Ezekiel himself *is* the living, walking Word of God. He is the Law written on tablets of flesh, which is perhaps why his tongue cannot be "loosed" to speak his own words until chapter 24. He becomes the tongue and lips and teeth of God Himself, his every action an articulation of judgment.

What does this mean for us today? The preaching, chanting and singing of the Words of God might feel like a constraint, but it is the Forming of the house, which we are then free to Fill. We do this not only in the composition of spiritual literature and worship music and sacred architecture, but also in secular music and our own stories in novel and films; in fact, we do this in every sphere. The binding of Israel under Moses resulted in the flourishing culture established under David and Solomon. As James Jordan observes, the Church is the nursery of all good culture.

Ezekiel's Vision (circa 1803-5)
William Blake

INQUIÉTUDE

The church is the first form of the kingdom. The church is also the nursery of the kingdom. It is within the institutional church that the fundamental principles of the kingdom are taught and learned. Christians learn government through the church government of elders. Having learned that, Christians are then ready to govern in more broad circumstances. We learn finances in the church, through the administration of the tithe. We learn charity in the church because we are starving and God feeds us bread and wine.

We learn music in the church. All of western music flows out of the music of the church. All of western theater flows out of the liturgy of the church. All of western literature flows out of the literature of the church.

The church creates civilization. The church is the nursery of culture.[4]

The notion that we could move away from God's *Forming* Words and remain culturally productive—or even *literate*—is proving to be an arrogant mistake. In an age when technology brings channels of communication crying out for quality content, our culture has nothing more to say. Our words are void. Originality is rare. Pop culture has become almost entirely self-referential. David P. Goldman writes:

4 James B. Jordan, *Ten Principles of Worship*, Lecture 1.
   Available from www.wordmp3.com

If one dispenses with the ambition to remake the world according to one's whim and accepts rather that the world is God's creation, then *imitatio Dei* consists of acts of kindness. In their urge toward self-worship, the artists of the twentieth century descended to extreme levels of artlessness to persuade themselves that they were in fact creative. In their compulsion to worship themselves in the absence of God, they produced ideas far more ridiculous, and certainly a great deal uglier, than revealed religion in all its weaknesses ever contrived. The modern cult of individual self-expression is a poor substitute for the religion it strove to replace, and the delusion of personal creativity an even worse substitute for redemption.[5]

We have become tinkling cymbals. Only by becoming saturated in Scripture once again will we bring a new age of culture-building which remains a blessing for future generations.

In Jordan's lectures on Ezekiel, he speculates about the sound that the "wheels within wheels" of the Lord's chariot would have made, being angled at 90 degrees to each other. Perhaps their "spirit-filled" sound was like the blades of many helicopters, a terrifying "Filling" of the sound of the Lord going "to and fro in the Spirit of the [judgment] day" in Genesis 3:8. But

---

5   David P. Goldman, "Admit It, You Really Hate Modern Art," in *It's Not the End of the World, It's Just the End of You: The Great Extinction of the Nations*, 121-122.

our Western chariots have lost their Spirit. Our world conquest, despite its faults, was carried on the wings of the Gospel. Like Israel, we have turned to the chariots of Egypt instead of relying upon the Lord of hosts. Likewise, declining education standards are not remedied by more borrowed money but by a return to the Bible. *Ichabod* is written over every public school. Our culture is like a ceiling fan after the power blacks out: the blades are still spinning, giving the impression that the *animus* remains, but the movement is merely residual inertia. The life is ebbing away with every slowing revolution. In medical terms, this is the death rattles. To be loosed from the Bible is to be bound by barbarism.

The education, literacy and culture enjoyed but taken for granted by many of Christianity's harshest critics was a direct result of Christianity. They assume such blessings will continue. Or do they?

"You are not educated if you don't know the Bible."
— Christopher Hitchens

"A native speaker of English who has not read a word of the King James Bible is verging on the barbarian."
— Richard Dawkins

3
EDUCATING JESUS
WISDOM BEYOND OUR YEARS

And the Lord was sorry that he had made man on the earth, and it grieved him to his heart. (Genesis 6:6)

But concerning that day and hour no one knows, not even the angels of heaven, nor the Son, but the Father only. (Matthew 24:36)

The relationship between the Father and the Son is an eternal *to-and-fro*. It is this primary "chiasm," *Forming* and *Filling*, which gave shape to the Creation Week and every event in the Word of God. Every facet of human life is also a "there-and-back-again."

Most importantly, it is also the shape of human history. All of antiquity up to the Ascension of Christ was a *Forming* which resulted in a Glorified Adam, the blameless Firstfruits. Pentecost began the *Filling*, the maturity of humanity in the maturity of Christ. But what if all of history, not just the incarnation, was also part of the process of perfecting the Son?

27

INQUIÉTUDE

TRANSCENDENCE

Creation - **Adam to Noah:**
World united as one blood

HIERARCHY

Division - **Abraham to Joseph:**
World divided by blood
(*Circumcision*)

ETHICS (LAW)

Ascension - **Moses to AD30:**
Centralized priesthood
EARTHLY MEDIATORS

Testing - **Christ:**
The harvest begins

Maturity - **Christ to AD70:**
Centralized priesthood
HEAVENLY MEDIATORS

OATH/SANCTIONS

Conquest - **AD70 to final judgment:**
World divided by water
(*Baptism*)

SUCCESSION

Glorification - **final judgment:**
World united by one Spirit

FORMING

FILLING

FUTURE

Creation - **Adam to Noah:** Let this mind be in you which was also in Christ Jesus, who, being in the form of God, did not consider it robbery to be equal with God, (Genesis 3:5)

FORMING

Division - **Abraham to Joseph:** but made Himself of no reputation, taking the form of a bondservant, and coming in the likeness of men. (Genesis 18:2)

Ascension - **Moses to AD30:** And being found in appearance as a man, He humbled Himself and became obedient to the point of death, even the death of the cross. (Exodus 4:22, 24:9-11; Hosea 11:1; Isaiah 53:7-9)

FILLING

Testing - **Christ:** Therefore God also has highly exalted Him and given Him the name which is above every name,

Maturity - **Christ to AD70:** that at the name of Jesus every knee should bow, of those in heaven, and of those on [the Land], and of those under [the Land], (Exodus 20:4)

Conquest - **AD70 to final judgment:** and that every tongue should confess that Jesus Christ is Lord,

FUTURE

Glorification - **final judgment:** to the glory of God the Father.

(Philippians 2:5-11)

INQUIÉTUDE

Based on this correspondence, it would appear that this *Forming* and *Filling* of Creation and Man was intimately linked to the One through whom all things were created. All of human history is also a single, but crucial, *to-and-fro* between the Father and His Son.

This implies that the full intentions of the Father during Old Testament history were only revealed stage by stage not only to humanity (Hebrews 1:1-2) and to the angels (1 Peter 1:12) but also to the Son, who *submitted, suffered* and *matured* at every step. The ministry of the preincarnate Son in heaven began the *credo* which culminated in an *ut intelligam* for all humanity on earth.[1] "The faith of Jesus Christ" is something which began *before* the foundation of the world.

In Marilynne Robinson's *Housekeeping*, the narrator takes some literary license to describe a God who is appalled by the murder of Abel. He possesses Covenant authority, yet it is a delegated authority. He is a Lord-in-training, a Yahweh who is yet a young man:

> Cain killed Abel, and the blood cried out from the ground—a story so sad that even God took notice of it. Maybe it was not the sadness of the story, since worse things have happened every minute since that day, but its novelty that He found striking. In the newness of the world God was a young man, and grew indignant over the slightest things. In the

---

1   *Credo ut intelligam* is Latin for "I believe so that I may understand," a maxim based on a saying of Augustine of Hippo (*crede, ut intelligas*, "believe so that you may understand"; Tract. Ev. Jo., 29.6).

newness of the world God had perhaps not Himself realized the ramifications of certain of His laws, for example, that shock will spend itself in waves; that our images will mimic every gesture, and that shattered they will multiply and mimic every gesture ten, a hundred, or a thousand times.[2]

Is it possible that the reference to Yahweh's repentance concerning the creation of Man (Genesis 6:6) was more than a mere anthropomorphism? Is it possible that when Yahweh says that child sacrifice had never entered into His heart (Jeremiah 7:31, 19:5; 32:35) He was not condescending to human understanding?

THE FATHER WHO HIDES HIS FACE

The firmament of Day 2 *(Division)*, unlike the works of other days, was not deemed "good." Neither was it deemed "bad," which indicates that it was a *temporary* veil between heaven and earth, a division for the sake of a greater union. It was like the cutting of Adam's flesh that he might be united with Eve as "one flesh." Cells divide that they may be united in a greater way. The darkness and "deep sleep" are for the purpose of *multiplication*. They are not inherently good but for a greater good. The "deep sleep" of Abraham, a corporate cutting of flesh, served a similar purpose.

The veil is a *division* which hides God's face, God's glorious intentions, from Man. Just as Noah was naked

2   Marilynne Robinson, *Housekeeping*, 192.

INQUIÉTUDE

behind a veil, and Moses' face was veiled, so Yahweh's throne was hidden behind a veil in the tent. Wise rulers like Joseph temporarily hide their faces, veiling their intentions for the purpose of testing their brothers. This is exactly what the Lord did to qualify Adam.

What if the mind of the Father was also hidden by a "firmament" from the Son, the Creation itself being the greatest good for the Son yet wrapped in a riddle and not yet complete? This would mean that the process of bringing the Son to a "bridal" maturity began *not* at the incarnation *but at the Creation*.

Although this is speculation, we do know that the glory Christ received at His enthronement was *not* the glory which He put off at His incarnation but that which He possessed *before the Creation*. Take note of Jesus' own words:

> "I glorified you on earth, having accomplished the work that you gave me to do. And now, Father, glorify me in your own presence with the glory that I had with you *before the world existed*." (John 17:4-5)

Nothing was created without the Son, yet not all was revealed to the Son from the beginning. His gradual perfection was not only prefigured but expressed—united inextricably—in His guidance of the human figures of Messianic history. Yahweh was *always* Jesus.

The implications of such a vision of the full obedience of the Son, *blind* obedience in the Creation of Light, are worth meditating upon.

St Joseph the Worker
Michael O'Brien www.studiobrien.com

INQUIÉTUDE

What perfect trust the Son demonstrated as He continued to obey the Father despite the horrors of Old Testament history. The events were as heartbreaking a revelation to the Son as they are to humanity. Yet His faith in the Father did not waver.

Since the Old Covenant was administered by angels, the servants of God, the Son Himself was humbled as an angel, "the angel of the Lord," that is, a heavenly *servant*.[3] He was *like* the angels in His submission, but *unlike* them because He was the Son (Galatians 4:1-7).

> No longer do I call you servants, for the servant does not know what his master is doing; but I have called you friends, for all that I have heard from my Father I have made known to you. (John 15:14-15)

From the act of Creation, the Son's submission would continue by degrees until His death on the cross. His obedience in entering history as a man and obeying "unto death" is breathtaking. Most heartbreaking of all is His willingness to actually *become* the veil, the flesh that was torn away to reveal the "naked" mind of the Father, the unhidden face of His mission for a bride for His Son (Hebrews 10:20). The firmament, as a veil between heaven and earth, was an image of the delegation of the Son by the Father, a garment "stretched out" like Joseph's robe, a covering that would be bloodied and torn throughout history until the death of Jesus.

---

3 For more discussion, see "Better Angels" in Michael Bull, *Sweet Counsel: Essays to Brighten the Eyes.*

THE SON WHO REVEALS THE FATHER

Since true wisdom comes only through faithful obedience, it makes sense that Jesus did not know all the Father's will. We ourselves are justified by "the faith of Jesus Christ," and faith assumes an absence of sight. As "Israel," Jesus obeyed God step by step, day by day. He did not know Lazarus was going to die. He did not know that He was going to be abandoned on the cross. The Father's will was revealed only on a "need to know" basis. His entire life was the *credo ut intelligam* experienced by all the sons of God. Perhaps even the knowledge of His coming death was obscure, revealed in a "dark saying" just as Paul's fate was revealed to him by the prophet Agabus (Numbers 12:6-8; Acts 21:11).

As an earthly prophet, Christ was told what to say. He only spoke face to face with the Father, thus becoming a "better Moses" (Hebrews 3:3) at His ascension, when He opened the sealed scroll containing His inheritance. He was always the voice which spoke from heaven, but only now does He speak His own mind.

Jesus is the truth, but the truth is a *process* because it is *relational:* submission before dominion, humility before exaltation. The fact is that all the Scriptures used to prove a *stasis* in the glory of Christ before and after His incarnation were written *after* His ascension. Jesus did not simply leave the perfection of heaven and become flesh. He had submitted to the Father *at every step of history* from the foundation of the world.

35

INQUIÉTUDE

In His earthly life, Jesus demonstrated the good *nature* of the Father. In His death, Jesus as the torn veil revealed the good *intentions* of the Father. He showed us God's true face.

THE HIDDEN WISDOM

Before you charge me with "open theism," this divine "education" concerned *only* the Son. All the authority of the Father over the Creation has *now been given* to the Son, indicating that He did not previously possess full authority over it. He served as a steward, doing only what the Father instructed Him to do (John 10:22-39). The Father's *omni*-potence in history (Forming) is now fully realized in the wisdom of His *pleni*-potent Son (Filling).[4]

All has now been revealed *to* Him, and *in* Him. He obeyed from the very beginning, and now He is a better Solomon, a king of peace who has sought God with all His heart and obtained an even greater glory, the glory of His Bride (Proverbs 25:2).

It is no longer the mystery of the mind of *God* which needs revealing. All has been revealed to those who possess the mind of *Christ* by the Spirit (1 Corinthians 2; Colossians 2:1-7). In the one who served faithfully in heaven and fulfilled the Law on earth, we, like David, have a wisdom beyond our years (Psalm 119:100).[5]

---

4   For more discussion, see "Images of God" in Michael Bull, *Sweet Counsel: Essays to Brighten the Eyes.*
5   As expected, this essay provoked some discussion among friends, some of which been included as Appendix 1.

36

4
GOD'S GAMBLE
PLAYING FOR A WHITE STONE

And in the breastpiece of judgment you shall put the Urim and the Thummim, and they shall be on Aaron's heart, when he goes in before the Lord. Thus Aaron shall bear the judgment of the people of Israel on his heart before the Lord regularly. (Exodus 28:30)

O pen theists teach that God cannot know the future. They deduce that since He gave human beings a will that is truly free, then anything is possible, and nothing can be predetermined. Covenant history has thus been a gigantic gamble on God's part. And we do know that God gambles. After all, He commanded His priests to "throw the dice."

TABERNACLE TWO-UP

The Urim and Thummim were basically a set of dice: two engraved stones, a black one and a white one, indicating *yes* and *no*, innocent or guilty, kept in a pouch on the ephod worn by the High Priest. Since the

INQUIÉTUDE

High Priest, from *Vestitus Sacerdotum Hebraeorum*, Volume 2. The illustration shows how the different vestments were worn together to form a complete outfit. The vestments (in the order in which they were worn): linen breeches *(Michnasayim)*, tunic *(Ketonet)*, sash *(Avnet)*, robe *(Me'il)*, vest *(Efod)*, breast-plate *(Hoshen)* and headdress and golden crown *(Mitznefet and Tzitz)*.

This book was written at 1680 in Amsterdam by Johanne Braunio (1638-1708), and is thought to be the most comprehensive historical research on vestments of the Jewish priests.

clothing of the High Priest corresponded to the coverings and furnishings of the cruciform Tabernacle, the
stones were simplified miniatures of the Siniatic
stones in the Ark of the Covenant. As miniature tablets
inside this miniature "Ark," God promised to speak
through this arrangement as He had spoken on Sinai.
The process, also known as "the lot," boils down to
"heads or tails," or a game of Two-up.[1]

A stone was withdrawn and whether it was black or
white signified the will of God. On the Day of
Atonement, this is how the choice was made between
the goat which would *ascend* to heaven as smoke, and
the goat which would symbolically *descend* into the
abyss as dust and ashes.[2] Black and white were disobedience or obedience,[3] cursing or blessing, death or life,
outer darkness or the presence of God.[4]

For us, the future *is* unknown. It *is* a risk. We can
identify and quantify all of the variables and speculate
on the outcomes, but we can never be entirely sure of

---

1 Two-up is a traditional Australian gambling game, involving a
designated "spinner" throwing two coins or pennies into the air.
Players gamble on whether the coins will fall with both heads
(obverse) up, both tails (reverse) up, or with one coin a head, and
one a tail (known as "odds").

2 Since both goats died, I suspect this is the meaning of the phrase
"the second death" in Revelation 20:6. The martyrs had ascended
to heaven (the first death, followed by the first resurrection) so the
second death had no power over them.

3 In Revelation 2:17, the "hidden manna" in the Most Holy Place and
the white stone in the ephod are images relating to obedience, the
"hidden food" of Jesus (John 4:32).

4 The black and white birds in Genesis 8 and 15 served a similar
purpose. See the chapter "Return of the Raven" in Michael Bull,
Sweet Counsel: Essays to Brighten the Eyes.

how they will combine to produce the end result. If we could, we would not need crash test dummies. We would not need insurance cover.

The Old Testament looks like a lot of risky business. Men fail God time and time again, but He simply keeps on "betting the farm," staking everything on the hope of another windfall.

However, what many fail to notice is that as this apparently compulsive behavior continues throughout history, God actually brings humanity to greater and greater levels of *maturity*. Every failure, every loss, is a cloud turned inside out to reveal a silver lining. Every attempt to steal from or oppress the patriarchs resulted in their enrichment, not only spiritually but also materially. Likewise, slavery in Egypt gave riches to Israel. Even Israel's scattering by Assyria and Babylon was used to sow the seeds of truth across a greater territory, a process which also entailed the plundering of all Israel's enemies from India to Ethiopia.

So, the Lord builds a house of worship out of people, brick by brick, throughout history, and then He bets it *all*—every chip—on the newcomer—His Son. To us, it seemed insane. To God, it was a sure thing. Was there ever any chance that His Son would fail?

THRILLS AND SPILLS

There is a certain thrill in risk. Gambling is as addictive to some personalities as adultery and embezzlement are to others. Stolen waters are sweet only temporarily, but sweet nonetheless. We will take risks for pleasure, and often the heart of the pleasure is the risk. But will we take risks *for the kingdom?* God repeatedly asks His people to take ridiculous risks for Him.

The history of the New Covenant is a similar history of insane risks. Some paid off immediately. Others paid off over time. But all involved some kind of initial loss, and the resulting increase is rarely given in a way that might have been foreseen. Jim Elliot prayed for the salvation of many people, but without much success. It was his death at the hands of the Waorani tribe of Amazonian Ecuador that inspired thousands of people to join Christian missions. Many other missionaries labored for years without seeing a single convert. Yet their work broke up the fallow ground, and those who followed them reaped a harvest.

As Christians, we want the thrills without the spills, but God is too crafty to give the game away. A veil is drawn behind us and another ahead of us. We are Moses between Pharaoh and the Red Sea, or Israel between the Red Sea and the Jordan. Like the Levite priests carrying the Ark, we must step into the water *before* it parts. Like Peter, we must step out of the boat *before* the miracle. Or, like Jesus, we must *refrain* from throwing ourselves from the pinnacle of the Temple, which is just as much an act of faith.

Miracles always follow risks taken in faith. Missionaries see more miracles because they take obedient risks. In the kingdom of God there is a miracle at the center, and miracles at the frontiers. In between these two, there is obedient service.

I heard a father once ask if Christian parenting came with any guarantees. He has two daughters. One is a faithful and dedicated Christian. The other trod it all underfoot. The girls are close in age and had identical upbringings. He wanted an explanation.

The answer is that planting and watering is the only way to achieve a harvest. But there is no guarantee that a storm or a fire or some pestilence will not wipe out the crop. We might produce a Jacob and an Esau, or a bride and a harlot, or two Jacobs and two brides, or nothing. But in the long run, the Word never returns empty. We are to be faithful witnesses because others are witnessing *our* faithfulness.

The Urim and Thummim was a ritual which expressed a "calculated risk" of faith in a God Who promised an abundant, if not miraculous, increase. The only guarantee is that God is a rewarder of those who diligently seek Him. Risk is inherent in faithfulness because it is a bet on the character and promises of God, and if we know Him, we will take that risk.

The Urim and Thummim were also a picture of the Holy Spirit-filled man, the tablets of the Law of Moses written on the fleshy tablets of the heart. The last time God's representatives used the lot was when the disciples had to choose a replacement for Judas. Immediately after this, Christ sent the Holy Spirit from heaven to indwell them. They no longer needed the dice. Just as the "elder-gems" on the breastplate of the High Priest sat above the stones in the ephod, when the disciples gathered together, Jesus was there in their midst giving them the white stone. When we gather together, and examine our hearts as Israel did before *Yom Kippur,* He does the same for us.

> We are of God. He who knows God hears us; he who is not of God does not hear us. By this we know the spirit of truth and the spirit of error.
> (1 John 4:6 NKJV)

Our endeavors might look like risky gambles, and there will be apparent failures, but as on Calvary, the spills *are* the thrills. As Herbert Schlossberg said:

> The Bible can be interpreted as a string of God's triumphs disguised as disasters.[5]

History is *open* in one sense, since we have been freed from every chain and weight to carry out God's work in His power. There are risks and variables, thrills and disappointments. We are free to play the table, work the room, attempt great big risky things for God. That is the freedom of Man under a sovereign God.

But, as always, it is a freedom *bound by Covenant.* Our Father *owns* the casino. Since Pentecost, Christ is the ultimate match-fixer. When we are united, the table is rigged in our favor. All the Covenants in the Old Testament were conditional and in some sense they all

5   Herbert Schlossberg, *Idols for Destruction,* 304.

ended in human failure. The New Covenant is no less conditional, but its success rests upon the faithfulness of Jesus Christ, and that is imparted to us, with His wisdom, by the Spirit. Where the little white ball lands on the roulette table is up to Him. But He knows exactly where it is going to land from the beginning.

The future is an open scroll, a history to be written, but one day, when the work is done, Jesus will roll up it, hand it back to the Father, and sit down again (Luke 4:17-20). Then we will see it was written by His hand.

Faithful witness for Christ is always a gamble, and it is a game of numbers. Returning to the insurance metaphor, we have a reliable policy, underwritten by God, with a clause for every possible contingency. And the cover provided was dark red. Jesus gives those who overcome (or *Conquer* in Bible Matrix terms) a white stone with a new and larger name (Genesis 17:5; 35:10; Revelation 2:17). This is because those who conquer are *living sacrifices,* chosen to ascend into His presence.

The world is open for conquest, but as with every good comedy, the conclusion of the matter is already settled. The last judgment is yet to come, but as far as the Father is concerned, the case is already *closed.* When the Gospel's "tour of duty" comes to an end, as all Covenants do, the riches of the wicked will be given to the righteous. That fact is certain.

Open Theists tell us that they have open minds when it comes to the Scriptures, but it seems to me that they have closed Bibles.

5
SEX AND ARCHITECTURE
THE FATHERHOOD OF ADAM

"This man shall not be your heir;
your very own son shall be your heir."
(Genesis 15:4)

When Paul refers to Abraham as the father of all who believe, the one through whom all nations would be blessed (Romans 4:9-22), we must interpret his inspired words through the lens of the architecture of Eden, the Sanctuary of our first father, Adam.

THE NAME OF THE FATHER

God's household in heaven was a tent of servants—the angels—but there was only one Son, through whom came all Creation. This means that the first verses of John's Gospel, which describe the pre-incarnate Word, can tell us a great deal about God's intentions for Adam, the incarnate image of God. All that Jesus was to the Father in heaven, Adam was to be on earth:

45

INQUIÉTUDE

In the beginning was the Word, and the Word was with God, and the Word was God. He was in the beginning with God. All things were made through him, and without him was not any thing made that was made. In him was life, and the life was the light of men. The light shines in the darkness, and the darkness has not overcome it. (John 1:1-5)

In the beginning, Adam was with God, made in the image of God. All things on earth were to be made through him. He was to be the light of all men by overcoming the darkness. The expansion of God's household rested upon the shoulders of Adam as an earthly son of God (Luke 3:38; Exodus 28:9-12).

By trusting in God's Word, exercising faith in His character, *servants become sons,* sharing God's mind by the Spirit. And then, also by the Spirit, *sons become fathers.* The ministry of Adam was designed to bring many sons to glory. Just as from the spring of Eden flowed the life-giving blessing of four *physical* rivers, so from Adam's body were to flow not only "rivers of men" in abundant *social* streams, but also the Law of the Spirit in an *ethical* succession.

The Covenant process began with the Word from the Father and was to end with Adam himself as a Great Father. We see this transformation replicated in Genesis 17:5, which moves Abram from the promise of being Covenant Head to a promised Covenant Body:

Annunciation (1481)
Sandro Botticelli

INQUIÉTUDE

"No longer shall your name be called Abram *[exalted father]*, but your name shall be Abraham *[father of the multitude]*."

Only through children does Man possess the Future, which is why the Covenant process ends with *Succession*.[1] As the Covenant process is expressed in the Bible matrix, the promise of children exalts the Man as Firstfruits *(Ascension)*. His fatherhood, the fulfillment of the promise, comes at Booths *(Glorification)*. The Man begins as a "single coded cell," a wall between sacred and profane. Only through *Testing* does he become a house. God then sends the promised increase and Adam becomes "a household," that is, a social body lifted up (erected), sealed (made safe) and then filled with the future (inhabited).

We see this very process in the life of Abraham. God called Abram out *physically* (feeding and protecting his house as a priest), then *socially* (conquering kings), before the promised child arrived.[2] Abraham was a barren man until he qualified as a Prophet. As a "triune man," he was then asked to give up his only son as a Firstfruits offering so that God might send a greater harvest. In this final great act of faith, Abraham became a Covenant shelter for all nations.

With the life story of Abraham in mind, let us

---

1   See the Covenant-literary charts at the end of this book.
2   Many commentators believe that Abram failed morally when he lied to Pharaoh, but in the context of the Covenant promises, he, and Jacob, faithfully outcrafted their respective serpents.

consider the intended ministry of Adam in the Garden and how it relates to his offspring as architecture. Via *Ethical Testing,* Creation becomes *pro*-creation.

THE FATHERHOOD OF ADAM

INITIATION
Creation: God the Father
(Day 1 - Light - Ark of the Testimony - Sabbath)

FORMING

DELEGATION
Division: Adam is made flesh
(Day 2 - Waters Divided - Veil - Passover)

PRESENTATION
Ascension: Priesthood – Father by PROMISE
(Day 3 - Land - Altar & Table - Firstfruits)

PURIFICATION
Testing: Kingdom – Father in NAME
(Day 4 - Lights - Lampstand - Pentecost)

FILLING

TRANSFORMATION
Maturity: Prophethood – Father in NATURE
(Day 5 - Swarms/Clouds - Incense - Trumpets)

VINDICATION
Conquest: Great Prophethood – Adam cuts flesh
(Day 6 - Animals & Man - Mediators - Atonement)

FUTURE

REPRESENTATION/PROCREATION
Glorification: Great Father – Adam is multiplied
(Day 7 - Rest & Rule - Shekinah - Booths) [3]

---

3   Genesis 1, 2 and 3 each follow the Bible Matrix independently, but chapters 2 and 3 also follow the pattern as a single unit.

INQUIÉTUDE

SPRINGS AND OFFSPRING

The children promised in Genesis 1:28, the "innocents" yet in Adam's loins, are silent but crucial characters in Genesis 3. Like Abraham, Adam was called to offer his firstborn son, not to God but to the original Molech.

Adam's dominion was linked to procreation, hence the serpent's attack upon Eve. It seems that Satan, an administrator of the Covenant (Acts 7:53; Galatians 3:19; Hebrews 1:14; 2:2), despised the fact that these "children of God" would inherit the house in which he was a mere servant. Like an indignant butler, or a jealous pet, his attack in the present was an attempt to hijack the future. Like Pharaoh and Herod after him, he would cut off the heirs of a rival kingdom. By God's mercy, his attempted murder of mankind was foiled.

However, through Adam's failure as Covenant Head to judge Satan, the future was nevertheless filled with widows and orphans.[4] And in Adam's place, the world's first false teacher became the corrupt tutor of all living, the father of lies (John 8:44). Nazis and Communists removed children from Christian parents for indoctrination. They understood, as do secularists today, that children are the key to dominion.[5]

---

4   For more on the biblical theme of widows and orphans, see Michael Bull, *Bible Matrix II: The Covenant Key*, chapters 2 and 6.
5   Since secularism has led Western cultures to voluntary infertility, state education is a means of stealing the minds of the children of people of faith. For more discussion, see David P. Goldman, *How Civilizations Die (and Why Islam Is Dying Too)*, chapter 2, "Faith, Fertility, and the World's Future."

An understanding of how this legal-relational situation models the architecture of heaven (as revealed in the Tabernacle) is eye-opening.

The Lord

The Glory Cloud

The Serpent

Eve

Adam

The Spring and Rivers of Eden

Dominion over the Earth

- God's Law was the Ark. Satan, as an "angel (messenger) of light" was the secondary lightbearer, the Lampstand.
- In his self-sacrifice as a priestly guard, Adam was to be broken bread and poured out wine, the Table.
- Between them, Eve, the mother of all living, was the fragrant Altar of Incense. As element 5, Day 5, she is a "multitude" in one body, "awesome as an army with banners" (Song of Solomon 6:4, 10). Women possess all their ova from birth.
- Thus, in the Tabernacle we see the battle for the future presented as a tug-o'-war between the serpent and the Man in which Adam did not even pick up the rope. It was victory by default for the serpent.

INQUIÉTUDE

OPENING ADAM

The Man was called to be a *wall,* a PRIESTLY divide between sacred and profane. God's life-giving authority created a single "coded" human cell, with Adam's submission to the Law of God as its life-protecting cell wall. This "clean cell" would be the source of all future life—but this was not possible if he remained alone.

Adam was divided to become a *house,* a head and a body, that is, a hierarchy of love. Serving as a KING who incarnated the Law would multiply Adam's "wall of flesh" into a purifying "wall of fire." He would be God's eyes on earth, discerning by the Word the intent of any invader, and protecting those in his care.

Finally, speaking as a PROPHET to those inside (men) and for those outside (at this point, the animal kingdom) would effectively unite them, the priestly and the kingly, creating a *"household of faith,"* of which Adam would be the door. Speaking the mind of God would tear down the wall of enmity between inside and outside, making everything sacred (Zechariah 14:21; Ephesians 2:14). The wisdom gained as plunder from the serpent would be ministered not only to Eve, but to all her offspring.

The serpent promised the end without the lawful means. He became the first "household god," setting himself up as a rival authority in the Sanctuary. Speaking as the first false prophet, he promised exaltation without ethical qualification, peace on earth without submission to heaven (Jeremiah 6:14).

Adam's failure in response was threefold. His failure to internalize the Law as a priest led to his failure in judgment as a king and his "prophetic voice" was silenced. Adam ministered life to the murderer and executed his sons (Mark 15:6-11). When called before God, instead of interceding for himself and for Eve (his "people") as a High Priest (Great Servant), Adam instead called for a sword, for *vengeance* (Genesis 4:24; Matthew 18:21-22; Luke 9:54). As his counterpart, and thus his potential co-regent, Eve followed Adam's example.[6] Instead of God's good Law being used in love to promote and protect life, it became an instrument of tyranny in the hand of an ethical child.

Be infants in evil, but in your thinking be mature.
(1 Corinthians 14:20)

SEX AND THE FUTURE

In all cases, ethics is architectural, and architecture is a result of ethics. As in Eden, and in Israel, the nature (Forming), name (Filling) and longevity (Future) of every nation depends not simply upon fertility but upon faithful obedience to God. Whether the multiplication of the Bride would be a Babylon or a Jerusalem, a pure bride who bore righteous armies or a spiritual harlot whose infants were offered to a false god, was all down to the Man in the Sanctuary.

---

6   It should be noted that Eve's call for vengeance upon the serpent was truly prophetic. She prefigured the Covenant Body, so her legal testimony here, despite the situation, was not in fact false witness.

INQUIÉTUDE

Consequently, we find a strange barrenness imped-ing the future of God's people, while the other nations were abundantly fruitful. For the nations, sex was the future, and they revered it as a god. For God, sex that results in true cultural longevity is inseparable from Covenant *Ethics*. This brings us to a consideration of the "Covenant shape" of sex.

SEX AS AN ACT OF DOMINION

TRANSCENDENCE

Creation: Adam, as Word, initiates the act of procreation that will change history

HIERARCHY

Division: Eve is chosen and cherished. Adam's self-sacrifice in foreplay leads to...

ETHICS

Ascension: arousal of the holy fire of desire. He "overshadows" Eve ("nearbringing")

Testing: Man and Woman are flesh united by fire as "Ish" and "Isha"

Maturity: Climax: Adam's is singular and Eve's is "multiple." Eve is "filled with a swarm"

OATH/SANCTIONS

Conquest: As Eve was chosen by Adam, so an ovum as "Body" chooses her "Head"

SUCCESSION

Glorification: Passion subsides and the united couple enter into godly rest.

FORMING

FILLING

FUTURE

You might notice that an erection is indeed architectural in nature. The Babelic tower is always phallic.

In Genesis 2:23, "Man" and "Woman" are "Ish" and "Isha," designating a relationship, (as do the words "father" and "son"). *Adam* is thus what a man is *physically*, and Ish is who he is made *socially*. According to James Jordan, these words may have been used because they sound like *eish* ("fire"). Adam was an Altar made of earth, and with his obedience comes the "fire" of Isha, the woman as the shining on the altar. Unholy sex is thus a response to "strange fire," which is why Israel's adultery in Numbers 25 was the outcome of her idolatries (Exodus 32:24, Leviticus 10:1). Some modern linguists believe "Ish" is derived from a root word meaning "strength." *Testing* is where we usually find the "mighty men" in the Bible Matrix, the kings who like Cain have usurped true worship, or who like Boaz are strong in the Lord.

Threshing wheat, the threshing floor and the grinding of the mill are biblical euphemisms for sex, both licit and illicit. As in Eden, the fruitfulness of the Land and the Bride are corresponding facets of God's Law, hence the "collection" of Boaz' seed by Ruth speaking of fruitfulness for Adam on the Land, and then miraculous life from the womb of Eve in Ruth's generational surrogacy on behalf of Naomi. Interestingly, the meaning of Boaz is "strength is within him."

INQUIÉTUDE

SEX AS A NEW CREATION

FORMING

Creation: As with the Sabbath, the pattern of the sexual act prefigures the act of gestation. Of many ova, one is chosen *(Sabbath)*

  Division: called out and cut into, *(Passover)*

    Ascension: freed from barrenness by Adamic fertilization, (the flow of blood is stopped) (Single Coded Cell) *(Firstfruits)*

FILLING

      Testing: and "opened" in cell division (Code Applied). *(Pentecost)*

    Maturity: Eve "shines" in pregnancy. Multiplication leads to a new body (Multiplied Coded Cells) *(Trumpets)*

    Conquest: Birth pangs, water and blood. The child is "divided" from its mother and the "old house," the placenta, is expelled *(Atonement)*

FUTURE

Glorification: The pain of childbirth subsides. There is rest, a new family, and a "larger tent." *(Booths)*

A new body "knitted together" in the womb by God is a Covenant "legal" process and relies upon a "code."

The correspondence of Atonement with the separation of not only the child from the mother, but also the child from the placenta, makes sense of Jesus' reference to "birth pangs" concerning the Jewish War (Matthew 24:8). Just as Mary's birth pangs heralded the first Christmas (Covenant Head), so the tribulation in the AD60s heralded Jew and Gentile in one new Man, a New Covenant Body.

56

OPENING EVE

As noted, Man is a "physical" name. Ish and Isha (Genesis 2:23) are "social" names. If we read a three-fold architecture into the first couple, the words father and mother (Genesis 2:24) give us the third level. This means that parenting is tied to Covenant *Ethics*, that is, obedience to God. For Adam to become a *physical* father, he must obey the Father as an *ethical* son.

Most Holy Place – Head
Man & Woman *(Physical)*

Holy Place – Hands
Husband & Wife *(Social)*

Courts – Feet
Father & Mother *(Ethical)*

A fruitful marriage is thus the complete "temple," which leads to some interesting conclusions.

It seems Adam's *Ethical* "firstfruits" in the Garden would allow God to pour out a miraculous harvest in the Land and open Eve's womb for innumerable children in the World. Neither the ground nor Eve, could be fruitful until *after* the serpent was crushed underfoot (or substitutionary blood was shed).

The different curses upon Adam and Eve at *Sanctions* reflect their delegated stations before God. The curse upon Adam relates to his head, the sweat of his brow (literally, his nose). He is the initiator in charge of providing food and protection for those who would otherwise be widows and orphans—*Forming*. When they are threatened, his prophetic nostrils are to be kindled. The curse upon Eve relates to her *body*—*Filling*. Food and offspring were necessary for the Future, the *Succession*, but these were dependent upon Word. Unlike the animals, Man also requires a steady diet of truth to survive (Deuteronomy 8:3).

Adam was created in the Land, then lifted up and "placed" in the Sanctuary as a physical Firstfruits, but his faithful obedience was to be a firstfruits of righteousness, which would allow God not only to pour out a harvest from the Land but also to open Eve's womb.

This means that the curses upon the brow (Covenant Head) and the womb (Covenant Body) were actually miraculous openings from the hand of God, made possible by the first Day of Coverings. They were thus Covenant *Sanctions* in both the negative *and* positive senses. God sanctioned, that is, allowed, the fruit of the Land and the fruit of the womb and moved the primeval Covenant narrative from the Garden to the Land. In terms of the "above, beside, below" order of the Decalogue, this second tier concerns a Sabbath for the Man who works the Land, and the honoring of parents by their offspring that the abundance of the Land might be retained.[7]

7 See the diagram of the Ten Words in the Covenant-literary charts at the end of this book.

DELEGATION

6
THE SPIRIT OF ADAM
EVERYTHING THAT HAS BREATH

There are heavenly bodies and earthly bodies, but the glory of the heavenly is of one kind, and the glory of the earthly is of another. (1 Corinthians 15:40)

Did Adam receive the Spirit of God? And if he *did* receive the Spirit, was the Spirit taken away from him when he sinned?

The answer is found in the fact that Adam's body was not only constructed as a tabernacle, a dwelling place for God, it was also a physical body which represented every living, breathing thing on earth.

THE FIRST PENTECOST

Adam's creation is not only a recapitulation of Genesis 1, and thus a "precapitulation" of the Tabernacle, it also prefigures Israel's festal calendar, which in turn is a microcosm of all history. The reception of spirit/breath by Adam corresponds to the Day of Pentecost.

INQUIÉTUDE

TRANSCENDENCE
Creation: "...then the Lord God
(Day 1 - Light - Ark of the Testimony - Sabbath)
HIERARCHY
Division: formed the man
(Day 2 - Waters Divided - Veil - Passover)
ETHICS
Ascension: of dust from the ground
(Day 3 - Land - Altar & Table - Firstfruits)
Testing: and breathed into his nostrils
(Day 4 - Lights - Lampstand - Pentecost)
Maturity: the breath of life,
(Day 5 - Swarms/Clouds - Incense - Trumpets)
OATH/SANCTIONS
Conquest: and the man became
(Day 6 - Animals & Man - Mediators - Atonement)
SUCCESSION
Glorification: a living creature."
(Day 7 - Rest & Rule - Shekinah - Booths)
(Genesis 2:7)

Adam was the Firstfruits of the Land he was to called to conquer. Once formed, he was lifted up as a "Levitical gift" into the Garden Sanctuary, which is why the construction of his body is an "order of service" for worship. At *Maturity,* the "breath of life" in his nostrils corresponds not only to "fragrant" testimony (the "burial spices" of resurrection) and a ministry of courageous prophecy, but also to the leading of corporate

Elohim Creating Adam (1795– c. 1805)
William Blake

worship, making Adam's frame the first "wind instrument." He was intended to be a vessel for the Spirit of God. Here, however, we will focus on the "Pentecost" of this stanza, the imparting of "breath."

THE GO-BETWEEN

We know that all Creation is upheld by the Word of God. Every heartbeat, every breath, we receive from Him and give back to Him. Is it, then, correct to speak of all men being animated by, or possessing, the Spirit of God to some degree? Or is the gift of the *spirit* here not the same as the gift of the *Spirit* at Pentecost?

The triune sacred architecture of the Scriptures implies that there is a heavenly breath and an earthly breath, and between them is one who possesses *both*, serving as the mediator between heaven and earth.

The first union of heaven and earth was an illegal one. It was the hybridizing, or possession, of an animal by an angel with grand designs. This angel invaded the Sanctuary by speaking through the serpent. Judgment upon this intruder divided its heavenly spirit from the created order; but the same spirit tempted Cain.

The angels who administered the Covenants also appeared in flesh, taking on human form as tutors and guardians. Heaven could visit earth but due to the corruption of the flesh (and the dust from which it came) nothing from earth could ever visit heaven. The "sacrifice of praise" was thus unacceptable without a prior sacrifice of blood.

THE FALSE PROPHET

So, there is a natural breath and a supernatural breath. Once made alive "naturally," it was intended that Adam would also be made alive "supernaturally," as a qualified mediator. Just as Adam possessed blood before he was given breath, in order to receive the Holy Spirit Adam would have to be blameless. So the "natural Pentecost" at Adam's creation was only a prefiguring of a supernatural Pentecost which did not eventuate.

By submitting to the words of a lying spirit, Adam failed to speak for God, and thus blasphemed the Holy Spirit. He became a man of unclean lips, a false prophet proclaiming a "peace" that was not from God, establishing a godless confession, an idolatry. When pressed on the matter, he still failed to confess, and resorted instead to blame, to "bearing false witness."

But substitutionary blood was shed, and Adam's life continued without the Spirit of God.

> For who among men knows the thoughts of a man except the spirit of the man which is in him? Even so the thoughts of God no one knows except the Spirit of God. (1 Corinthians 2:11)

Breath and lips are a means of communion, of a "shared life." Adam shared the same natural breath as the animals, and with his lips he named them. With his lips he also named his wife, with whom he shared not only breath but also flesh and bone.

INQUIÉTUDE

But Adam did not receive the Spirit of God, and so was incapable of true "face to face" communion with God, that is, conversation without some kind of veil. Heaven and earth were no longer on speaking terms without the shedding of blood.

GIVING UP THE GHOST

Since Adam possessed only the breath of the animal kingdom, Man and beasts were eventually destroyed.

> For behold, I will bring a flood of waters upon the earth to destroy all flesh in which is the breath of life under heaven. (Genesis 6:17)

The "Adamic" Covenant was fundamentally *physical* in nature. All flesh, all natural breath, was repossessed. Only the true prophet, Noah, and the remnant he sheltered, were redeemed. The world returned to the state described at the beginning of Genesis 1.

Before the flood, God gave a warning concerning "breath." The microcosmic pattern of Adam's *physical* creation is discernible in the entire process of Adam's *ethical* qualification, but also in the "Covenant cycle" from Adam to Noah,[1] at the center of which God says,

> "My Spirit shall not abide in man forever, for he is flesh: his days shall be 120 years." (Genesis 6:3)

---

1   See the detailed charts on pages 65 and 73 of Michael Bull, *Bible Matrix: An Introduction to the DNA of the Scriptures.*

This "Pentecostal" judgment predicts the deluge but its placement relates it to *Testing*. Since the word rendered "abide in" in the ESV is a legal term, better translated *judge, rule,* or *contend with,* the "breath" here is not *physical* but *ethical,* not earthly but heavenly. Because Man could no longer be reasoned with (Isaiah 1:18), there was no avenue of fellowship, which also implies that the sacrifices had ceased (Hebrews 10:26). God "gave up" these would-be gods to their delusions. He withdrew His Spirit from the work of conviction (Genesis 4:6), allowing men to fill up their sins before the earthly breath was extinguished.

The 120 year span of Noah's ministry is significant, since it is echoed in the lifespan of Moses, the mediator who spoke with God "face to face" and became the giver of the Law at the first Pentecost.[2]

APOSTASY IS NATURAL

Adam was given a natural breath, an earthly life, with the opportunity to receive a supernatural life, the heavenly Spirit. The curse of death was not only the loss of the promised inheritance, but also of the natural life which he already possessed.

---

2   "'Therefore his days shall be 120 years': this means, not that human life should in future never attain a greater age than 120 years, but that a respite of 120 years should still be granted to the human race. This sentence, as we may gather from the context, was made known to Noah in his 480th year, to be published by him as "preacher of righteousness" (2 Peter 2:5) to the degenerate race." – Keil and Delitzsch Biblical Commentary on the Old Testament.

> For to the one who has, more will be given, and he
> will have an abundance, but from the one who has
> not, even what he has will be taken away.
> (Matthew 13:12)

We see the same process in the Israelites whose idolatry cursed them to die in the wilderness, and also in the Jewish rulers whose "Covenant sorcery" and eventual destruction were the consequence of their rejection of the Spirit at Pentecost. Their kingdom—and their Lampstand—were removed, destroyed by the "breath" of Jesus' coming against Jerusalem in AD70 (2 Thessalonians 2:8). This is the context of the book of Hebrews, which was a warning to Jewish Christians.

> For it is impossible, in the case of those who have
> once been enlightened, who have tasted the heavenly
> gift, and have shared in the Holy Spirit, and have tasted
> the goodness of the word of God and the powers of
> the age to come, and then have fallen away, to restore
> them again to repentance... (Hebrews 6:4-6)

Adam is always the firstfruits of a greater harvest. Faithfulness would have seen his entire house filled with an Edenic *Shekinah*, praise from everything which has breath (Psalm 150:6). Instead, a rejection of the Spirit of heaven led to the end of life on earth.

Jesus breathed on His disciples a blameless life in the flesh (John 20:22), making them acceptable mediators. But those who rejected the Spirit of Pentecost eventually came face to face with consuming fire.

7
THE MEEKEST MAN

SUBMISSION AND DOMINION

"Who made you a ruler and a judge over us?" (Acts 7:27)

According to Numbers 12:3, Moses was the meekest man "on the face of the ground [*'adamah*]."

Psalm 37:11 says that the meek will inherit the Land [*erets*] and delight in abundant prosperity.

Isaiah 11:4 tells us that

> with righteousness
> [God] shall judge the poor,
> and decide with equity
> for the meek of the Land;
> and he shall strike the Land
> with the rod of his mouth,
> and with the breath of his lips
> he shall kill the wicked.

But what is meekness? And why is it connected to the "face of the ground" (Adam), or the Land?

INQUIÉTUDE

MEEKNESS IS A TOUR OF DUTY

Every time God makes a new Covenant, He puts a man, an "Adam," between heaven and earth as a mediator. The requirement for success is *passivity* towards God (obedience to the Covenant *Ethics*) and then *activity* towards the Creation. This is why God tested Adam before opening the Land and the womb. God required the *Ethical* fruit of righteousness before He would give Adam dominion over a greater domain.[1] Submission to heaven results in dominion over the earth.

The important thing to notice is that being *meek* does not make one *weak*. Meekness towards God is not passivity towards men. Meekness is a willingness to be pliable under godly authority, and an unwillingness to be pliable under ungodly authority. The famous words of the disciples in Acts 5:29 about obeying God rather than men are a display of meekness as *strength*. They were *passive* under the Spirit of God that God might be *active* in the hearts of men. This text is not just about the disciples' commitment to Christ. It tells us what it takes to allow the power of God to go to work in the world. Meekness in prayer results in power in ministry.

This is why Jesus presents the centurion as an example of faith in Matthew 8. As a mediator between the throne of Caesar and the nations of the world, he

---

1   See Michael Bull, *Bible Matrix II: The Covenant Key* for an explanation of how a Covenant is a mission, an ethical tour of duty.

Moses Kills the Egyptian (1860)
Julius Schnorr von Carolsfeld

understands the relationship between submission and dominion, and he recognizes true authority in Jesus' submission to God.

The Gentile centurion, and the Jewish disciples, humbled themselves under the almighty hand and were exalted. And between these two events, Jesus, as a better Adam, did exactly the same thing and changed the course of history.

Bold witness is what Paul meant when he said he was "filling up" the sufferings of Christ for the sake of the Church. The death of Paul's body *(passivity)* gave life to Christ's Body *(activity)*.

A GODLY INHERITANCE

This sheds a great deal of light on Jesus' promise about the meek inheriting the Land. Inheritance is Covenantal. It is the "good success" that the obedient man receives for persevering through faith in God's promises. He obeys, and God gives him a territory (Land), an offspring (womb), and the future, which is what God promised to both Adam and to Abraham, picturing the worldwide ministry of Jesus.

So how do we take this promise of Jesus in its historical context? He is saying that the current rulers of Judah, those who claimed to be children of Abraham, would be *disinherited,* and that those Jews who had circumcised hearts, who were found to be pliable by the Spirit, would inherit all the promises currently held by the Jewish rulers. The swap would be as sudden as the leprosy of Naaman finding a new home in Gehazi. Since Christ fulfilled the Law, and all the promises were wrapped up in Him, a modern Jew has no inheritance unless he turns to Christ.

So, Man is called to be *passive* towards God and *active* towards Creation. This is the role that Jesus currently fills, representing us before the Father as the Mediator between heaven and earth. His submission to the cutting hand of the Law qualified him for total dominion, and opened a new channel for the work of the Spirit in the world. An Adam governed by God is an Adam fit to govern. Since Jesus now rules the nations with a rod of iron, meekness does not mean gentleness. It is simply a submission to authority that one might be given authority, and it brings us back to Moses, the meekest man who ever lived.

THE MINISTRY OF MOSES

The reference to Moses as the meekest man on the "face of the ground" ties him to Adam. Adam was, as mentioned, the firstfruits of the Land. God *made* him out of the dust and *placed* him in the Garden. Thus, he was not made in the Garden. He was made out of the place that he was being qualified to rule over and to make fruitful. Adam was made out of earth to be filled with heaven, the perfect hybrid, like Jesus.[2]

---

2   For more discussion on the "holy hybrids" of the Bible, see the chapter "Elementary Things" in Michael Bull, *Bible Matrix II: The Covenant Key.*

The "face" of a true Adam is later represented by the Table of Facebread in the Tabernacle, the promise of a blameless man, qualified to face God and to see His face. God veiled His face to Moses, and Moses' face, as mediator of the Law, was likewise veiled to Israel until Christ came, the Man who did not hide from God.

Like the centurion, Moses understood submission and dominion. He was trained in the ways of Egypt, and, as Stephen tells us, he was "mighty in word and deed" (Acts 7:22). This means that he was not only a *hearer* of the laws but a *doer* of them. He was mighty because he was not only submissive (under authority) but he acted upon what he heard with kingly authority. What was his first act as a ruler? The execution of an Egyptian!

Because modern Christians are taught that all the Old Testament histories are morality fables, and not taught the Covenant context of the accounts, they miss the point of many stories. Like Noah, Moses possessed the authority to pass judgment (Genesis 9:6). Apparently he also possessed the authority to execute the sentence. James Jordan writes:

> The Bible never criticizes Moses for this, but presents his action as righteous and faithful (Acts 7:24ff.; Heb. 11:24ff.). The execution of criminals is never said to defile the land, or to require atonement; such execution is itself the atonement required."[3]

3 James B. Jordan, *The Law of the Covenant*, 254-255.

This sounds strange to our ears, but Moses acted with the authority delegated to him by Pharaoh. And whom did God punish for this incident? Since the Hebrews would not have Moses to rule over them, they suffered for another forty years under the direct authority of Pharaoh. Likewise, when Israel rejected the testimony of the faithful spies, they suffered and died in the wilderness. Moses was not to blame.

However, if Moses was acting with Pharaoh's authority, why did he "look this way and that," and bury the body in the sand? If he was confident in his authority, he would not have done these things.

Perhaps Moses merely feared the unjust reaction of Pharaoh, under whose authority he still served. When Moses slew the Egyptian, he was doing the will of God but not with the authority or power of God. Moses was torn between obeying God and obeying a man. This would not be the case one generation later when he would return to slay many more Egyptians. In that day, he would not do it by his own hand. Through the meekness of Moses, the Land of Ham would be struck with the rod of God's mouth.

Moses' judgment is recapitulated in Christ's ministry in the first century. He warned a new dynasty of Pharaohs—the Herods—and then returned one generation later to slay many more "Egyptians." But Christ waited until He was entirely qualified before passing judgment, which leads to an interesting observation about the lifespan of Moses.

INQUIÉTUDE

THE FACES OF GOD

Priesthood pictures a willingness to be obedient, so that one might then minister the authority of God (as a king) and speak for Him (prophetic). As a priest, God's face is *"against you"* in the Law, to discipline and train you. As a king, God's face *"shines upon you"* to enlighten you, as the Law did for David. As a prophet, you *become* the face of God, representing Him among men as His mouth. This is what we see in the 120 year life of Moses.

Moses, the Levite saved from the sword of Pharaoh, spent 40 years learning under authority (Table of Showbread). When he exercised sound judgment, he was forced to flee. For the next 40 years he was a shepherd. In this, God showed him the true nature of Kingdom, as He later showed David. He prefigured Israel's most famous king until he saw the burning bush, a Lampstand. When he returned to Egypt, he fulfilled his original judgment in the power of God as a prophet, and spent 40 years speaking the Law as an elder with access to God (the Incense Altar). Priest, king and prophet are the three "faces" of the Law, and this puts an interesting spin on the final words between Moses and Pharaoh. In the structure of Exodus 10:28-29, Pharaoh claims authority over the priestly and kingly "faces" (steps 3 and 4) and then predicts Moses' death in Deuteronomy (step 5). However, as the truly "triune" man, Moses claims the *Succession*.

TRANSCENDENCE
Creation: Then Pharaoh said to him,
(Initiation - Genesis - Ark of the Testimony)

HIERARCHY
Division: "Get away from me;
(Delegation - Exodus - Veil)

ETHICS
PRIESTHOOD
Ascension: take care never to see my face again,
(Presentation - Leviticus - Altar & Table)

KINGDOM
Testing: for on the day you see my face
(Purification - Numbers - Lampstand)

PROPHECY
Maturity: you shall die."
(Transformation - Deuteronomy - Incense Altar)

OATH/SANCTIONS
Conquest: Moses said, "As you say!
(Vindication - Joshua - Mediators/Laver)

SUCCESSION
Glorification: I will not see your face again."
(No Representation - Judges - Shekinah)

(Exodus 10: 28-29)

INQUIÉTUDE

Moses' threefold life prefigured Israel's history, and the shape of the entire Old Testament. And all because he was the most pliable, the most truly "circumcised" Jew. He heard God's Words and acted upon them. He was not merely a hearer but a *humble* hearer and thus a mighty doer.

> Therefore put away all filthiness and rampant wickedness and receive with meekness the implanted word, which is able to save your souls. (James 1:21)

Finally, we must note that it was Moses, the meekest Adam on the face of the ground, who brought Israel out of the dust of Egypt, the land of grain, and presented him, as "God's firstborn son" (Exodus 4:22) at the gate of the new Garden Sanctuary, the Tabernacle. But it would be a "meek" generation of Israel which would inherit Canaan and "delight in abundant prosperity."

8
THE SPIRIT OF PROPHECY

KEEPING JESUS TOGETHER

...the testimony of Jesus is the spirit of prophecy.
(Revelation 19:10)

The Creation Week, although sevenfold, consisted of three days of Forming, three days of Filling, and then a Future, the dominion of the world promised to Adam. But before Adam could be considered qualified to rule the world as the representative of God, Adam himself would have to be a new creation.

The pattern of every Covenant is fivefold, with the Covenant "Ethics" as step 3 at the center. This pattern becomes sevenfold, a new Creation, when the Man fulfills God's requirements in a threefold office, often called the Triune Office.[1] The three parts of this office are the Priest *(listen to God)*, the King *(act for God)* and the Prophet *(speak for God)*.

Adam heard the Law from God, but failed to act, to

---

1   See the Covenant-literary charts at the end of this book

INQUIÉTUDE

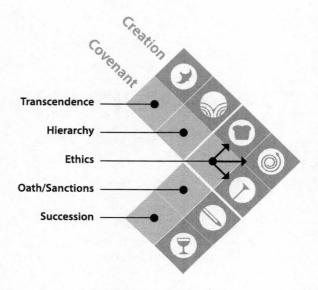

rule over the serpent, and he also failed to testify against the serpent on behalf of his wife.

So, at the center of this "expanded" Covenant pattern is the Man who is himself *Forming* (Priesthood), *Filling* (Kingdom) and *Future* (Prophecy). Where the first Adam failed, the last Adam was faithful. Christ at the center of history is the entire Creation Week in one Man.

The furniture and the rites of the Holy Place were images of the Triune Office, a threefold mediatory role between heaven and earth, past and future. The Table spoke of Priesthood *(Firstfruits)*, the Lampstand of Kingdom *(Pentecost)*, and the Incense Altar of Prophecy *(Trumpets)*. Combined, these three elements represented the flesh, the fire and the smoke of the sacrifice, a death-and-resurrection.

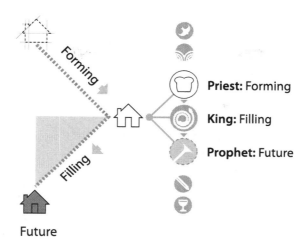

Priest: Forming

King: Filling

Prophet: Future

Forming

Filling

Future

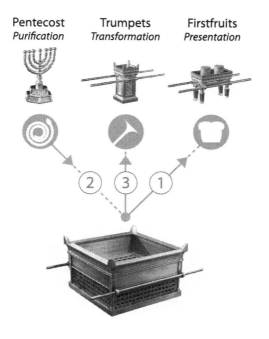

Pentecost
Purification

Trumpets
Transformation

Firstfruits
Presentation

A SINGLE SACRIFICE

An obedience which is truly sacrificial is losing one's life that it might be saved, and we see that in the flesh, the fire, and the ascending fragrant smoke.

Mediating for the nations, Israel's history worked through Priestly, Kingly, and Prophetic stages, but in the larger picture, the Aaronic Order was Priesthood, Christ brought the Kingdom at Pentecost, and the apostles began the era of global Prophecy. Where the Old Israel concerned the offering of the *Firstfruits,* the ministry of the New Israel (beginning at *Pentecost)* was instead a ministry of *Trumpets,* a body whose fundamental purpose is prayer (to heaven above) and witness to the resurrection (testimony to the nations below).

The transformation of the Old Israel into the New required the fulfillment of the Triune Office in one Man, the High Priest of a new order, whose sacrifice ended all sacrifices (Hebrews 7:27; 10;12). Revelation thus describes Him as a *Lamb* with seven *horns* and seven *eyes,* features which symbolize the Table, the Incense Altar and the Lampstand combined in a single minister. Christ listened to His Father, acted perfectly upon what He heard, and testified accordingly. The Tabernacle architecture thus provides much of the structure for Jesus' testimony to the Pharisees in John's Gospel.

Since the Tabernacle was cross-shaped, cruciform, with the Ark and Altar as heaven and earth, and the threefold Mediator in between, it was the crucifixion

The Angel Gabriel Appearing to Zacharias (circa. 1799–1800)
William Blake

which finally linked Hearing, Ruling, and Witness—as a single process—for all men. The unity of the Triune Office in Christ is the foundation of all Church history.

As we saw in chapter 5, the deliberate separation of these three offices began in Eden with Adam's failure as a Priest, the Serpent's usurping of Adam's intended dominion as a false King, and Eve, the embodiment of Adam's future, between them.

Likewise, we see Christ, as Prophet, condemned by both Jew (Priest) and Gentile (King), and His Church eventually prey to the rebellious Jews (Herodian Priesthood) and the Romans (Neronic Kingdom).

Although Christ fulfilled the Triune Office, humbling Himself and being exalted above every name, the Adamic nature, with every encouragement from Satan, desires to pull these three apart. We focus on Hearing at the expense of Ruling and Witness, or Ruling at the expense of Hearing and Witness, or Witness at the expense of Hearing and Ruling. This internal "sacrificial" logic reveals the cause of some of our theological differences and denominational philosophies.

SACRAMENTALISM, PENTECOSTALISM, AND EVANGELISM

Sacramentalists focus on Hearing at the expense of Ruling and Witness. They want to take us back to childhood, putting us under the constraints of a written "Covenant" before calling us to new life in Jesus. For them, a Christian is one under obligation to *hear,* as

Israel was, immature children rather than qualified prophets commanded to *go and tell*. A Christian is not someone identified by personal profession but by "flesh," by blood ties (familial or tribal), all part of a picture of a Church *under* guardians instead of a Church *of* guardians. Receiving the sacraments is thus seen as equivalent to *hearing* the Word, rather than the sacraments being the means of initial and continued *testimony*. Sacramentalism is Abrahamic, relating to the Bronze Altar and the offering of the Firstfruits of the womb (Isaac). This is misguided, and in fact presents a distorted picture of the Gospel of Christ to the world. It rests upon the elementary principles *(stoicheia)*, which the Church has outgrown, and restores demarcations of obligation which Christ died to tear down. They claim to be "Trinitarian" in their worship, but horizontally at least, they focus on the Table, on getting people "into the Covenant" rather than on simply going out and telling them about Jesus. Certainly, this is "pre-Pentecostal," but focusing on Pentecost alone is also a problem.

Pentecostals focus on the Spirit, but at the expense of first listening to the Word. Because of this, they often lack biblical judgment, failing to discern between light and darkness, and it follows that "kingly" excesses such as adultery and covetousness are more common.

Adam heard from God before he was expected to Rule *with understanding*. Expecting to hear from God without first studying His Word, many Pentecostals fall prey to false spirits as Adam did. This is why the kings of Israel were commanded to copy out the Torah by their own hand. Kingdom requires wisdom.

Finally, we come to Evangelism (as distinct from evangelicalism, which arguably includes all three of these "separate tabernacles," Matthew 17:4). This "triune voice" is the true focus of the New Israel. Many Sacramentalists and Pentecostals minimize its importance and some even ridicule it as unnecessary. Baptists (for want of a broader term) get this emphasis right, yet even they often fail to see evangelism as the end of a *triune process*. Evangelism without first Hearing and Obeying the Word, and receiving the boldness of the Spirit, is not Evangelism. What is purported to be the "fragrant smoke" of faithful testimony (in both deed and word) is very often merely the product of manipulation or coercion. It is either the result of a guilt-trip *(Priestly)*, or authoritarianism *(Kingly)* rather than an outflow which is truly *Prophetic*.

So what is Evangelism that is truly *Prophetic*? A faithful Word that burns in your belly as a result of study and obedience, and bubbles over in a divine confidence, a holy boldness that resembles the lack of inhibition enjoyed by drunkards (Acts 2:13; Ephesians 5:18). This is pictured in the priestly bread and kingly wine of weekly Communion, which are united in us before we are recommissioned to a ministry of confident testimony in the world.

This process also explains the "balance" between

testimony in word and deed. Some Christians focus on the Word, and others on the deeds (such as social justice). If we apply the threefold process here, it becomes clear that we earn the right to be heard through sacrificial deeds. We put ourselves on the Altar, are animated by the fire of the Spirit, and the fragrant Gospel of Christ, already pleasing to God, is offered by Him to our hearers. In doing this, Hearing, Acting, Speaking, we are not only "living sacrifices," we are "keeping Jesus together" in the union of His Triune Office, a Prophetic body which makes redundant the blood-guilt of false Priesthood and tears down the bloodthirsty, adulterous, greedy Kings of the World as Jesus and the prophets did.

THE CROSS OF REALITY

The continual temptation is to revert to immaturity (Sacramentalism) or seize a false maturity (Pentecostalism). I am sure you will think of other applications for this process. It is everywhere in Creation because it images the Creator. But this process is also the God-given means of reuniting one with the other.

Sacramentalism is all about the earth (the Land and the womb: *Forming*). Pentecostalism is all about heaven (spiritual gifts, visions, *Filling*). But the Spirit of Christ is the Spirit of Prophecy, of the *Future*. Unity in the "horizontal" offices of the mediatory body brings "vertical" unity between heaven and earth.

Heaven

Kingdom   *Prophecy*   *Priesthood*

Ministry

Earth

9
BOWING THE HEAVENS

THY WILL ON EARTH

...who alone stretched out the heavens
and trampled the waves of the sea... (Job 9:8)

What do the Psalms mean when they speak of the Lord "bowing the heavens"?

He bowed the heavens and came down;
thick darkness was under his feet. (Psalm 18:9)

Bow thy heavens, O Lord, and come down: touch
the mountains, and they shall smoke. (Psalm 144:5)

The word "bow" is also used to describe the Lord *stretching out* the heavens like a tent in Psalm 104:2. It carries the idea of *extending* the government of heaven.

The language is architectural, based on the original cosmic "Temple" constructed in Genesis 1. The heavens and earth were created as places distinct from one another, just as God is distinct from His Creation. The duality at the very beginning of the Creation is a physical image of the *Transcendence* of God. He who initiates is *distinct* from that which is initiated, as a teacher is distinct from his class.

A division between light and darkness follows, then on Day 2 there is another putting asunder. The "heavens and earth" duality is replicated in the waters, divided into "above" and "below," an entirely physical, yet still Covenantal, heavens and earth. This act delegated *authority* to the heavens above the earth *(Hierarchy)*. The firmament was a Veil that hid the face (and intentions) of heaven from the earth. When this Veil was "torn," men came face to face with God (Genesis 7:11).

The Abrahamic "waters above" was a crystal sea, the court of angelic government, witnessed by Moses and the elders of Israel when they ascended Sinai.

> There was under his feet as it were a pavement of sapphire stone, like the very heaven for clearness. (Exodus 24:10)

Yet this crystal sea was no longer in the heavens, at least for this occasion, but temporarily upon Sinai. Seated in (or just below) His heavenly court, these representatives of Israel were free, in a preliminary sense, from the curses upon the dust of the earth.

Israel had passed through the depths of the Red Sea, the waters of the abyss, and by this baptism was being prepared for legal witness to the nations, an office of heavenly government on earth. This is what was celebrated in the divine feast atop Sinai.

This journey from the waters below to the waters

The Midianites Are Routed (1866)
Gustav Doré

above lifted up Israel as "dry land" (Genesis 1:8; Exodus 14:22). The elders were then lifted up as representatives of the "holy seed" (Genesis 1:11-12). The roles of all the people were then replicated in the architecture of the Tabernacle. The Bronze Altar imaged the earth and the Bronze Laver imaged the heavenly sea.

The request by the Psalmist to "bend" the heavens is thus a plea to bring this crystal sea down once again onto the top of Sinai, to make it smoke. In a limited sense, it calls on God to take up His warbow from the clouds once again and become a hunter of beastly men, as He did when Israel sinned. Thus we observe this sea in Ezekiel as part of the "Tabernacle" architecture as it was delegated in the war chariot of the Lord.

> Over the heads of the living creatures there was the likeness of an expanse, shining like awe-inspiring crystal, spread out above their heads. (Ezekiel 1:22)

Since the Tabernacle elements correspond to specific points in the Covenant process,[1] there is not only a symmetrical correspondence between the separation of the waters *(Division)* and their "reunion" in the Day of Coverings *(Conquest)*, there is also a correspondence between the purifying Laver in which all mediators, both human priests and animal substitutes, were washed, and the *Sanctions* (blessings and curses) of the Covenant. Those who would not be purified by the mercy of heaven would be purified from the earth.

---

[1]   See the Covenant-literary charts at the end of this book.

When mediation failed, the waters above and below would reunite in a symbolic flood. In Tabernacle terms, this is the union of the Bronze Laver "above" with the Bronze Altar "below," together forming a purifying lake of fire. This is the Day of the Lord, when Yahweh finally comes down from heaven in judgment (Genesis 11:7; Exodus 3:8; Acts 1:11; Matthew 24:37). Since it is likely that the Great Flood is the event which began volcanic activity on earth, it would be fitting— architecturally-speaking—if the initial bursting forth of the fountains of the deep was an outpouring of *boiling* water, the original "lake of fire" of the primeval cosmic Temple.[2] Likewise, Elijah "flooded" the twelve stone altar on Carmel and God made it smoke.

Like Noah, the Psalmist himself thus serves as the faithful Covenant Man who has kept the *Ethics* and is now, like Habakkuk, "suing God" to keep His part of the bargain.[3] He is asking the Lord to redeem His people and take vengeance upon His enemies. When Babylonian and Roman armies came like a flood, the Lord "touched" Zion and it smoked like Sinai.

When Israel obeys, she is enlightened and united, but the flip side for the wicked is a confusion, a thick darkness, which the Lord sends among her enemies, as He did at the battle of Midian. The eyes of the enemies are darkened, but the Bride sees God (to some

2 A terrifying fusion of hot and cold is also found in Jesus' judgment of the "kingly" church of Laodicea in Revelation 3:15-16.
3 For more discussion, see "Man Sues God" in Michael Bull, *Bible Matrix II: The Covenant Key.*

degree) with unveiled face. A request to "bow the heavens" is to bring on a Day of Judgment in which God's will is done on earth as it is in heaven. It *opens* the waters for Israel and *closes* them upon Pharaoh.

In the first century, because Jesus had finally taken humanity beyond the barrier, above the sea, the martyred saints stood upon it in a position of authority (Revelation 15:2). Like the Psalmist, they could call down Covenant curses upon the enemies of God, in this case the Circumcision (the Herodian Land Beast) and those with whom the rulers of the Land had conspired against the Church (the Gentile Sea Beast). This event took the Mosaic feast upon Sinai one step further, from just *below* the sea to just *above* it. The burning Sinaitic Altar-mountain was thrown down (Revelation 8:8), replaced by a bridal city, with the fire now *inside* it as internal Law, a slain lamb as the light of Zion. In Exodus, and indeed in the Psalms, the upper barrier of water was yet to be broken. But in the ascension of Christ, as firstborn from the dead, the waters were broken, and we are seated with Him in heavenly places. As it was at the baptism of Jesus, the heavens have been bowed *in us,* the baptized, "the camp of the saints, and the *beloved* (Davidic) city," giving us the authority to call for God's will to be done on earth as it is in heaven. The crystal sea is now a crystal city. When it finally touches down, the last enemies will be destroyed by fire, and heaven and earth will be united fully and forever (Revelation 20:9-10).

10
ROBED IN THE SEA

THE GLORY OF 'TACHASH'

Now Israel loved Joseph more than any other of his sons, because he was the son of his old age. And he made him a robe of many colors. (Genesis 37:3)

The Tabernacle was covered in three layers: an inner covering of linen, then red-dyed ramskin, and finally an outer layer of *tachash*.

But what is *tachash*? There have been many suggestions as to its meaning, from the skins of dolphins and dugongs to unicorns. But perhaps the mystery has now been solved, and this possible identity may shed light on a thread of biblical imagery meant for the eyes.

Following are some fascinating excerpts from a book entitled *Sacred Monsters: Mysterious and Mythical Creatures of Scripture, Talmud and Midrash*, by Natan Slifkin, a man known popularly as the "Zoo Rabbi." One by one, he knocks out the popular contenders for the meaning of *tachash*, and then suggests something surprising, which, since it relates to other images in the Bible, is likely the correct one.

THE TACHASH

Slifkin writes:

> Although the *re'em* is no unicorn, there is another fascinating potential unicorn mentioned in the Torah. This is the *tachash,* whose skin was used as a cover for the Tabernacle:
>
>> And rams' skins dyed red, and *tachash* skins, and acacia wood. (Exodus 25:5)
>
> The *tachash* also appears later as a material used to cover the vessels of the Tabernacle when they were transported from place to place [Numbers 4:6, 8, 10-12, 14]. We also find one other context in Scripture in which the *tachash* is mentioned, where it is described as something from which shoes were made:
>
>> I clothed you also with embroidered cloth, and shod you with *tachash,* and I girded you with fine linen and covered you with silk. (Ezekiel 16:10)
>
> Opinions differ widely as to the identity of the *tachash*. In part, this is due to the scarcity of clues given by the Torah. [One opinion, from the Talmud is] that the *tachash* was a kind of kosher animal. The Talmud proceeds to describe this as a unicorn [Talmud Yerushalmi, Shabbos 2:3]... But what was this mysterious unicorn?

Rabbi Natan Slifkin, with a black-and-white ruffed lemur.
Photo: DRosenbach

INQUIÉTUDE

One clue given by the Talmud as to the identity of the *tachash*-unicorn is that it was variegated in its coloration:

> It is translated (in Aramaic) as *sasgavna* because it glistened (or "rejoiced") in its many colors *(gavnin)*...
> [Talmud, Shabbos 28a]

After a summary of various "unicorns" of history, including the narwhal, and whether this *tachash* was a kosher animal, Slifkin continues:

> A completely different approach began with the Hebrew-English dictionary of Brown, Driver and Briggs, which traced the word *tachash* to the Arabic *tukhush* meaning porpoise. Over time, this was changed to a seal in many English Bibles, perhaps out of the desire to find a porpoise-like animal that had fur. But Canon Henry Tristram, who traveled throughout Israel in the nineteenth century as part of his efforts to research the natural history of the Bible, pointed out that the Arabic word is actually a generic term that includes not only dolphins and seals, but also the dugong. This large aquatic mammal sometimes swims up the Red Sea. Tristram cites several reports of Bedouin making sandals from the hide of dugongs, and as we saw, this is exactly what the Book of Ezekiel stated *tachash*-skin was used for. The dugong, sometimes called sea-cow, thus gained great popularity as the bearer of the name *tachash*. The German naturalist Eduard Rüppell (1794-1884) even gave the dugong the Latin name

Halicore tabernaculi—"dugong of the Tabernacle"—
and in Modern Hebrew, it bears the same name:
tachash ha-Mishkan.

But there is a difficulty with identifying the *tachash*
as the dugong. The account in Ezekiel of *tachash* hide
used in sandals seems to be referring to a decorative
upper part of the sandal, as the surrounding context
indicates:

> I clothed you also with embroidered cloth, and
> shod you with *tachash,* and I girded you with fine
> linen, and I covered you with silk. I also decked
> you with ornaments, and I put bracelets upon
> your hands, and a chain on your neck. And I put
> a ring on your nose, and earrings in your ears,
> and a beautiful crown upon your head. Thus were
> you decked with gold and silver; and your garment
> was of fine linen, and silk, and embroidered cloth;
> you ate fine flour, and honey, and oil; and you were
> very beautiful, and you were fit for royal estate.
> (Ezekiel 16:10-13)

The hide of dugongs, however, is very coarse and stiff.
This makes it ideal for the soles of sandals, but it
would hardly be a decorative upper cover to be praised
together with embroidered cloth, fine linen and silk.
And as a decorative covering for the Tabernacle, it is
singularly inappropriate.

There is a recent proposal as to the identity of the
tachash that seems the most promising of all. It has
been suggested that the word *tachash* was based on
the Akkadian *duhsu,* which refers to colored beadwork

that was often attached to leather.[1] Not only is there a case to be made for the name being a cognate (as was the basis for identifying the *tachash* as the badger, swift antelope, porpoise, seal, and dugong), but there are further varied lines of evidence to support this identification. The background to this patterned work was usually deep blue or turquoise, which fits with both the *tanyon* of Rabbi Yehudah in the Jerusalem Talmud and also the hyacinth-blue of the Septuagint. *Duhsu* beadwork was also often used in conjunction with red-dyed leather, which is exactly how the *tachash* hide was used in the Tabernacle. And beautiful sandals that were decorated with *duhsu* beadwork were found in the tomb of Tutankhamen, which supports the description in Ezekiel of beautiful *tachash*-sandals. As we saw in the Talmud Yerushalmi, there are views that the *tachash* was not an animal but rather the name of a way of decorating the rams' hides that covered the Tabernacle.

Slifkin concludes:

...Amidst the great variety of suggestions that have been offered as to the identity of the *tachash*, including the ermine, narwhal, porpoise, dugong, seal, badger, okapi, zebra, black leather, antelope, and giraffe, a very likely candidate is the far less exciting beadwork. But the truth is not always exciting.[2]

---

1   *Encyclopedia Mikra'it;* Stephanie Dalley, "Hebrew *Tahas*, Akkadian *Duhsu*, Faience and Beadwork."

2   Natan Slifkin, *Sacred Monsters: Mysterious and Mythical Creatures of Scripture, Talmud and Midrash,* 55-79.

A TRIUNE COVERING

Unlike Slifkin, I find this possible "truth" to be *very* exciting, at least once it is plugged into a biblical theology which is sensitive to images.

If the outer covering was indeed beadwork with a turquoise background over red leather, the three coverings relate to the three domains of the Tabernacle:

Garden / Most Holy:
priestly linen

___

Land / Holy Place:
ramskins dyed red

___

World-Sea / Bronze Laver:
variegated beadwork

The High Priest wore **linen** on the annual Day of Coverings, standing in the open veil before the Ark of the Testimony to sprinkle blood for the priesthood and people. This is the domain of the Father.

The priestly linen represents Adam's death in the Garden, or at least the death which he deserved. The whiteness relates to biblical "leprosy," which is scaled skin like a covering of dust. These are all serpentine symbols.[3] The burial clothes which were discarded by

3   For more discussion, see "Scales of Justice" in Michael Bull, *Sweet Counsel: Essays to Brighten the Eyes.*

INQUIÉTUDE

Christ picture for us the removal of the "shining" skin of the serpent, an uncovering of the angelic deception.

> The Hebrew word rendered "serpent" in Genesis 3:1 is *Nachash* (from the root *Nachash, to shine),* and means *a shining one.* Hence, in Chaldee it means brass or copper, because of its *shining.* Hence also, the word *Nehushtan,* a piece of brass, in 2 Kings 18:4.[4]

Saul's first victory was the defeat of "Nahash" the king of Ammon. Goliath of Gath is also presented as such a shining serpent, one who desired to curse Israel:

> He had a helmet of bronze on his head, and he was armed with a coat of *mail* [literally "scales"], and the weight of the coat was five thousand shekels of bronze. And he had bronze armor on his legs, and a javelin of bronze slung between his shoulders.
> (1 Samuel 17:5-6)

This is also background for the scales which fell from the eyes of Paul, a man who, like Satan, presented as an angel (messenger) of light with a false Gospel— circumcision—on his mission to slay the Bride. He who defeats the serpent is robed in white, the skin removed from the serpent.

> And as he prayed, the appearance of his countenance was altered, and his clothing was white and glistening." (Luke 9:29, King James 2000 Bible)

---

4   E. W. Bullinger, *The Companion Bible,* Appendix 19.

Ramskins represented the threefold sacrifice of the firstborn, Isaac *(Presentation:* Genesis 22:13), all Israel *(Purification:* Exodus 4:22), and the Levites who substituted for all the firstborn of Israel as a kind of "firstborn from the dead," resurrected and able to serve in the court of God *(Transformation:* Numbers 3:12). Since Adam and Eve were clothed in animal skin before they could enter into the Land and conceive children, the skins of the sacrifices were given to the Levite priests' (Leviticus 7:8). The red ramskins speak of the threefold office of the Son as a living sacrifice.

Faithfulness in the Garden results in a white robe *(Priesthood:* Luke 9:29; Revelation 19:8). Dominion over the Land results in a robe dyed red, or dipped in blood *(Kingdom:* Matthew 27:28; Revelation 17:4; 19:13). Detailed beadwork, however resembles a gathering or "host" of scales, a variegated or "rainbow" covering *(Prophecy:* Genesis 9:13; Revelation 4:3; 10:1).

The **tachash** thus represents the ministry of the Spirit, the promise of dominion over the World. He who defeats the *nachash* must be splashed with blood to wear the *tachash.* The High Priest wore linen on the Day of Atonement, since He had to sprinkle blood. But when finished he was reinvested with robes of glory, which included the variegated colors of the gemstones of the breastplate, the glory of the tribes of Israel. This "Aaronic" dominion over the tribes was the "Land" version of Jesus' coming dominion over the nations through a reinvested Noahic order of Melchizedek.

INQUIÉTUDE

The glory of the king of kings is a white robe refracted through a glass, a crystal city, into bridal rainbow colors. Adam's purity is white light. Eve's glory is multicolored. The ministry begun in Eve must become global. The woman in the Garden is destined to become a city in the World. This is why the Bible speaks not only of serpents but also of dragons.

DINOSAUR SKIN

Since serpents are generally "Land" animals, creatures to be kept from the Garden, the *tachash* must represent the integrated (Forming) and colorful (Filling) skin of a beast which ruled the Land and Sea. Pharaoh is likened to such a beast in Ezekiel 32:

> "Son of man, raise a lamentation over Pharaoh king of Egypt and say to him: 'You consider yourself a lion of the nations, but you are like a dragon in the seas; you burst forth in your rivers, trouble the waters with your feet, and foul their rivers. Thus says the Lord God: I will throw my net over you with a host of many peoples, and they will haul you up in my dragnet.'" (Ezekiel 32:-3)

Many assume this beast to be a modern crocodile, but numerous remains of something larger have been discovered. The *sarcosuchus imperator* ("flesh crocodile emperor") weighed up to ten tons, had a 1.8 meter long skull with over a hundred teeth, scales like roofing tiles, and a bulbous structure at the end of its snout

The Destruction of Leviathan (1865)
Gustav Doré

with an enormous cavity under the nostrils. This could have been part of a biological mechanism to produce flames and smoke, as does the bombardier beetle. If so, this beast, often referred to as "Supercroc," is possibly the Leviathan of Job 41, a *fire-breathing* dragon.

> I will not keep silence concerning his limbs,
> or his mighty strength, or his goodly frame.
> Who can strip off his outer garment?
> Who would come near him with a bridle?
> Who can open the doors of his face?
> Around his teeth is terror.
> His back is made of rows of shields,
> shut up closely as with a seal.
> One is so near to another
> that no air can come between them.
> They are joined one to another;
> they clasp each other and cannot be separated.
> His sneezings flash forth light,
> and his eyes are like the eyelids of the dawn.
> Out of his mouth go flaming torches;
> sparks of fire leap forth.
> Out of his nostrils comes forth smoke,
> as from a boiling pot and burning rushes.
> His breath kindles coals,
> and a flame comes forth from his mouth.
> In his neck abides strength,
> and terror dances before him.
> The folds of his flesh stick together,
> firmly cast on him and immovable.
> His heart is hard as a stone,
> hard as the lower millstone.

In social terms, a dragon is a "corporate" serpent, the lie in the Garden rising from the dust on new legs in multiple nations *gathered together* by this deception. This was the situation before the flood, and the potential situation in the Tower of Babel. In festal terms, it is the inversion of the Feast of Booths: not the nations bringing their "variegated" glory into the Temple of God, but the nations gathering "on the sand of the sea" as a single army against the Church. The progression from serpent to dragon, from Land to Sea, is thus a progression of dominion. Remy Wilkins writes:

> My thesis is that the two words which my online sources transliterate as *nachash* (serpent) and *tanniyn* (dragon) are not interchangeable, but that it shows a progression. Serpents are little dragons over which man receives dominion early on, but man must wait before dominion over dragons, giant serpents, can be achieved.
>
> In the Creation account, God makes seven categories of creatures, the teemers (fish), the birds, dragons *(tanniyn)*, cattle, creepies, beasts, and man. There are some deep waters here, since the teemers *(sherets)* and creepies *(remes)* seem to be interchangeable, perhaps because some sea creatures creep (shrimp and crabs).

Genesis 1:26 says:

> Then God said, "Let us make man in our image, after our likeness. And let them have dominion over the fish of the sea and over the birds of the heavens and over the livestock and over all the earth and over every creeping thing that creeps on the earth."

Wilkins notes that the dragons *and* the beasts of the earth are missing from this particular list, and the list in Genesis 1:28 does not mention the beasts of the earth explicitly, and dragons are entirely omitted.

> Perhaps beasts are not explicitly mentioned because to tame a lion is much more difficult than to tame a cow. Dominion is always a work in progress, so some things come farther down the line than others. Both the beasts and particularly the dragons are at different levels of difficulty.

Wilkins then notes that in Genesis 9:2, concerning Noah, the cattle are left off the list presumably because they were by now domesticated. Unlike Genesis 1:28, here the beasts of the earth are now under Covenant, but the dragons are still out of reach. He then moves from Genesis to Exodus, where a similar pattern appears:

> A curious event happens in Exodus that needs to be considered. In Exodus 4, God tells Moses to cast his rod down and it becomes a serpent *(nachash)*. In Exodus 7 in the showdown with Pharaoh and his magicians, Moses tells Aaron to throw down his rod and it becomes a dragon *(tanniyn)*, though your Bible may translate it serpent.
>
> Pharaoh's men cast down their rods and they too become *tanniyn,* but we know they are smaller because Aaron's rod swallows them.
>
> In verse 15, God tells Moses to take his rod, which turned into a serpent *(nachash)* and to smite the river. So Moses' rod turns into a serpent, but Aaron's

turns into a dragon. I'm not sure why. But it does fit the pattern of serpents first, then dragons.

Dragons seem to be beyond man's ability to deal with. God asks Job (in chapter 41) if he can handle Leviathan, the great sea beast, and the answer is clearly no. But in Psalm 74 we learn that Yahweh breaks the dragons and feeds us the meat of Leviathan. Moreover, there are hints that things will change. Psalm 91:13 says: "Thou shalt tread upon the lion and adder: the young lion and the dragon shalt thou trample under feet" [KJV]. While this primarily refers to Christ, we no doubt partake of this in Him.

Wilkins then notes that Psalm 8 also speaks of a time when dragons would be under the foot of Man.

The verse that connects serpent to dragon is Isaiah 27:1, where Leviathan is described as a serpent:

> In that day the Lord with his hard and great and strong sword will punish Leviathan the fleeing serpent, Leviathan the twisting serpent, and he will slay the dragon that is in the sea.

We learn from the Greek testament that Satan is the serpent of old and the dragon of later. In the Hebrew testament, even though serpents are afflictions, they are under man's feet, but man does not mess with dragons until Jesus comes.

The change from serpent to dragon also means a change in tactics. The serpent seeks to win through deceit, but the dragon through violence. The serpent lies then tries to devour, which is a perversion of the

Word then Food pattern. He lies then tries to devour us, whereas Jesus speaks the truth and feeds us.[5]

The process of maturity in the saints is replicated, or perverted, in the maturity of sin. Both holiness and sin grow and bear fruit. So the move from serpent to dragon is the maturation of the demonic. All sin begins with a lie. Ideas have consequences. Ideas take on a body. False ideas, if heeded, eventually cause carnage.

THE TYRANT KING

As discussed, the dragon is a *corporate* serpent, a body gathered to "incarnate" his lie, a false Church-State— the sin of Eden grown to full maturity expressed in open rebellion against God. In the Revelation, the serpent deceives the Woman and attempts to devour her children as a dragon. The seed of the serpent multiplied against the multiplied seed of the Woman.

What, then, is the significance of this "dragon" robe upon the Tabernacle? I suggest that it has the same meaning as the multicolored robe given by Jacob to Joseph, a robe of office which conferred not only Covenant authority but also a promise of Covenant *Succession*. Thus, Joseph's rule in Egypt was the third "layer" of the dominion of the patriarchs:

---

5   Compiled from comments by Remy Wilkins on the Biblical Horizons forum in 2011. Reproduced with permission.

Garden / Most Holy:
SERPENT (Adam - Purity - Word)
**Abram plants trees, and rescues Sarai from
Pharaoh, the serpent king, by outcrafting him**

Land / Holy Place:
SHEPHERDS (Cain - Sacrifice - Sacrament)
**Isaac's firstborn wears animal skins, is named Edom
("red") and like Cain attempts to murder his brother
after Jacob outcrafts him**

World-Sea / Bronze Laver:
DRAGON (Noah - Dominion - Government)
**Joseph is the wisest man in all Egypt, who through
faith becomes a blessing to all nations, and
outcrafts his brothers to test their hearts**

The success of the patriarchs moves from the domain of the father (Abraham), to his sons, to a man who is filled with the Spirit, who not only becomes wiser than a serpent, but also subdues and gathers "all nations" in his realm, who bring their riches to him that they might be saved. Joseph is the Tree of Life (Priesthood) and the Tree of Knowledge (Kingdom) combined as a Tree of Righteousness (Prophecy). This brings us to the significance of Joseph's bones as the foundation for a new "bridal" Israel.

The Egyptians despised the Hebrews since they were

shepherds, alluding once again to Cain's hatred of Abel, and of Joseph's brothers' jealousy of his dreams and his authority. So, like Joseph's original robe, this covering of beadwork was a *promise* of dominion:

Garden / White Linen: **The bones of Joseph**

Land / Ramskin: **The priesthood of Levi**

World-Sea / *Tachash:* **The armies of Israel**

The promises to Abraham were fulfilled in the glory of the hosts of Israel and their possession of the Land.

> Thus the Lord gave to Israel all the land that he swore to give to their fathers. And they took possession of it, and they settled there. And the Lord gave them rest on every side just as he had sworn to their fathers. Not one of all their enemies had withstood them, for the Lord had given all their enemies into their hands. Not one word of all the good promises that the Lord had made to the house of Israel had failed; all came to pass. (Joshua 21:43-45)

Since the dragon is a "corporate serpent," only a "corporate Adam," the Bride, has a footprint great enough to subdue it. A *totus Diabolus* can only be crushed by the *totus Christus,* so this promise of dominion is of course finally fulfilled in Jesus and His Church.

Jesus crushed the serpent in the Garden, but the defeated serpent formed an army of false brothers in the Land (the Judaizers), and eventually called up a beast from the Sea, gathering Jew and Gentile against the Jew-Gentile Church. This "variegated" dragon was defeated by the Firstfruits Church—a "variegated" or corporate foot (Romans 16:20).

The movement from deception, via legislation, to violence is craftily employed by God as an "eye for eye" judgment upon the evil one. Satan was deceived and defeated at the cross (Garden), then a strong delusion was sent upon those who rejected the Pentecostal Spirit (Land). Finally, Jesus gathered the Roman armies, and the beast devoured not the true bride but the false one (World).

Even though this first century pattern was indeed threefold, this Abrahamic "World" of the *oikoumene* was representative of an even greater world. On a global scale, Jesus' death and resurrection in the Garden (AD30) led to the death and resurrection of Israel (AD70), and will finally lead to the resurrection of all the Japhethite nations. Revelation 20 describes the final gathering of the nations against the people of God.

BEAUTIFUL FEET

After each conquest, the victorious Adam invites His Bride as co-regent to place her foot upon the neck of the defeated serpent. In Joshua 10:22-26, after the king of Jerusalem gathered five other kings to fight with him against Israel, Joshua's men rolled away the stones from the cave in which they were hidden and then trapped (Garden), placed their feet upon their necks (Land), then hung them from trees until evening and threw their bodies back into the cave (World). In Christ, the Bride is given not only the wisdom to judge angels, but the authority to execute them.

Since detailed beadwork represents the scales of serpents and dragons, the sandals covered in *tachash* in Ezekiel 16 are the biblical equivalent of crocodile skin shoes. The Bride of Christ plunders all the glorious attributes of the beasts through the *Ethical* work of the Spirit. The beadwork shoes are the feet of Eve, who stands on the neck of the enemy, and walks on the sea.

This explains Revelation 20's use of imagery from the book of Esther and its prediction in Ezekiel 38-39. Haman gathered all nations against the people of God, Gog and Magog, but was defeated by the Bride of the King of Kings. Whereas the elders of Israel saw their God with a pavement of sapphire under his Priestly feet, "like the very heaven for clearness" (Exodus 24:10), the court of Ahasuerus is described as a crystal sea of variegated color, "a mosaic pavement of porphyry, marble, mother-of-pearl and precious stones" (Esther 1:6). Esther's approach to the throne through this multinational court brought rest to Israel in every province.

The beadwork is a glorious "bridal" body of all nations, like the gemstones of the High Priest, but drawn from the Sea as well as the Land, gathered not by a lie but through worship in spirit and truth.

PRESENTATION

11

THE MEANING OF MANGER

A CHILD FOR THE BEAST

"For my flesh is true food, and my blood is true drink."
(John 6:55)

In English, the word *manger* is archaic, preserved for us by the Christmas tradition. In French, the word is still in use, being the infinitive "to eat." As with every detail in the Scriptures, the fact that the One who would give Himself to us in the elements of a meal was placed in a food trough invites contemplation.

BIRDS AND BEASTS

Firstly, there is the significance of this infant's cradle being a food trough for *animals*. The Covenant curse repeated throughout the Old Testament was the threat that one would be slain and left for the scavengers, the birds and the beasts, instead of being buried in the Land. What is the meaning of this? That the dead would be "scattered" instead of "gathered" to the fathers

INQUIÉTUDE

(Genesis 25:8; 35:29).[1] Gathering is the work of the husbandman and the shepherd. Indeed, the final annual feast in Leviticus 23 is Tabernacles, otherwise known as Booths and *Ingathering*. It corresponds to the *Succession* step of the Covenant pattern, arrangements for either future generations, or the future itself. The wicked are scattered, cut off and have no future.[2]

The Levitical curses for disobeying the Law included the threat of the wild beasts returning to the Land and devouring Israel's children. This is the reason for Elisha's calling of bears upon the children of Bethel, a town which was a center of false worship.[3]

Of course, the beasts which use a manger are not wild beasts but *domesticated* beasts, animals from the Land, servants of Man, rather than animals from the "Sea," or the World, which were yet to be tamed. These animals symbolized faithful Israelites, and a "priestly" selection of these served as sacrificial substitutes. The placement of the incarnate Son in a manger not only freed faithful Israelites from the Covenant curse, and Levites from priestly service, it freed the domestic animals from the continual bondage of slaughter for sin. Here was the first blameless man, an individual fit for sacrifice, entirely without blemish, one who would

---

1   For more discussion, see "Birds and Beasts" in Michael Bull, *God's Kitchen: Theology You Can Eat & Drink*.
2   See the Covenant-literary charts at the end of this book.
3   For more discussion, see "I Will Kill Her Children With Death" in Michael Bull, *Sweet Counsel: Essays to Brighten the Eyes*.

A stone trough in Tel Megiddo, Israel, which sits above the Jezreel Valley, indicating that horses and chariots were kept here. However, the domestic manger in Bethlehem would have been situated in the family room of the house, where some of the animals would be taken to spend the night.

make "human sacrifices" acceptable to God in the ministry of the Apostolic Church.

The manger was thus a miniature altar, but also a *reversal* of the ministry of the altar. Here was the true Isaac, the firstfruits of the womb of the Woman, lifted up as the firstfruits of the Land. Being blameless, He would taste death, but would not see corruption. He would be consumed, but not by the birds and the beasts. Jesus would be gathered first to the true fathers, then, once enthroned, He would gather the true sons. Those who would not eat His flesh and drink His blood would indeed be eaten by the birds and beasts, the armies and looters which ransacked Jerusalem seventy years later (Revelation 19:11-21).

BREAD AND WINE

The fruit in the Garden was ready to eat, but the grain and grapes of the Land required the contribution of godly men, the labor and wisdom of the sons of Adam. Abel was as shepherd, and Cain a husbandman. Abel offered the fruit of the flock to cover the curse on the womb, and Cain's offering covered the curse on the Land. The murder of Abel by Cain reversed the ministry of substitution, as did the murder of Christ by His false brothers. The relationship of flesh and blood to bread and wine begins in the earliest chapters of the Bible.

Indeed, we can trace it back further. Bread is morning food, providing energy for work, and wine is evening food, bringing on rest. Bread and wine are thus the culinary sign of a new beginning: morning and evening, light and darkness. It is no coincidence that the blood of Passover and of Atonement was presented in the darkness, where only the eyes of the Lord could see. The two trees in the center of the Garden were "Sanctuary" versions of bread and wine, which is why consuming the fruit of the second tree would "open" one's eyes as a judge between good and evil, light and darkness. The Lord's table is not food for children, but for wise judges whose eyes have been opened by the Spirit of God. Those who allow children at the Lord's table commit a grievous error. Their sin is an image of that committed in the Garden, a grasping of Kingdom before God's time.

> When he was at table with them, he took the bread and blessed and broke it and gave it to them. And their eyes were opened, and they recognized him. And he vanished from their sight. They said to each other, "Did not our hearts burn within us while he talked to us on the road, while he opened to us the Scriptures?" (Luke 24:30-32)

The scales of judgment carried by the third horseman in the Revelation condemn the "grain" of the Old Covenant and protect the "oil and wine" of the New (Revelation 6:5-6). Bread pictures the daily work of the priests, those who stand in God's house and wait upon Him as servants, cooks and butlers. Oil and wine are for kings and prophets, those invited to sit enthroned and dine with God. Throughout the Aaronic era, although the priests ate meat and bread from the sacrifices, they never drank wine in God's presence. It was poured out like blood.[4] No one drank with God until Christ offered both bread and wine to His disciples and promised that they would sit on twelve thrones and judge Israel. As with the exaltation of Christ, their own exaltation would require humiliation and death. This is what the book of Revelation is all about. The firstfruits Church is harvested as grain and grapes (Revelation 14:14-20) and later enthroned as the Bride, co-regents of the New Covenant (Revelation 19:9; 20:4).[5]

This process of Priesthood and Kingdom, humility and exaltation, morning and evening, light and darkness, is the biblical backdrop surrounding the manger in Bethlehem. *Beth-lechem* means "house of bread." A manger is a place for grain and similar fruits of the Land. It is not the place for either grapes or wine. The elements of the narrative are all consistent with Priesthood, with the immaturity of the Old Covenant and its guidelines for "children." The Christ would have to grow into a Man for there to be wine, and wine was the product of His first miracle (John 2:11).

After His baptism, Jesus was thrown by the Spirit into the wilderness, tempted with bread and with

4   For more discussion, see "The Forbidden Feast" in Michael Bull, *God's Kitchen: Theology You Can Eat & Drink.*
5   Most, if not all, of these observations are from James B. Jordan, *From Bread to Wine, Toward a More Biblical Liturgical Theology.*

tainted offers of Kingdom and Prophecy, and threatened by wild beasts (Mark 1:12-13). After gathering His disciples and a ministry of testimony and suffering, His blood would be offered in a noonday of darkness, visible to the eyes of the Father and His true sons.

The manger was a sign to Jews, to a nation of shepherds and husbandmen (Luke 2:12). It was the showbread offered to all by the house of David.[6] The Gentile *magi* did not need to see the child in a manger wrapped in cloths. They did not come to see a priest but a king, a monarch who was nothing like the Herods, a ruler who would shepherd Israel like priestly Abel, and not devour them like beastly Cain (Matthew 2:16; Revelation 13:11).

As did Cain, the Herods and Pharisees would lose their fields and vineyards, (Genesis 4:12; Matthew 21:33-46; Mark 12:1-12; Luke 20:9-19) which would instead be given to nation that would bear the "fruits" God requires first: not the fruit of the womb or the Land, but the fruits of the Spirit.

---

6   David is twice described as "ruddy" of face, a word which means "blood-filled," a fulfillment of the Table in the Tabernacle, a kingly firstfruits of the priestly nation.

12
UNCIRCUMCISED JEWS

BRIDEGROOM OF BLOOD

At that time the Lord said to Joshua, "Make flint knives and circumcise the sons of Israel a second time." (Joshua 5:2)

Was Israel disobedient in its failure to circumcise every male born in the wilderness (Joshua 5:1-9)? Israel was not chastised, so what was the purpose in the plan of God for this lapse in the practice?

Since Israel's forty years in the wilderness were preceded by Moses' own forty years in the wilderness, the circumcision of Gershom, the firstborn son of Moses (Exodus 4:24-26), might hold the answer.

The account follows the Lord's threat against the firstborn of Pharaoh, thus the "him" whom the Lord sought to kill was not Moses but Gershom, but the ambiguity reminds us of Moses' own deliverance from Pharaoh. The inn in verse 24 is "a halting place for the night." Like Passover, the attempted slaying of the son took place in the darkness.

INQUIÉTUDE

TRANSCENDENCE
And it came to pass *(Genesis - origins)*
   on the road *(Exodus - journey)*
      at the lodge, *(Leviticus - house)*
         and encountered him *(Numbers - sight)*
        the Lord *(Deuteronomy - legal authority)*
      and sought *(Joshua - mission/mediation)*
to kill him. *(Judges - rest & rule forfeited)*
HIERARCHY
Then took Zipporah *(Initiation)*
   a sharp stone *(Delegation)*
      and cut off *(Presentation - Altar)*
      the foreskin *(Firstfruits - Table)*
         of her son *(Purification - Peace)*
      and struck it *(Transformation - Plague/"stroke")*
   at his feet, *(Vindication - Cleansing)*
and said, *(Representation)*
ETHICS
"Truly, *(Transcendence)*
   a son-in-law *(Hierarchy)*
      of blood-guilt *(Ethics)*
   you are *(Oath/Sanctions)*
to me." *(Succession)*
OATH/SANCTIONS
So He withdrew *(Sabbath)*
   from him *(Passover)*
      at that time. *(Firstfruits)*
SUCCESSION
She said, *(Transcendence)*
   "a son-in-law *(Hierarchy)*
      of bloodguilt" *(Ethics)*
   because-of-the-circumcision. *(Oath/Sanctions)*
(No Succession)

The fact that the son was *not* slain reminds us of the offering of Isaac. Each event was a deliberate "passing over." But the missing *Succession* also reminds us that the inheritance promised to Abraham had not yet been possessed. Canaan (the fruit of the Land) was bound by Covenant to circumcision (the fruit of the womb).

After the birth of Ishmael, Abraham was rescued from oblivion by circumcision. This circumcision was a prelude to the cutting off of Sodom. Likewise the circumcision of Moses' son was a prelude to the cutting off of Egypt.[1]

The Bible Matrix pattern can be identified in each era of Moses' life, and in all three there is some kind of atoning blood at *Division* and again at *Conquest*.

Pharaoh slaughtered Hebrew infants, but Moses was spared. He was *trained* as a Gentile, and this period ended in the bloodshed of the guilty Egyptian. His people, who had been worshiping the gods of Egypt, rejected him, and there was no rest from their slavery.

Pharaoh then sought to kill Moses, but he fled and *lived* as a Gentile under the godly ministry of Jethro, a tribal Priest-King after the order of Melchizedek. The circumcision of Gershom is the "Passover" of the pattern between Moses' call and his return to the mountain of God.[2]

The cutting off of Egypt and the cutting off of Jericho are the bookends to the corporate un-circumcision of

---

1   James B. Jordan, *Lot*, Biblical Horizons No. 116.
2   See Appendix 2.

Israel. The sons born in the wilderness needed to be circumcised, but it would be a "new" circumcision. Hence the Lord refers to it as "a second time." The old house was now entirely cut off.

> When the circumcising of the whole nation was finished, they remained in their places in the camp until they were healed. And the Lord said to Joshua, "Today I have rolled away the reproach of Egypt from you." And so the name of that place is called Gilgal to this day. (Joshua 5:8,9).

The reproach of Egypt was sourced in Israel's uncircumcised, Canaanite heart. The reinstitution after each lapse coincides with a new circumcision of Israel's hearts, followed by a *Conquest* in which Israel possesses the riches of her enemies. At this point we must remember the curses of Noah upon Ham's son Canaan in Genesis 9. In Egypt, Israel's God conquered "the Land of Ham" (Psalm 78:51; 105:23,27; 106:22; 1 Chronicles 4:40), the domain of *the father*. In the conquest of Canaan, beginning with Jericho, under the Captain of the Lord's hosts, Israel took possession of the domain of *the son*.

The act of seizing an inheritance (Kingdom) before God's time was not only the sin of Ham but the sin of Cain and the sin of Adam. The reproach of Egypt was a failure not only to distrust Egypt's gods, but to trust the true God and "go up" to possess the Land.

The lapse by Moses and the lapse by Israel were both

The Firstborn of the Egyptians are Slain (1866)
Gustav Doré

129

related to the death of the old "carnal" Israel and the birth of a new, "spiritual" one. The old circumcision *itself* had to be cut off.

So, incredibly, this "uncircumcision" entailed the *death* of the Covenant with Abraham, an *end* to the era of the patriarchs, and its restitution as a kind of "new Covenant" under Moses and Joshua. The husks of faithless old Israel were "threshed" in the wilderness, harvesting a new seed, one with the *faith* of Abraham.

Joshua and Caleb were the only remaining faithful "leaven" from the old circumcision. All the "Isaacs" who were rescued at the Passover were now dead. So this leaven of Joshua could be put into new "meal."

The result of this new circumcision was Israel's qualification to "cut off all flesh" in Jericho as a Firstfruits of the Land. Israel was circumcised and his reproach "rolled away" like the stone sealing a tomb. The children of Abraham then "circumcised" the city of Jericho, cutting around it for seven days. The walls fell and the army cut off all flesh.

During the exile in Babylon there was a similar lapse. The Aaronic Priesthood was cut off. Genealogies were of little importance, and many Israelites took Canaanite wives who did not convert. In Ezra, it is no longer merely the priests, but all Israel, for whom genealogy suddenly became important. For this "new Covenant" with Israel and Judah (Jeremiah 31:31-40), physical descent was crucial for every Israelite male who wished to partake in Israel's revived ministry under a new Aaronic Priesthood established in Joshua, who is rendered clean in Zechariah 3. His filthy garments are removed (deconsecration) and he is given new ones (reconsecration).

When we get to the New Covenant in the blood of Jesus, we have an even sharper fulfillment of this "un-circumcision" and "recircumcision," one which did away with the import of genealogy *altogether*. Heart circumcision, that is, faith, became the *sign* of the Covenant rather than merely its goal.

> For no one is a Jew who is merely one outwardly, nor is circumcision outward and physical. But a Jew is one inwardly, and circumcision is a matter of the heart, by the Spirit, not by the letter. His praise is not from man but from God. (Romans 2:28-29)

If we superimpose the 40 years of wandering onto the 40 years from AD30-70, the final generation of Israel according to the flesh, we can see that it is the Jews who followed a Herodian Pharaoh who were cut off, and the uncircumcised "new Israel," that is, the Jew-Gentile Church, the *re*-generation, who inherited the promises. This sheds some light on Paul's use of Hagar (Egypt) and Sarah (Canaan) to argue against any remaining significance of circumcision in his letter to the Galatians.

What is the principle here? Moses could not judge Pharaoh until the Egyptian heart in Moses was cut off in the wilderness. Israel could not judge Canaan until the Canaanite heart in Israel was cut off in the wilderness. David could not inherit Saul's kingdom until the "uncircumcised" heart of Saul in David was cut off in the wilderness. Adam could not rule the beasts until the beastly heart of Adam was cut off. Christ could not judge the world until Christ was handed over to the Gentiles, and cut off for the world.

In every case, the first "cutting" was a prelude to a greater one. The Man, or the people, pass *under* the sword that he or they might be qualified to *bear* the sword. Each death was the "deconsecration" of the old order, rendering it unclean, that a greater one might be established.[3] In Christ, not only the old Aaronic Priesthood died, but also the Adamic heart.

So, how was a "second circumcision" established before the "cutting off" of Jerusalem? It was certainly not a revival of Abrahamic circumcision, since the "seed" had come and ascended to heaven. What bloody event occurred just before the destruction of the last Canaanite city, the Jerusalem of the Herods? It was the slaughter of the Apostolic Church, the true sons of Abraham, outside the city walls, those who were the "firstfruits" for God and the Lamb (Revelation 14:4).

3   See Appendix 3.

13

INNER PARTS

THE MISSING HEART

"For the life of the flesh is in the blood..." (Leviticus 17:11)

Why does the book of Leviticus never mention the hearts of the sacrificial animals? Peter Leithart writes:

Ancient Israelites offered the inner organs of sacrificial animals—entrails, kidneys, a portion of the liver. The heart is never mentioned. In all of the complicated sacrificial instructions of Leviticus, the word *leb* never appears, even once. We learn what happens to the stomach (Deuteronomy 18:3) but not the heart.

This is all the odder when we realize that the heart is often associated with one of the sacrificed organs—the kidneys *(kilyah).* Yahweh examines heart and kidneys (Psalm 7:9), tests the mind and heart (Psalm 26:2); when the Psalmist's heart is embittered, it is as if something has pierced his kidneys (Psalm 73:21; cf. Jeremiah 17:10; 20:12).

And it is odd because the heart is so central to Hebraic anthropology. Out of it come the issues of

133

life (Proverbs), and Israel is commanded to be devoted to Yahweh with the heart (Deuteronomy 6:5). What better way to express this than to offer the heart ceremoniously into the altar fire?

Perhaps the heart is implied in the *qereb,* the "inner parts" that are placed on the altar (the "inner parts" and heart are juxtaposed in, e.g., Psalm 64:6). Even so, why not make it explicit?

No theories here. Only questions.[1]

The answer to Leithart's very good question concerning the "missing heart" might be found in the layout of the Tabernacle. The three articles of furniture in the Holy Place picture a union between heaven and earth through the falling of holy fire and the "ascension" of sacrificial smoke as a "ladder" or tower. The Table is the flesh, the Lampstand is the fire, and the Incense Altar is the smoke. These three not only represent the *Ethical* steps in the Covenant process, they also picture the offices of Priest, King and Prophet, a microcosm of the Old Testament, united as one in the Christ.

To relate this to "sacrificial" anatomy (the animals and humans of Day 6), we should notice the sacred architecture inherent in the text which describes the Creation of Adam. It not only recapitulates the "Forming and Filling" of the Creation Week, it prefigures both the furniture of the Tabernacle and the rite of sacrifice:

1   Peter J. Leithart, *Heartless,* First Things blog, May 31, 2014.

INITIATION – *Animal Chosen*
Creation: "...then the Lord God *(Sabbath)*

  DELEGATION – *Animal Cut*
  Division: formed the man *(Passover)*

    PRESENTATION – *Flesh and Blood*
    Ascension: of dust from the ground *(Firstfruits)*

      PURIFICATION – *Fire*
      Testing: and breathed into his nostrils
      (Pentecost)

    TRANSFORMATION – *Smoke*
    Maturity: the breath of life, *(Trumpets)*

  VINDICATION – *Acceptable Savor*
  Conquest: and the man became *(Atonement)*

REPRESENTATION – *Land and Womb opened anew*
Glorification: a living creature." *(Booths)*

(Genesis 2:7)

If the heart were to be identified in this passage, where would it feature? It seems that "all flesh" would correspond to the Bronze Altar. (On the stone altars before the establishment of the Levitical law, it was indeed *all flesh* which was consumed. Men did not eat with God.) Adam's lungs were filled in a prefiguring of Pentecost. Only then did he become a living being.

Perhaps the reason the heart is not mentioned is because the Lord will not separate it from the lungs. The central three *"Ethical"* steps of this Covenant-Man are a symbolic union of heaven and earth, dust from below *(Ascension)* and "spirit" from above *(Testing)*. They result in the first use of a human windpipe as an instrument *(Maturity)*. Only after this Priest-King-Prophet process occurred did Adam's heart beat.

The Babylonian Talmud, however, *does* refer to the heart. It is attached to the lungs and the windpipe.

> HE HOLLOWED OUT THE BREAST AND GAVE IT TO THE ONE TO WHOSE LOT IT HAD FALLEN. HE CAME TO THE RIGHT FLANK AND CUT INTO IT AS FAR AS THE SPINE, WITHOUT HOWEVER TOUCHING THE SPINE, UNTIL HE CAME TO THE PLACE BETWEEN TWO SMALL RIBS. HE CUT IT OFF AND GAVE IT TO THE ONE TO WHOSE LOT IT HAD FALLEN, WITH THE LIVER ATTACHED TO IT. HE THEN CAME TO THE NECK, AND LEAVING TWO RIBS ON EACH SIDE OF IT HE CUT IT OFF AND GAVE IT TO THE ONE TO WHOSE LOT IT HAD FALLEN, WITH THE WINDPIPE AND THE HEART AND THE LUNG ATTACHED TO IT.[2]

The Tabernacle layout is humaniform (and indeed cruciform), so Adam's torso and arms correspond to the Holy Place. The heart, which is situated slightly to the left of the human body, would correspond to the Golden Table, which symbolizes the Firstfruits offered to God (flesh and blood, bread and wine). The Lampstand is the receiver of breath, the "fire" of heaven, the

---

2   Babylonian Talmud, Tractate Tamid 31a, Soncino 1961 Edition, 23-24.

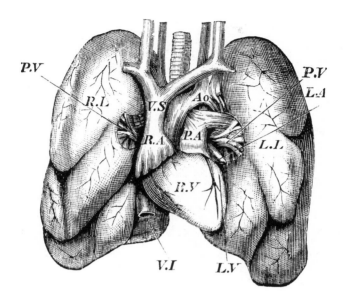

Law-Spirit of God, and thus is the windpipe. But there are two lungs, not just one, so the Tabernacle imagery breaks down. Or does it? Forming results in Filling. The filled lungs picture "the house filled with smoke," two legal witnesses, the clouds of incense as the testimony of a good conscience, the fragrant witness of an accepted sacrifice, the law written on two tablets of flesh. Indeed, after his deep "sacrificial" sleep, Adam's first spoken words name his bride.

The heart is not missing but is "one flesh" with the lungs, an indivisible tryst, a *marriage* between dust and air, an ascension from earth to heaven by the Spirit.

137

INQUIÉTUDE

> "...the heart in biblical physiology [is] the seat of understanding rather than of feeling."[3]

The life is in the blood, but that earthly life is sourced in heaven. The blood is the *mediator* which makes life possible, and must never be consumed, but like the wine on the table, poured out as water (Numbers 28:7; Deuteronomy 12:16, 24; 15:23).

It is believed that Jesus collapsed under the weight of the cross due to hypovolemic shock after being flogged. Low blood pressure causes the heart to race, which in turn gathers fluid in the sack around the heart and around the lungs. When the Roman soldier thrust the spear into Jesus' side, he pierced both the lungs and heart, "the heavens and the earth," *together.* Blood and water, "Land and Sea," came from His side (John 19:34). The end came with a flood.

The blood is forbidden because it is "Ichabod," a sacrificial testimony to the "ghost" leaving the house of flesh. By faith, the flesh and blood of submission become the bread and wine of dominion (Matthew 4:4; John 6:53; Luke 22:18). Only spiritual harlots, the murderers of the prophets, actually drink blood.

> For the word of God is living and active, sharper than any two-edged sword, piercing to the division of soul and of spirit, of joints and of marrow, and discerning the thoughts and intentions of the heart. (Hebrews 4:12)

---

3   Robert Altar, *The Art of Biblical Narrative,* 196.

14
TOKENS OF VIRGINITY
THE TEARING OF THE VEIL

"But if the thing is true, and evidences of virginity are not found for the young woman, then they shall bring out the young woman to the door of her father's house, and the men of her city shall stone her to death with stones, because she has done a disgraceful thing in Israel, to play the harlot in her father's house. So you shall put away the evil from among you." (Deuteronomy 22:20-21)

In his discussion of slavery in Exodus 21, James Jordan's "interpretive maximalism" is in full swing. He claims that because doorposts could be likened to legs, the Passover blood smeared on doorposts corresponds to the blood of circumcision. He writes:

> ...a few words about the boring of the ear at the doorpost. The Passover blood was placed on the doorposts (Ex. 12:7, 22, 23), and Israel was to remain in their houses all night (12:22). Exiting through the bloody doorway, the place of birth, was a token of

new birth or resurrection for Israel. Similarly, when God tried to kill her son, Zipporah understood that blood needed to be placed on the "doorposts" of the "house" of the firstborn, for the redemption of the firstborn was the redemption of the whole household, and the destruction of the household was the consequence of not circumcising and dedicating the firstborn, as God had just finished telling Moses (Ex. 4:22, 23). Thus, Zipporah cut off her son's foreskin and touched it to her son's legs, thereby putting blood on the "doorposts of his house," and the angel of death stopped trying to kill him.[1]

If that is not enough to offend modern sensibilities, Jordan later says that this blood is equivalent to the token of virginity from the wedding night. Since a virgin was more valuable than a non-virgin, the bed sheet was to be carefully wrapped and preserved by the parents of the bride, the blood on the sheet serving as a certificate of authenticity, proving that the parents had not presented their daughter to her prospective husband under false pretenses.

Jordan explains that God demands that *His* bride be a virgin. To symbolize this, the wife of the High Priest had to be a virgin (Leviticus 21:13). Since Eve lost her "spiritual virginity" when she listened to the serpent, and began bearing his seed alongside her own, she had played the harlot. Spiritually-speaking, she could provide no blood on the wedding night. He writes:

[1]   James B. Jordan, *The Law of the Covenant,* 82-83.

Stained glass window in St John's Church, Chester, England
(1900) showing Hiram, the architect of the temple in Jerusalem,
and the two pillars of bronze, Jachin and Boaz.
Photo: Wolfgang Sauber.

141

What will be done for such a woman, if her husband truly loves her? He will provide his own blood to stain the sheet, to provide her with tokens of virginity. Just as it was blood from her "private parts" which would have been her token, so it must be blood from his, for it is at this part of their bodies that they become "one flesh"... Thus, one of the (many) meanings of circumcision was this: Since Israel was a harlot, her Husband would give His blood for her covering and as a sign of their union. The circumcision of each male child provided a continuing reminder to Israel that she deserved to be put to death for playing the harlot in her father's house, and that a substitutionary atonement was the only way she would find judicial righteousness. Also, circumcision provided not just a reminder, but an actual covering until the crucifixion of her Lord would provide the final circumcision, and her definitive justification.[2]

Jesus and Paul tell us that the human body is a Tabernacle, a Temple. This means that the strange and apparently barbaric stipulations in the Torah pertaining to the human body were in fact sacrificial images. Just like the laws which required Israelites who served at the Tabernacle to have *skin without blemishes*, so this token of blood was likewise a symbol of purity for all Israel. This was not a new thing. Jacob's wounded hip was memorialized in Israel's meat eating practices

---

2   James B. Jordan, *The Law of the Covenant*, 257-258.

(Genesis 32:32), and the blood of a goat stood in for the blood of Joseph as a false testimony of his death to his father (Genesis 37:31). Personal types play out as corporate antitypes right to the end of the Bible. One man dies for all the people. But one *woman* dies, also.

The Tabernacle was nomadic, and thus "Adamic," a house as yet unestablished, picturing Israel's reliance on Yahweh for the fulfillment of the Abrahamic promises. Like Jesus, who had nowhere to lay His head, it was a Levitical ministry without rest.[3] Having no "legs" of its own, it was carried around on human legs, borne on the shoulders of Levites (Numbers 4:15).

The Temple, however, was an "Evian" Body with legs, two great bronze pillars: Jachin (Priesthood) and Boaz (Kingdom). Covered in beautiful stone, it was *immovable*. In it, not only did the Ark of the Testimony finally find rest, but all the other furnitures were "multiplied."

These two are the natural body and the resurrection body. But they are also a Head and a Body, structure and glory, order and beauty, Forming and Filling.

Leviticus 1 is the Creation week recapitulated in blood as a sacrificial rite.[4] It made *all things* new. The "clean" head ascended, then the body was washed and ascended. Only the body was washed, but *both* were bloodied. This pictures the covering of God's people through the ministry of the High Priest. A righteous

---

3   Leviticus ends with curses, so the "Day 7" rest, the promised Land inheritance, and the Covenant *Succession* are missing.

4   See the chapter "God's Kitchen" in Michael Bull, *Bible Matrix II: The Covenant Key.*

INQUIÉTUDE

Adam will rescue His Eve from the serpent and cover her sin through self-sacrificial service. This is why Paul pictures himself, a minister of the Spirit, as the "matchmaker" between the Lamb and the nations.

> For I feel a divine jealousy for you, since I betrothed you to one husband, to present you as a pure virgin to Christ. But I am afraid that as the serpent deceived Eve by his cunning, your thoughts will be led astray from a sincere and pure devotion to Christ.
> (2 Corinthians 11:2-3)

This gives us a clue to what is going on in the book of Revelation. Jesus is presented as a glorified Tabernacle, a priest who has completed His duties once for all, and His bride as a glorified Temple, that is, a holy city.

The "head" of the sacrifice ascends first, so John sees the Lamb who is worthy to open the Covenant scroll. Christ was without blemish *(Initiation)*, then bloodied in His crucifixion *(Delegation)*. He *became* circumcision, preparing Him for *divine* marriage by the Spirit. So, how was the Bridal Body "bloodied"? What was the evidence of *her* faithfulness? What was the legal witness? It was the blood of martyrdom.

The seals on the scroll were broken, but the New Covenant believers were then sealed as *human* scrolls. The seals of the Spirit were not merely seals of safety, they were seals of authenticity which were intended to be *broken* when their messages reached their destinations. They were signs of judicial "virginity."

144

After being sealed as "blameless" lambs, these holy ones were then sacrificed, martyred, washed (presumably by passing through the sea of crystal, as imaged in the Tabernacle Laver) and finally ascended to rule with Christ. The marriage supper of the Lamb followed.

Just as circumcision was fulfilled in the tearing of the "veil" of Jesus' flesh, so the token of virginity was fulfilled in the removing of the veil of Moses through the destruction of the Temple in Jerusalem and the now unholy city, the harlot whom Jesus calls Egypt, Sodom and Babylon.

> It is these who have not defiled themselves with women, for they are virgins. It is these who follow the Lamb wherever he goes. These have been redeemed from mankind as firstfruits for God and the Lamb, and in their mouth no lie was found, for they are blameless. (Revelation 14:4)

In Jesus' death, He became a door, a *bloodied* door, and then a "Davidic" Tabernacle. In the death and resurrection of His Bride, He became a complete household, a Temple, a Lamb at the center of a holy city.

Likewise, Israel entered the Land, was recircumcised, then the razing of the walls of Jericho was proof of the "virginity" of the betrothed Land. The triumphal entry of the Ark from the "skins" Tabernacle into Solomon's "robed" Temple was also a mark of authenticity, a picture of heaven and earth becoming "one."

The Bible is full of such "marks." The first were the

kingly "signs" in heaven in Genesis 1:14, which established the seasons, days and years. God put a mark upon Cain, the firstborn, in Genesis 4, that he might escape vengeance for his bloodshed. The "bow in the clouds" is also said to be a "mark" which restrains vengeance, maintaining the seasons, days and years in Genesis 8:22; 9:12-17. And circumcision was also a "mark" (Genesis 17:11), a sign which made the children of Israel God's firstborn, witnessed to *corporately* in the blood on the doorposts at Passover.

What was it that *restrained* God's vengeance at the crucifixion of Christ, postponing the immediate destruction of the city (Daniel 9:26; Revelation 7:1)? It was Jesus' forgiveness and the *tearing* of the Veil.

Then who was the *restrainer* who held back the *tearing down* of the Temple during the persecutions of the saints (2 Thessalonians 2:1-8)? It was the Spirit who *sealed* those saints, the bloody *marks* of martyrdom serving as tokens of their spiritual "virginity."

> For neither circumcision counts for anything, nor uncircumcision, but a new creation. And as for all who walk by this rule, peace and mercy be upon them, and upon the Israel of God. From now on let no one cause me trouble, for I bear on my body the marks of Jesus. (Galatians 6:15-17)

When these sealed ones were broken, like the seal on Christ's tomb, the glory departed. Israel was stoned with stones, but the true Bridegroom and His Bride were naked and unashamed before God.

15
A CASTRATED HEART

THE EUNUCHRY OF GREATER ADAM

> *Now as a concession, not a command, I say this. I*
> *wish that all were as I myself am. But each has his*
> *own gift from God, one of one kind and one of*
> *another.* (1 Corinthians 7:6-7)

Reliance upon rules and regulations is a sign of immaturity. There is nothing wrong with them, of course, just as there is nothing wrong with the "gutter guards" used to keep the ten pin bowling ball moving towards the pins for children's parties at the bowling alley. Likewise, there was nothing wrong with creeds, rosary beads or religious paintings in their early days. They were simply mnemonic devices for the illiterate.

But, just as it was with the Pharisees in the first century, these lifeless, inflexible *"stoicheia"* become a problem when they turn into legislation and become mandatory. Failing to tithe one's kitchen herbs leads inevitably to certain destruction.

The celibacy of certain prominent men in the Bible

is part of this discussion. The question is not "Is celibacy holier than marriage?" but why were these spiritual giants, including Jesus, celibate at all?

What started me thinking was a friend's observation that James Jordan wrote at one time that Daniel and his three friends were all eunuchs.

> Those who maintained faith, however, and saw through the crisis, received the blessing. They trusted God's good purposes and submitted to His plan. Foremost among these were Daniel and his friends, who wound up with the highest glory and influence among the Gentiles, though they were made eunuchs, thereby receiving a form of Jacob's "foot" wound. ("Feet" in the Bible sometimes refers to or represents the privates; Judges 3:24; Ruth 3:7; 1 Samuel 24:3. Jacob's was a literal foot wound, of course.)[1]

Now, before you write this off as mere speculation, this is exactly the kind of symbolism the Bible consistently employs. Ethical truths are frequently presented to us as social and physical, and even physiological, signs. The correspondence between circumcision (physical/social) and a circumcised heart (ethical) is the prime example. They are not the same thing, but one points to the other. As it is with the members of the Trinity, all of God's signs are self-effacing, pointing to another member's glory.

---

1   James B. Jordan, *Crisis Time: Patriarchal Prologue, Part 3*, Biblical Horizons No. 111.

Daniel in the Lions' Den (1896)
Henry Ossawa Tanner

INQUIÉTUDE

More recently, however, Jordan has written that Daniel and his friends could *not* have been eunuchs.

> ...the young men were without blemish. The word "blemish" here is used in Leviticus 21:17-23 and 22:20-25 and elsewhere to refer to blemishes on priests and sacrifices. (On the basis of Leviticus 21:20, Daniel and his friends could not have been eunuchs, and since being without blemish was a qualification for the post into which they were being educated, we can be sure that they were not made eunuchs.) The young men were from the tribe of Judah, not Levi, so they were not priests in the sense of being servants of Yahweh's household. The word "priest" *(kohen)*, however, actually means "palace servant," and is used occasionally for the servants of a human king (2 Samuel 8:18; 20:26). The young men were being made priests in the sense of being royal servants of Nebuchadnezzar, and thus Daniel uses the Levitical term for "blemish" to alert us to the parallel.

> The parallel is important to the theology of Daniel. We have already made the point that the four men are corners of a new house, a new economy, in God's history. That house is going to be the empire within which Israel is going to live. God intends to convert Nebuchadnezzar and turn his empire into God's house.[2]

---

2   James B. Jordan, *The Handwriting on the Wall: A Commentary on the Book of Daniel*, 145.

From the standpoint of palace service, the roles of wise men and eunuchs were very different, as different as elders are from servants. Daniel and his friends were in the charge of the chief of the eunuchs, but when promoted, Daniel did not *become* the chief of the eunuchs. Also, the eunuchs lived in the palace (as the "neuter" Spirit inhabiting the house, taking care of the Bride on behalf of the Bridegroom, as we see Hegai doing in the book of Esther), whereas the wise men, since they possessed their own houses, presumably had their own wives, children, servants and animals.

> The king answered and said to the Chaldeans, "The word from me is firm: if you do not make known to me the dream and its interpretation, you shall be torn limb from limb, and your houses shall be laid in ruins. But if you show the dream and its interpretation, you shall receive from me gifts and rewards and great honor. Therefore show me the dream and its interpretation." (Daniel 2:5-6)

In Daniel 6, many decades later, the prophet Daniel has his own house (Daniel 6:10), support for the fact that he is not a eunuch, but there is still no mention of his household, of a wife or children. The only wives and children mentioned in the text are those of the men who intended Daniel harm.

> And the king commanded, and those men who had maliciously accused Daniel were brought and cast into the den of lions—they, their children, and their

wives. And before they reached the bottom of the den, the lions overpowered them and broke all their bones in pieces. (Daniel 6:24)

So although Jordan has changed his view, I believe that he was correct, in a sense, all along. The difference is the same as the shift from a circumcised penis to a circumcised heart. Here, however, we are not dealing merely with circumcision but castration. In that case, what is a castrated heart?

Although Daniel and his friends were not eunuchs by decree, they were eunuchs by choice, just as there is the rite of circumcision of the flesh and the rite of circumcision of the heart (baptism). The corporal sign signified a time of childhood instruction, but the response of a willing heart is the sign of ethical maturity.

Thus, Daniel was likely a "spiritual eunuch." Like Jeremiah, Christ and Paul, he was denied marriage by God, cut off symbolically from the social order of the people of God and offered up as a kind of firstfruits so that a greater harvest might be given. Instead of being bound by marriage, these men were servants of a broader vow, bound as living sacrifices that Israel might be loosed.

These men had no physical children because God was using them to bring spiritual children to Himself under a Covenant that was matured through a process of death and resurrection. This helps us to make sense of the use of Isaiah 8:18 in Hebrews 2:

"Here am I and the children whom God has given Me."

Like Jeremiah, Daniel, and Paul, Jesus Christ had no children, which is unthinkable in Jewish terms, even today. He was thus a "corporate Adam" whose bride was a corporate Eve, the people of God. If you find this difficult to comprehend, think of Captain James T. Kirk from *Star Trek,* who although not celibate, once bemoaned that the only kind of "marriage" available to him was a commitment to his ship, crew and career.

The celibacy of these men was not the result of legislation. If anything, it went *against* the laws and customs of the Covenant people. Perhaps this is why Paul's advice concerning marriage was not a command but a concession. Just as married couples might choose to separate themselves temporarily to God to wage spiritual warfare, these men were forever devoted to intercession for the greater family. The love of a greater bride was their fire.

> And everyone who has left houses or brothers or sisters or father or mother or children or lands, for my name's sake, will receive a hundredfold and will inherit eternal life. (Matthew 19:29)

PURIFICATION

16
GUNS, GIRLS, AND GOLD

THE HEART OF KINGDOM

This calls for wisdom: let the one who has understanding calculate the number of the beast, for it is the number of a man, and his number is 666. (Revelation 13:18)

Moses gave Israel three laws for her future kings (Deuteronomy 17:14-20). As moderns who wrongly assume the Bible is merely an obsolete container for "propositional truth," we not only fail to see these three laws as a continuum, a *process,* and thus fail to identify them in Bible history, we also fail to interpret contemporary history in their brilliant light.

As we should expect, the text which presents to us these laws for kings also follows the pattern of biblical Covenants, exhibiting the shape of the entire book of Deuteronomy in microcosm.

INQUIÉTUDE

<u>TRANSCENDENCE</u>
Creation (Genesis – Ark of the Covenant)

"When you come to the land
(Ark scatters enemies: Joshua 3:13)
    that the Lord your God is giving you,
    (Veil – circumcision: Joshua 5:3-7)
        and you possess it and dwell in it
        (Bronze Altar – inheritance: Joshua 21:43-45)
        and then say,
        (Table: 1 Samuel 8: unworthy to open the scroll)
            'I will set a king over me,
            (Lampstand – law opened: Psalm 119)
        like all the nations that are around me,'
        (Incense – prophetic ministry)
    you may indeed set a king over you
    (Mediator – New Adam, a priest-king like David)
whom the Lord your God will choose.
(Rest and Rule: Solomon, king of peace)

This first stanza predicts the historical events to come as "sacrificial architecture." However, Israel was not yet humble, not yet ready for Kingdom. The sin of the tribes was the sin of Adam. They saw Kingdom (equality with God, Philippians 2:6-7) as something to be grasped, not something to be received as a gift after being qualified through humble obedience. A true Adam would be God's legal representative, His "image," speaking for Him from a great white (ivory) throne.[1]

---

[1] For more discussion, see "Images of God" in Michael Bull, *Sweet Counsel: Essays to Brighten the Eyes.*

HIERARCHY

Division (Exodus – Veil/Circumcision)

One

(Animal chosen – INITIATION)
    from among your brothers
    (Animal cut – DELEGATION)
        you shall set over you a king.
        (Animal lifted up – PRESENTATION)
            You may not
            (Holy fire – PURIFICATION)
        set over you a foreigner
        (Holy smoke – Witness/TRANSFORMATION)
    who is not your brother.
    (Mediation – VINDICATION)

—

(No Rest – REPRESENTATION)

Israel's kings were to be Priest-Kings, so the selection of a blameless king was "sacrificial." The chosen one would be set apart from his brothers as "a son of the herd" just as Israel was set apart from the nations. The "triune" nature of the world found in the Edenic fruit was a microcosm of the Abrahamic architecture:

Ethical	Garden	Seed	Priest-King
Social	Land	Flesh	Israel
PHYSICAL[2]	WORLD	SKIN	GENTILES

2 It might be argued that circumcision was a Physical sign, and the Gentile nations were the Social world, but circumcision *divided* the Social world, so the nations *represented* the Physical Creation. More on this in chapter 18.

INQUIÉTUDE

Israel was a skinned sacrifice, a "peeled fruit" which carried the seed. If the king was a Gentile, there would be no Covenant *Succession*. This goes beyond the circumcision of the flesh (Social) to the circumcision of the heart (Ethical: Leviticus 26:41). Saul was rejected because he became like an uncircumcised Gentile king, a spear-thrower, an authority unto himself.[3]

Notice that the king was the center of stanza 1 as the source of Law (Day 4), but in stanza 2 the command of the Lord is at the center. And there is no line 7, no *Succession*. Israel's problem was kings who did not act like brothers, but who instead behaved like Pharaoh.

ETHICS
Ascension (Leviticus – Bronze Altar)

Only he must not *(Genesis - Creation)*
   multiply horses *(Exodus - Division)*
      or cause to return *(Leviticus - Ascension)*
         the people *(Numbers - Testing)*
      to Egypt *(Deuteronomy - Maturity)*
   to multiply horses, *(Joshua - Conquest)*
since the Lord has said, *(Judges - Glorification)*

The people were not to return to Egypt *Ethically* (in their hearts, desiring a golden calf), *Socially* (through intermarriage with idolaters), or *Physically* (through political alliances, as they did in fear of Babylon). The placement of Egypt at step five relates it to Gentile

---

3   The 200 foreskins before Saul's throne in 1 Samuel 18:27 is akin to the piles of heads and corpses left by Assyrians at city gates.

The Idolatry of Solomon (circa 1720)
Nicolas Vleughels

armies (hosts) and plagues. Note the symmetry of the horses at *Division* and *Conquest*. Joshua's strength was not in chariots but in the Captain of the Lord's hosts. A failure in the faithfulness of the priesthood would lead to a loss of dominion over the "four-horned" Land, which is what occurs in the book of Judges. For Israel, Kingdom depended upon Priesthood.

Ascension has two stanzas, the second one presenting the Covenant Law given on the mountain, although here it is not sevenfold but fivefold. This means it is not an inheritance scroll as it is in Revelation 5, but a stone tablet, a commandment.[4]

Ascension (Leviticus – Table of Facebread)

'Never *(Transcendence - Genesis)*
    shall you *(Hierarchy - Exodus)*
        again return *(Ethics - Leviticus)*
    this way *(Oath/Sanctions - Numbers)*
in the future.' *(Succession - Deuteronomy)*

Interestingly the "return" at the Levitical step of the Bronze Altar is still at the Levitical step here, which reflects the relationship between the fivefold pattern of Moses and the sevenfold pattern of Israel.[5]

---

4   At this point in the Revelation, Jesus opens the scroll, His legal claim upon not only the Land but also all the nations of the World. Four "Spirit horses" ride out, and by chapter 19, Jesus has multiplied horses. None of Jesus' horses are the armies of men, but angelic hosts serving human prophets. The curse upon those who trusted in horses was to be invaded by the Gentile hosts.

5   For a comparison, see the chart on page 279 of Michael Bull, *Bible Matrix II: The Covenant Key*.

Testing (Numbers – Lampstand)

And he shall not *(Transcendence)*
   multiply wives, *(Hierarchy)*
      lest his heart turn away, *(Ethics)*
     nor silver and gold *(Oath/Sanctions)*
  increase greatly. *(Succession)*

Women and gold appear at the center of the structure for typological reasons. Incorruptible gold and refining fire are both symbols of pure desire, thus both are represented by the Lampstand. Numbers is the book which tells us of Israel's harlotry (a personal sign in chapter 6, then the nationwide sin in chapter 25). Whereas the multiplication of horses occurs in the Land, wives and gold appeal to the heart. In that sense, their multiplication is "Sanctuary" sin. Polygamy promises many sons (an instant dynasty), and silver and gold are wealth from the ground. So perhaps here we have not only the womb and Land promises of Eden represented, but also Abel, whose offering substituted for the firstborn, and Cain, a worker of the ground.

This fivefold stanza follows the Covenant pattern, with the Law at *Transcendence,* an uncircumcised heart at *Hierarchy,* a deceived heart at *Ethics,* a deluded heart at *Sanctions* (plunder allowed to become a plague), and a self-sufficient "Laodicean" inheritance at *Succession.*

The word "multiply" is used repeatedly, and true "multiplication" is not supposed to come until *Maturity,* from the hand of God. You might remember

that it was the line of Cain which possessed all the gifts
and temptations of Kingdom without reference to God:
wisdom in such things as animal husbandry, music,
and metalwork.

It is interesting that these five lines also echo the
architectural progression of the Ten Words (above,
beside, below), which means they also correspond
thematically to the entire Old Covenant history:

<u>TRANSCENDENCE</u>
And he shall not
(1 Word from God; 2 Oath to God – Adam to Noah)
   <u>HIERARCHY</u>
   multiply wives,
   (3 Land; 4 Womb – Abraham to Joseph)
      <u>ETHICS</u>
      lest his heart turn away,
      (5 Murder; 6 Adultery – Moses to David)
<u>OATH/SANCTIONS</u>
nor silver and gold
(7 Theft; 8 Legal Witness – Solomon to Jeremiah)
<u>SUCCESSION</u>
increase greatly.
(9 House; 10 Household – Daniel to Esther)[6]

Silver and gold together speak of multiplication. Not
only did Solomon amass so much gold that silver was
treated like almost like refuse (1 Kings 10:21), the ten
("multiplied") lampstands in Solomon's Temple were

---

6 See the diagram of the Ten Words in the Covenant-literary charts at
the end of this book.

made of gold, but there were also lampstands of silver, perhaps for use in rooms other than the Holy Place. The gold speaks of the Bridegroom (the light of the sun) and the silver of the Bride (the reflected light of the moon). Appearing at this point in the stanza, such plunder accords with the Bride being either redeemed or sold, harking back to Adam's failure to protect Eve, Abraham's purchase of a field from Ephron for Sarah's burial, and also Achan's theft of gold, silver and a robe after the "redemption" of Rahab's house.

Maturity (Deuteronomy – Incense: Legal Witness)

"And when he shall come *(Creation)*
   and sit on the throne *(Division)*
      of his kingdom, *(Ascension – Land)*
      he shall write *(Ascension – scroll opened)*
        a copy of this law *(Testing – legal image)*
      likewise on a scroll *(Maturity – scroll received)*
     before the faces *(Conquest – Veil opened)*
  of the Levitical priests. *(Glorification – Representatives)*

James Jordan has noted that the reason we find the wisdom literature so mysterious is that unlike Jewish children we have not had the books of Moses and Samuel drummed into our memories prior to reading David and Solomon. They require the earlier texts to be hidden in our hearts for easy reference.

The placement of this directive at *Maturity* is significant. It corresponds to Deuteronomy, which means "Second Law," because Moses repeated the Law to a new generation of Israel. It was the macrocosm of the second set of tablets given to old Israel after her golden calf sin at Sinai. Not only this but the phrase "a copy of this law" appears at the center. The king was to be a son of God on earth, an image of the Father in heaven. His obedience was to be a sign of the goodness of God, a visible demonstration that Israel's God not only spoke (unlike idols), He was also worthy to be obeyed.

The king shows his submission to God through his submission to Levitical priests. As the king watched over Israel (as her shepherd), so God watched over the king through his priestly angels. It is noteworthy that this stanza reverses the process of *Ascension*: the king is exalted in the first half, yet he *remains* humble.

OATH/SANCTIONS
Conquest (Joshua – Mediators)

And it shall be with him, *(Transcendence)*
    and he shall read in it all the days of his life,
    (Hierarchy)
        that he may learn to fear the Lord his God
        (Ethics)
    by keeping all the words of this law
    (Oath/Sanctions)
and likewise the statutes, diligently, *(Succession)*

This is the "Day 6" of the cycle and the theme is Adam in the Garden of God. The Law of God humbles the Man so that God might keep His promises to him. Of course, Adam was only given a single prohibition. Israel's kings, like all rulers, were faced with manifold decisions. The complete canon, as it stood at the time, needed to be internalized that it might be applied wisely in new or unforeseen situations. In sacrificial terms, if the flesh of the king was continually put on the altar under the guidance of the priests, then the fire of sound judgment would fall from heaven. After this, God would be with him as he subdued the Land and the nation would be at peace.

The fear of the Lord is the beginning of wisdom and it appears at the center of numerous "matrix" cycles, sometimes as "trembling." If Israel's kings continued to fear God, they would have nothing else to fear.

SUCCESSION
Glorification (Judges – Representing God to the Nations)

that his heart may not be lifted up
(Transcendence)
 above his brothers,
 (Hierarchy)
  and that he may not turn aside
  (Ethics – Priest)
   from the commandment,
   (Ethics – Kingdom)
  either to the right hand or to the left,
  (Ethics – Prophecy)
 so that he may continue long in his kingdom,
 (Oath/Sanctions – blessing)
he and his children, in Israel.
(Succession – offspring)

INQUIÉTUDE

Finally, we come to Covenant *Succession*, the inheritance of the faithful man. This one is mostly explained by the subtitles in the chart, but I would also note that the "right hand or left" is a reference to Kingdom and Priesthood, both of which are under the authority of the Prophet. It is at this step *(Maturity)* that Moses sits on a rock and Aaron *(Priest)* and Hur *(of Judah: King)* hold up his arms. All three were there at *Ascension,* but they were not yet united. Separate elements refers to the Levitical divisions of just about everything under the Mosaic Law; this is what the apostles call the *stoicheia*. At *Maturity,* however, the Priest, King, and Prophet are of one mind; Aaron and Hur are physically united with Moses so that Joshua might conquer Amalek. Of course, this pictures for us the ministry of Christ in the Church, and the exaltation of a nation where there is spiritual unity under God.

THE FALL OF SOLOMON

In his downfall, Solomon actually reversed the order of these three prohibitions, which began a process of "de-Creation." He amassed 666 talents of gold so that silver became commonplace (hence the symbols 666 and "wisdom" are used to signify the temple-building Herods in the Revelation), he took many idolatrous wives, and then became a trader in Egyptian horses. His fall was Ethical, Social, then Physical, as the Land was taken away.

A similar degeneration can be observed in the past

few centuries of modern Western Culture. Faithfulness to God brought global conquest, faithfulness in marriage, then prosperity and great wisdom (science). Once prosperous (gold), we forgot God and dismantled marriage (girls) and then relied upon military power rather than God's guidance and protection to maintain peace with our enemies (guns).

17
BABYLONIAN BOOKENDS

THE OFFSPRING OF DANIEL

> *Now after Jesus was born in Bethlehem of Judea in the days of Herod the king, behold, wise men from the east came to Jerusalem, saying, "Where is he who has been born king of the Jews? For we saw his star when it rose and have come to worship him." When Herod the king heard this, he was troubled, and all Jerusalem with him...* (Matthew 2:1-2)

An atheist friend once declared to me that a cumulative reading of the Bible makes no sense, since the Bible is not a single book but an anthology. Well, the Bible is indeed an anthology, but it was not only compiled but also *inspired* by a single Author.

Without such a foundation for hermeneutics, the significance of many of the historical details "planted" like seeds for us in the text goes unnoticed. One such overlooked "payoff" is the import of the appearance of the wise men from the east in Matthew 2.

INQUIÉTUDE

A NEW COVENANT

The period from the exile to Christ was a unique era in Bible history. Instead of considering this half-millennium as a limbo of oppression, stagnation and unfulfilled promises, James Jordan observes that this was instead a time of preparation for the Gospel, and Israel was given a special ministry under a new covenant:

> It is often overlooked that the restoration establishment was indeed a new covenant, and an advance in glory beyond the Davidic establishment. Whether we call the post-exilic establishment a new covenant or simply a "covenant renewal," the fact is that there were very great changes involved in the new cosmos, changes equivalent to the changes involved in previous new covenants...
>
> The Restoration is the least familiar and least studied phase of Old Covenant history. It is often assumed that the Kingdom of God went into the doldrums during this period, and that the people simply suffered until the coming of Messiah. Such an understanding of the postexilic era utterly fails to do justice to the case. The Restoration was actually a far more glorious time than ever before, in terms of spiritual power, though not in terms of outward glory and splendor.[1]

---

1 James B. Jordan, *Through New Eyes: Developing a Biblical View of the World*, 244, 254.

Human-headed winged bull and winged lion
(lamassu), Neo-Assyrian, Ashurnasirpal II; 883–
859 B.C. Mesopotamia, Nimrud (ancient Kalhu)
Alabaster (gypsum); 10' 3¹/₂" high (Metropolitan
Museum of Art). Photo: Dr Steven Zucker.

INQUIÉTUDE

Due to the failure of Israel's kings, God put the nation through a death-and-resurrection, elevating his people to a higher court than that of David and Solomon—a *Gentile* one. Since they would not submit to the court of heaven, they would learn to serve a king of all kings on earth. By this "sacrificial" act, the influence of Israel expanded via the court of the emperor to all the nations under his rule.

In the ministry of the synagogues run by laymen, the Jews would now serve God in a prophetic capacity as a nation of teachers and witnesses throughout the *oikoumene* (a "household" of nations). This ministry began in the testimony of Daniel and his friends in the court of Nebuchadnezzar, which led to the conversion of the emperor, much as the witness of Joseph had led to the conversion of Pharaoh.

THE TIMES OF THE GENTILES

This new "social architecture" is set up in the book of Daniel. The thrones of the ancient kings, including that of Solomon, were often surrounded by beasts, the symbolic meaning of which can be traced back to Genesis 1-2, the dominion over all flesh which was promised to Adam. Like the beasts in Genesis, these beasts were wild and intended to be subdued, but they were not inherently evil. James Jordan writes:

> Daniel 7 first presents four composite beasts. These are not presented all at once, as in Ezekiel 1, but they

are presented first in the order of the vision, as in Ezekiel 1. They are one beast, for each beast incorporates the previous, just as the statue of Daniel 1 had four sections or historical phases, but was one statue. The cherubim guard God's throne, and also with their wings form a boundary for the Chariot. Similarly, Daniel's beasts, as some kind of earthly form of cherubim, are to guard God's earthly people (the Jews) and form the boundaries of His Oikumene kingdom. Ezekiel's beasts came down from the sky; Daniel's come up from the great sea. The great sea is not the Mediterranean, because Babylon and Persia did not come from there. Nor is it some kind of mythological sea. Rather, in accordance with Biblical symbolism, the sea represents the Gentile world. These beasts are Gentile empires that are to act as guardian cherubim.

Some modern interpreters point to great "chaos beasts" as part of the ancient religions of the Near East, and assume that such dangerous and threatening beasts are in view. While educated Jews, like Daniel and his friends, would certainly know about such "chaos-monster myths," they would also realize that this vision came from the same God who had revealed His chariot and His four beasts to Ezekiel. With their Jewish background, and with Ezekiel clearly in mind, Daniel and his friends would not have been drawn off by the red herring of "chaos-monsters," but would have recognized the beasts of Daniel 7 as cherubic figures. Just as Satan was a fallen cherub, so these beasts might fall; but as Satan

175

was created good at the beginning, so were these beasts.

Daniel's beasts come in an historical order, each replaced in turn when it becomes evil and moves against God's people in a climactic way (compare Daniel 5-6). When the fourth beast and his Little Horn sidekick turn against God's people, the fifth and final kingdom, that of a man and not a beast, replaces it—just as the "stone cut without hands" replaced the statue in Daniel 2.[2]

Babylon was the first beast. Nebuchadnezzar himself, for cursing the children of Abraham, was humbled, subdued, by being transformed into a combination of "bird and beast," a minister of the Covenant curses (Deuteronomy 28:26; 1 Samuel 17:44-46).[3]

This 500 year "animal kingdom" was like the penultimate act of the Creation Week, the land filled with beasts but awaiting its human rulers, the Man and His Bride.[4]

The final guardian was Rome, and we see Roman authorities protecting Christians from Jewish persecution in the book of Acts. Under Nero and the Herods, the final beast turned bad. Jew and Gentile became

---

2   James B. Jordan, *The Handwriting on the Wall: A Commentary on the Book of Daniel*, 333-334.
3   The blessing for obedience to the Covenant was dominion over the beasts. The Covenant curse, however, was to be eaten by them. For more discussion, see "Birds and Beasts" in Michael Bull, *God's Kitchen: Theology You Can Eat & Drink*.
4   See the Creation Week recapitulated in Israel's history in Michael Bull, *Bible Matrix: An Introduction to the DNA of the Scriptures*, 191.

united in their persecution of the Church. In their removal, the "times of the Gentiles," through the removal of the Jew-Gentile distinction, circumcision and the law, came to an end (Luke 21:24; Romans 11:25; Revelation 11:2; 19:17-19).

What does all of this *"oikoumene"* background mean for Matthew 2? It reveals the significance of the visit of the wise men from the east.

READING THE STARS

This "Restoration Covenant" era began with young men of Judah taken as captives for training by the Chaldeans, the religious leaders of the Babylonian region. The book of Daniel presents them as characters similar to those in Pharaoh's court, the men who opposed Moses. Daniel not only trumps their wisdom but ends up ruling over them. He was taken captive to be taught, but rather than seeking their power, he humbled himself and became the teacher.

Since Daniel ruled the wise men, he taught them the true source of wisdom, the Word of God, and redeemed them from pagan star gazing, a practice condemned by God because only He can interpret the stars, and He does so only to His prophets (Genesis 15:5; 22:17; 37:9, Deuteronomy 1:10; 4:19; 28:62, Judges 5:20; Isaiah 14:13; Jude 1:13; Revelation 1:16). Daniel was such a prophet, and he led these Gentiles to the truth concerning the stars. Stars are signs of the sons of God, those who are destined to ascend and rule the heavens.

INQUIÉTUDE

Instead of seeking wisdom from the created heavens, the wise men now understood that "there is a God in heaven" who reveals such secrets. Daniel's first resort after Nebuchadnezzar's fury was to seek God, along with his brothers:

> Then Daniel went to his house and made the matter known to Hananiah, Mishael, and Azariah, his companions, and told them to seek mercy from the God of heaven concerning this mystery, so that Daniel and his companions might not be destroyed with the rest of the wise men of Babylon. (Daniel 2:17-18)

When summoned before the king in chapter 2, Daniel was as fearless concerning his testimony to the true God as he had been in chapter 1.

> Daniel answered the king and said, "No wise men, enchanters, magicians, or astrologers can show to the king the mystery that the king has asked, but there is a God in heaven who reveals mysteries, and he has made known to King Nebuchadnezzar what will be in the latter days." (Daniel 2:27-28)

It is unlikely that these events would have been forgotten, especially by the Chaldeans. This intervention by Daniel was a game changer. Indeed, it was remembered by the queen many decades later (Daniel 5:10-12), who advised that Daniel be called upon to interpret the handwriting on the wall for Belshazzar.

So, this era which began with Jews traveling to Babylon ends with a delegation of wise men traveling to Jerusalem. They were now far more enamored with the God of heaven than with the heavens themselves, and far more familiar with the Hebrew Scriptures than Herod and the rulers of Jerusalem. They would have known of Balaam's prophecy concerning the star of Jacob (Numbers 24:15-19), and also the timing of the coming of the Messiah (Daniel 9). The irony of the fact that this infant king was a surprise to the rulers of Jerusalem, who it seems had no reliable prophets in their employ, would not have been lost on Matthew's first readers. It is also the arrival of the wise men which sets the kingdom of the Herods against the kingdom of heaven. It was their testimony to Herod which brought about the massacre of the infants, an act which exposed the king as a man like Pharaoh, and his prophets as men like Jannes and Jambres (2 Timothy 3:8).

These believing wise men from the east understood the nature of *true* Kingdom. It was not in the study of the stars but in the knowledge of the one who *made* the stars "for signs and for seasons, and for days and years," to be "lights in the expanse of the heavens to give light upon the earth" (Genesis 1:14-15).

The Restoration Era is bookended by wise men, so we would do well to compare texts from the beginning with texts from the end. The first thing we might notice is that at the beginning, the wise men work for Nebuchadnezzar, but at the end they work for God:

INQUIÉTUDE

"And those who are wise shall shine like the brightness of the sky above; and those who turn many to righteousness, like the stars forever and ever. But you, Daniel, shut up the words and seal the book, until the time of the end." (Daniel 12:3-4)

In Matthew, the time of the end, the last days (of Israel and the Old Covenant) was at hand, only one generation away. The appearance of the Chaldeans is thus the beginning of the end. While those from the east were bringing their glory into the kingdom, the Herods were behaving like the sons of Joktan, the Shemites who "journeyed from the east" but ended up compromising with Nimrod's Babel project, seeking a name for themselves rather than seeking God (Genesis 10-11:9).[5]

Matthew's narrative begins with wise men who were "angels" from the courts of earthly kings, guardians who had protected Israel until she gave birth to the promised One. They remembered Daniel of the tribe of Judah, the humble man without a kingdom whose only boast was in his God:

---

5   James Jordan observes that the building of Babel always required a compromise by the people of God, a false witness, but that the building of the house and city of God always required the aid of a faithful Gentile sponsor. Melchizedek sponsored Abraham, Jethro sponsored Moses, Hiram sponsored Solomon, and Cyrus sponsored Ezra and Nehemiah. The gifts of the wise men from the east was thus a continuation of the necessity for a Gentile witness to the ministry of Israel.

Then the king gave Daniel high honors and many great gifts, and made him ruler over the whole province of Babylon and chief prefect over all the wise men of Babylon. (Daniel 1:48)

Thanks to Daniel, they were not like the wise men of Nebuchadnezzar:

The Chaldeans answered the king and said, "There is not a man on earth who can meet the king's demand, for no great and powerful king has asked such a thing of any magician or enchanter or Chaldean. The thing that the king asks is difficult, and no one can show it to the king except the gods, whose dwelling is not with flesh." (Daniel 2:10-11)

Now that they worshiped the God of heaven, He was not only pleased to speak to these converted wise men in dreams as He did to Daniel (Matthew 2:12), He was pleased to meet them in person, as a man on earth, a God who now dwelt in flesh.

18
COSMIC LANGUAGE

ETHNIC CLEANSING AS MERCY

"Immediately after the tribulation of those days the sun will be darkened, and the moon will not give its light, and the stars will fall from heaven, and the powers of the heavens will be shaken." (Matthew 24:29)

In Matthew 24:29, Jesus employs "cosmic language," signs in the sun, moon and stars, to predict the imminent end of the Old Covenant. His first century audience would have recognized His allusion to the prophecy against Babylon in Isaiah 13 and understood His discourse as a condemnation of Jerusalem as a contemporary Babel.

So, this "cosmic" language is clearly poetic, but why would the prophets—including Jesus and His apostles—deliberately cause so much confusion by using such language to describe non-cosmic events? The answer is found in the mercy of God.

INQUIÉTUDE

AN IMAGE OF THE WORLD

From Adam to Abraham, "the World" was the actual globe. Adam was the representative of all flesh, including the animal subjects in his kingdom, with whom he shared physical breath. Sin in the Garden led to sin in the Land and finally to the corruption of the entire World. Thus, the Covenant Sanctions wiped out all life in the entire physical world. Noah was not only the first man qualified to judge other men, he was also the first to offer an "ascension" for the whole world as an Adam in communion with God in a "new creation." It seems that unlike previous offerings, this was consumed by fire, creating a fragrant "ladder to heaven" as a testimony of mediation.[1]

This new priesthood which represented the entire world was a priesthood of all nations led by tribal Priest-Kings such as Melchizedek. After the sin of Ham (Garden) and the revival of the Cainite city in Babel (Land), the only way to avert another "macrocosmic" flood was to reestablish a sacrificial substitute, a "microcosmic" world, one which, like the offerings of Noah, would represent all Creation. Thus, to Abraham was promised a singular nation set apart from all others, not only fruitfulness in Land and womb (an echo of the curses in Genesis 3), but also an outflow of

---

1   See James B. Jordan, *The First Ascension, A Brief History of "Sacrifice" According to the Bible: Part 5,* Biblical Horizons No. 253.

blessing to all other nations. Israel would bear the curses for the sake of the world, which is why Genesis concludes with the barrenness of Sarah and the famines in Canaan reversed and united in the salvation of all nations under Joseph.

Once the Lord had qualified Abraham as a new kind of representative, the meal of bread and wine with Melchizedek was an investiture with priestly authority. Via symbols of death, Abraham's nation was given life. In circumcision his offspring became a Social Land, then in baptism they were given representative office over the Social Sea of the Gentiles.

Under Moses, God built a "penal substitute" for the world. The ark was the three-level world represented above the *Physical* waters and the Tabernacle was the three-level world represented above the *Social* waters. Just as Jacob's "tent" of seventy people moved from Canaan to Egypt and multiplied into a nation, at the Feast of Tabernacles, seventy bulls were offered for the seventy nations listed in Genesis 10.

The Tabernacle represented the Garden, Land and World in microcosm, but once in Canaan the Tabernacle represented the Garden, Canaan the Land, and the surrounding nations the World. Israel truly became a representative "Land" lifted up above the represented "Sea." The human "ascension" begun in the offering of Isaac on Moriah was now an entire nation.

As anyone who grew up before the advent of computer graphics knows, when a TV show or movie required the destruction of a building, an aircraft, a city, or a mountain, it was always cheaper to blow up a model, something which *faithfully* represented the original but on a smaller scale. The "waters" rising to cleanse the Land were Social, not Physical. In God's mercy, instead of a "Creational" flood, the cleansing was Social or "ethnic," as it was under Joshua.

Of course, when I say "ethnic," I refer to the nations. The "ethnic" cleansing ordered by God was never racial, but always Covenantal, and thus a judgment for sin. The Canaanites were evangelized by Abraham, who proclaimed the Lord to them (Genesis 12:8; 13:4; 26:25), and made sacrifices for them, yet they continued to fill up their sins. Although these judgments were local, they were substitutionary, that is, they represented the judgment of the entire Land.

Like the Great Flood, the military invasions were tragic necessities, but they were to be far preferred over another global deluge. Not only this, but like the Physical flood, they resulted in the benefit for mankind of greater judicial maturity. Just as Noah was the first man worthy to bear the sword, the sword of divine justice against Jericho was in the hands of men rather than God. Judgment was limited but judicial maturity was expanded.

For Canaanite sins, Israel would suffer similar floods. Assyria invaded Israel, covering the Land but reaching "up to the neck," leaving Jerusalem as a head above water (Isaiah 8:8). Solomon's and Herod's

Temples were destroyed under "floods" of Gentile armies (Daniel 9:26). Thus, it is no accident that the Revelation borrows much imagery from the conquest of Jericho, the original Social deluge.

The replacement "cosmos" after each judgment was not only "a new heavens and a new earth" in Covenantal terms, it was the investiture of a new order of sacrificial representation and broader prophetic responsibility.

So, this representative arrangement not only explains the strange references to earthquakes, stars, birds and fish in the prophets, it reveals the purpose of the "sacrificial" death of Judah and Jerusalem and the Temple for the sake of all nations: the prophets used cosmic language so that the cosmos might be spared.

THE IMAGE OF MAN

This brings us to a substitutionary atonement which we do understand, the fulfillment of the cruciform Tabernacle in the cross of Christ. Although Jesus' execution was Physical and Social, it was primarily Personal. Beginning in Galilee (World), working through Judah and Samaria (Land) and ending in Jerusalem (Garden), Christ alone ascended to rule all nations.

The murderous High Priest himself moved the focus from the Social to the Personal, predicting that one man should die for the people (John 11:49-53). The cross was the death of one man, but this man

INQUIÉTUDE

(Personal) represented not only Israel (Social Land) but also all nations (Social Sea). As James Jordan has observed, Christ was condemned by legal representatives of all domains, in the house of the High Priest (Garden), by Herod (Land) and then handed over to Pilate (World).

Christ ended the division of humanity in His own body, and the legal testimony of this microcosmic "deluge" was the blood (Land) and water (Sea) which flowed separately from His corpse (John 19:34-35). As a blameless substitute for all mankind, Jesus became the "model," the entire Creation magnified, concentrated in a single sacrificial "tabernacle" (John 1:14). Being the Creator Himself, Jesus was not a cheaper option but a very expensive model, the reverse of the substitution of Isaac on Moriah. As God in human flesh, Christ was heaven and earth made indivisible. The entire world is judged in and by Him, which is why He used cosmic language to describe His own death.

> Jesus answered, "This voice has come for your sake, not mine. Now is the judgment of this world (cosmos); now will the ruler of this world (cosmos) be cast out. And I, when I am lifted up from the earth (land), will draw all to myself. (John 12:30-32)

Notice that Jesus does not say "all people" but "all." This can mean all people, depending upon the context, but the word carries the idea of "all kinds." Certainly, His personal ministry resulted in a new Social order, but it will culminate in a restored Physical order. Covenant history is thus symmetrical or chiastic, shaped like an hourglass, with the cross of Christ at the center of reality.

Since every part of Bible history is a symmetrical "there and back again" (including Israel's journey from Canaan to Egypt and back to Canaan), Scripture itself invites us to compare each of these events with every other. When such comparisons are made, it seems that this entire process of *Physical – Social – Ethical – Social – Physical* was prefigured for us in the Torah. We can see it not only in the shape of biblical covenants, but also in the first five chapters of the Bible.

Perhaps most interestingly, it may also offer a clue to the structure of the book of Leviticus, where the subject matter appears to follow the journey of the High Priest on the Day of Atonement. He moves from the courtyard (Physical Place) into the Holy Place (Social Time) and finally alone into the Most Holy (Personal Holiness). Once his representative ministry was complete, the order was reversed: Holiness, Time, Place.

INQUIÉTUDE

COVENANT	GENESIS 1-5
TRANSCENDENCE	**Physical** Order *(World to Land)*
HIERARCHY	**Social** Order *(Land to Garden)*
ETHICS	**Ethical** Order *(Garden lost)*
OATH/SANCTIONS	**Social** Order corrupted *(Land lost)*
SUCCESSION	**Physical** Order condemned *(World lost)*

The Veil in the Temple was torn at the death of Christ, but the Temple itself was not. Not yet. A new "cosmic house" would have to be built before the old house was judged and torn down. God never leaves His people without a shelter, and never leaves the world without legal representation, either from earth to heaven (priest), or from heaven to earth (prophet).

The four "Gospel" horses in Revelation 6:1-8 carry the message of the resurrection from the Garden (Most Holy) into the Land (both the blessings and the curses), and establish a new representative house, the Church of Christ. Then the slain and exalted Apostolic Church accompanies Christ on white horses through the divided Abrahamic Land into the World (Revelation

LEVITICUS	CREATION
Place (Court) Lev. 1-7	**Physical-Social-Ethical** Cosmos *(Adam to Noah)*
Time (Holy Place) Lev. 8-12	**Social-Ethical** Cosmos *(Abraham/Moses to Christ)*
Holiness (Most Holy) Lev. 13-18/19/20-22	**Ethical** Cosmos *(The cross of Christ)*
Time (Holy Place) Lev. 23-24	**Ethical-Social** Cosmos *(Christ in the Church)*
Place (Court) Lev. 25-27	**Ethical-Social-Physical** Cosmos *(Restored Creation)*

19:11-21).[2] A generation after the three year ministry of Christ, the campaign of Titus Vespasian followed exactly the same "microcosmic" course, beginning in Galilee, moving through Judea, and finally conquering Jerusalem. The smoke of the Temple was an ironic ladder to heaven, ascending as an eternal memorial to its destruction (Revelation 18:18).

---

2   An offshoot of full preterism known as "Covenant Creationism" claims that since Jesus described the Jewish War as being like the days of Noah, the flood of Noah must have been merely local. However, the dichotomy is not global/local so much as Physical/Social. Their error results in Covenant history becoming entirely Social, with no Physical Creation at the beginning and no Physical Restoration at the end.

THE PERFECT STORM

This "hourglass" structure not only explains the differences and similarities between Israel and the Church as part of a process of judicial maturity (a transformation from flesh to smoke), it reveals why the "cosmic language" of the circumcision is no longer required.

From Abraham to AD70, the nations were the Sea and Israel was the Land. The divide was Social, and the means was circumcision. But after AD70, any cosmic language is again cosmic. The "Land and Sea" are again the actual land and sea. Or are they? If we want the pattern above to be truly chiastic, and for the final restoration to be truly Creational, the current "Sea" must still be representative, still "Social."

Just as the flaming sword of judgment was given to men, so the sword of the Word in the mouth of the glorified Christ is the "cosmic language" of the Gospel. The "tongues" of fire on the Day of Pentecost did not reverse the division of tongues at Babel. Rather, it was a sign that the Gospel would invade, inhabit and transform every tongue, every nation, as an inheritance for Christ. Apparently ceasing before AD70, this miraculous gift bore witness to the circumcision that there was a new universal language, the *esperanto* of the Gospel. The first "universal language" (Greek) and "worldwide travel" (Roman roads) were merely vehicles for something truly cosmic.

From AD70 until the final judgment, a process of

"ethnic cleansing" is being carried out, but this is not a battle against flesh and blood. Our weapons are spiritual. The sword is the Word, the "Covenant oath" in the mouths of the saints. The ministry is not representative destruction but irrigation, not blood but water, not Priesthood but Prophecy. The cleansing is not a bloody genocide, nor a conversion by coercion (a *jihad*), but a washing by the Word, a "purge" that wipes out the old enmities and unites us by giving us the one sound mind, the mind of Christ.

> For the earth will be filled
> With the knowledge of the glory of the Lord,
> As the waters cover the sea.
> (Habakkuk 2:14)

Revelation 20 describes for us this present age, in which Satan is bound from deceiving the nations. While the Gospel continues to gather the nations together, a boundary is set that the evil one might not gather them against the Church until this work is done. As it was in Leviticus, the focus of ministry has now moved from **Holiness** (Christ) to **Time** (1000 years), and this enigmatic span is an allusion to the history of Israel: a millennium of *tent* worship, and a millennium of *Temple* worship. The restoration of the Physical order (**Place**) will see the destruction of the last enemy, which is death.

> The times of ignorance God overlooked, but now he
> commands all people everywhere to repent, because

> he has fixed a day on which he will judge the world in righteousness by a man whom he has appointed; and of this he has given assurance to all by raising him from the dead. (Acts 17:30-31)

It is the Church which now holds back, or restrains, the judgment of the world. Not only are the saints salt and light, we are martyrs, that is, sacrifices without blemish. The saints in heaven and on earth are a "representative cosmos," models of kingdom citizens. The people of God are no longer the Land but the heavenly Sea, which is why the Covenant sign is no longer circumcision but baptism. Pentecost moved the people of God from a defensive ministry to an offensive one, from Priesthood to Prophecy, from being guarded by God to invading for God. As Israel was under Joshua, the Church herself is the oncoming storm, and the shipwrecks of various utopian dreams strewn throughout Christian history are evidence of the nations' failed attempts to protect themselves from her.

Whereas the "cosmic temple" language concerned the Forming of the house, the Gospel, a language of cosmic hope, is one concerned with the Filling of that house, a confession that unites all nations and will eventually lead to the Physical restoration of the Creation. It is the life giving decree of the resurrection of Christ, in whom all the world was plunged into the abyss and raised up to live a new life. Until then, His resurrection must be "preached to every creature."

19

HAPPY HOLIDAYS

NAILED TO THE MAST

The command of Queen Esther confirmed these practices of
Purim, and it was recorded in writing. (Esther 9:32)

Rachel Held Evans is a writer who likes the challenge of "asking tough questions about Christianity in the context of the Bible Belt."

The problem with her ministry on our behalf is that she takes the same road taken by King Saul. Since she will not listen to the voice of God in the Scriptures, she heads off to Endor for answers, looking for wisdom in a people who do what is right in their own eyes.

Evans ridiculed Christians who complained about the de-Christianizing of Christmas, expressed in the use of the greeting "happy holidays" in place of the highly offensive "Merry Christmas." In case we thought this was low level persecution, she prepared a helpful chart:

INQUIÉTUDE

Are you Being Persecuted?

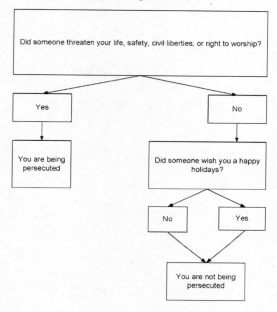

Image source: rachelheldevans.com/blog/holidays-persecuted

In response, Douglas Wilson commented:

First, persecution is defined by the Scriptures, and not by theological liberals who are in the process of shifting their loyalties over to the other side. The Lord Jesus defines persecution to include verbal abuse (Matthew. 5:11). And Paul says Isaac was persecuted by Ishmael because he was laughed at (Galatians 4:29). So we are not limited to an entirely arbitrary list on a chart of false alternatives.

196

But second, I quite agree that conservative Christians ought not to be whining about any of this. There is nothing here to surprise us, and subbing in Winter Holiday for Christmas is not exactly a fiery trial yet.[1]

Is *minor* persecution actually persecution or not? Do we have the right to complain about the *abortion* of Christ from Christmas? I believe the Bible gives us an entirely different perspective. Those who are whining *and* those who are whining about the whiners need a good dose of the Apostle Paul.

The modern mind desires mastery of all things through "classification." Labeling everything is fine, but this practice often blinds us to the relationships which still exist between all of these supposedly isolated things. For Paul, any suffering for the sake of the Gospel was something to be undertaken voluntarily *because of what it could achieve.* Defining graded levels of persecution is a sign that, unlike Paul, we wish to *avoid* it!

Paul did not see any level of persecution as an infringement upon his "life, safety, civil liberties or right to worship." He saw every persecution, at every level, as an opportunity for legal witness to the resurrection and the Gospel of Christ, and therefore rejoiced in it. The bigger the persecution, therefore, the bigger the opportunity. But neither did he pass up the little

1   Douglas Wilson, *Trigger Alert! Merry Christmas!,* www.dougwils.com, November 21, 2013.

ones. Paul's testimony, along with that of the other apostles, ended the false witness of Herodian Judaism. After AD70, the continued suffering of the Chuch eventually led to the end of pagan Rome, and the institution of the Christian calendar—and its holidays.

A millennium later, with the Roman Church now as corrupt as the Herods, it was the murders of many Reformers which resulted in the celebration of Reformation Day, a holiday which is seeing a revival in some quarters. As the old Euro-centric Christendom breathes its last, it is fitting to revive the remembrance of its foundation. It will bolster us to make the sacrifices which will be required to establish a new and even greater Christian age in Western lands.

The book of Esther gives us a wonderful example of the power of bold testimony. It shows us that persecution is most often a misunderstood opportunity.

After the exile, the Jews were living among other cultures in the same way as Christians do. However, under Mordecai's instruction, the heroine did not take advantage of the little opportunities. She refrained from revealing her Jewish identity. This deceit was the epitome of the attitude of the Jews, who were largely keeping their faith to themselves to avoid highlighting the enmity which still remained between Jew and Gentile. They failed to take advantage of the little opportunities for witness, so God sent a really big one: the threat of genocide, with the sanction of the Emperor.

Mordecai and Esther failed at the start but God

Die facht sich an gar ein grausem

liche erschrockenliche hystorien von dem wilden reütrich. Dracole wayde. Wie er die leüt gespist hat. vnd gepraten, vnd mit den haübtern, yn einem kessel gesoten. vñ wie er die leüt geschunden hat vñ zerhacken lassen als ein kraut. Jtez er hat auch den müttern ire kind gepratē vnd sy habēs müssen selber essen. Vnd vil andere erschrockenliche ding die in dissem Tractat geschribē stend. Vnd in welchem land er geregiret hat.

Woodcut from the title page of a 1499 pamphlet published by Markus Ayrer in Nuremberg. It depicts Vlad III "the Impaler" (identified as *Dracole wyade* = *Draculea voivode*) dining among the impaled corpses of his victims.

turned their failure into faithfulness. Added to this, there was the irony that Haman was not aware of the identity of the Queen, so God even used her *lack* of witness as the key to the persecutor's downfall.

The execution of Haman was a prophetic sign. He was impaled on a pole, lifted up as a serpent. Indeed, in Esther and Mordecai, the colors were nailed to the mast for every Jew from India to Ethiopia, for whom Esther bravely interceded. In the end, they passed with flying colors.

The end of the persecutors at God's hand resulted in a new festival, *Purim,* an extra "happy, holy day" which is still celebrated by Jews today.

Every seed that falls into the ground and dies results in a great harvest. Our God delights in "turning the tables." Secularists should learn from history that anyone who challenges God's work in any age always comes off second best. Those who bite and devour the saints ultimately bite the dust (Genesis 3:14).

So whether you are confronted with a sanitized "Happy Holidays" at the supermarket checkout or hauled before the courts (as you may soon well be), every level of persecution is an opportunity to move history forward, to let God's will be done on earth as it is in heaven, the only courtroom worth worrying about.

And, who knows, fresh persecution in the West might even result in a brand new Christian holiday. Wouldn't that be ironic?

20
THE LAST SIN
BLASPHEMY AGAINST THE SPIRIT

> *"For as in those days before the flood they were eating and drinking, marrying and giving in marriage, until the day when Noah entered the ark, and they were unaware until the flood came and swept them all away, so will be the coming of the Son of Man."*
> (Matthew 24:38-39)

Most disputes about the meaning of the Scriptures are not due to a lack of trying when it comes to hermeneutics. They result from a lack of *due process*. By this, I do not mean the process of interpretation, but rather the identification of the processes of God. He has a consistent way of doing things, and we must watch and learn.

A prime example is what we are supposed to make of Christ's words concerning the unpardonable sin. Viewed in the context of Covenant architecture, it becomes apparent that blasphemy against the Spirit is unpardonable not because it is the *worst* sin. It is unpardonable because it is the *last* sin.

INQUIÉTUDE

Firstly, the structure of Jesus' words is "sacrificial." In this case we might think of it as an Ascension Offering, since the entire animal is consumed by God, who "comes down" in the holy fire to "see" what man has built. The *Ethics* of the Law are the heavens bowed down to the earth to sift and thresh and refine.

TRANSCENDENCE – *Animal Chosen*
Creation: "Therefore I say to you, *(Initiation - Sabbath)*

> **HIERARCHY** – *Animal Cut*
> *Division:* every sin and blasphemy WILL BE forgiven men, *(Delegation - Passover)*

> > **ETHICS** – *Blood, Fire and Smoke*
> > *Ascension:* but the blasphemy against the Spirit WILL NOT be forgiven men.
> > *(Presentation - Firstfruits)*

> > > *Testing:* Anyone who speaks a word against the Son of Man, it WILL BE forgiven him;
> > > *(Purification - Pentecost)*

> > *Maturity:* but whoever speaks against the Holy Spirit, it WILL NOT be forgiven him,
> > *(Transformation - Trumpets)*

> **OATH/SANCTIONS** – *Acceptable Savor*
> *Conquest:* either in this age
> *(Vindication - Atonement)*

SUCCESSION – *Land and Womb opened anew*
or in the age to come."
(Representation - Booths)

(Matthew 12:31-32)

Some points worth noting concerning the structure:

- The passage divides neatly into a *Forming*, a *Filling*, and a *Future*. The word "blasphemy" is used in the *Forming* section. It means to misrepresent something, to bear false witness against it. The word "speak," however, is used in the *Filling* section, and this has the connotation of laying something to rest, bringing the matter to a close, having the last word as a prophet—in this case, a false one.
- If this structure is overlaid upon the first century history, it places those who cursed Christ at His crucifixion and yet repented after Peter's sermon right at the center, at the "Pentecost" step. Their sin was not high-handed, since they realized what they had done once their "judicial" eyes were opened. They had been led astray by the Jewish rulers.
- Within the threefold *Ethics* section, the WILL NOTs correspond to altars, the Bronze Altar and the Golden Altar. The WILL BE corresponds to the Lampstand, Pentecost, the Spirit of God, yet here there is no *mention* of the Spirit. It seems that being outside of Christ means one is exposed to holy fire, but those who are in Christ have the Spirit and cannot say that Jesus is cursed (1 Corinthians 12:3). The forgiveness of all Israel at the crucifixion *(Passover)* would be limited to those who believed when judgment came a generation later *(Atonement)*.

In the "Covenant-renewal" shape of this knife-sharp stanza of Jesus, there is no *Atonement* for sin (Step 6) and no *Succession*, no "Day 7," no *rest* for the Land.

Jesus is talking about the Jews in His day who, like their forefathers in the wilderness, would fail to enter into the promised inheritance of Israel. The blessings are missing from Step 6 because the end of old Israel was the expression of a self-maledictory oath.[1]

> So I declared on *oath* in my anger, 'They shall never enter my rest.'(Hebrews 3:11, NIV).

The fire of the Law (Steps 3-5) was intended to make the house clean for the fire of the Spirit, the Shekinah (Step 7). But if the Spirit was rejected, the house was left desolate. Instead of a pleasing savor—the pleasant smell of roasting meat on the altar below, or the smell of resurrection spices on the altar above—there was the "stink" of corruption (Amos 5:21).

In sacrificial terms, Christ ascended as High Priest, He sent the Spirit as holy fire to purify His people, and their apostolic witness "filled the house with smoke." Those who rejected and murdered Christ were forgiven, but those who rejected the Spirit of Pentecost became a house filled with demons. Pure fire makes the Bride. Strange fire makes the harlot.

It was the same with Israel in the wilderness. She was forgiven for the sin with the golden calf, spiritual harlotry. But God said He would visit her *again* for this sin. It was *not* over. In the book of Numbers, the same sin was committed on a greater scale. The judgment at

---

1   The self-maledictory nature of the oath explains the use of the conditional "if" in Greek in Hebrews 3:11; 4:3 and 4:5.

Sinai was a warning, so this later rebellion with pagan gods and pagan women was not a "wandering astray." This was the last straw, *the last sin,* for old Israel, the generation which came out of Egypt. The nation was threshed and the husks were blown away.

Likewise, all the crimes in the last days of the Old Covenant were committed in a society *saturated* in the Scriptures and the witness of the prophets. This means the sin was "high-handed," committed not merely by the leaders but also by the people in *full knowledge* of the Words of God. Blasphemy against the Spirit follows enlightenment. It is sin which is "epistemologically self-conscious," that is, "open-eyed" rebellion.

> But the person who does anything with a high hand, whether he is native or a sojourner, reviles the Lord, and that person shall be cut off from among his people. (Numbers 15:30)

The New Testament alludes to Exodus and Numbers to describe the sins of the Jewish leaders in the first century, but also to the days of Noah. The primeval history follows the same pattern. The sin of Cain was "covered" by a mark *(Passover),* but the Cainite line rejected the testimony of Enosh. Eventually, Enoch "ascended" as a kind of *Firstfruits. Pentecost* was the removal of the Spirit from earth, an initial *Trumpets* warning rather than a corporate execution. The last sin in that case was the rejection of the testimony of Noah, whose legal witness was their "last trumpet."

INQUIÉTUDE

FIRST WORLD **FIRST CENTURY**

TRANSCENDENCE
Creation (Initiation - Sabbath)

Adam's creation, The perfect life
sin and redemption of Christ

HIERARCHY
Division (Delegation - Passover)

Abel is slain. The death and
Cain is exiled. resurrection of Christ

ETHICS
Ascension (Presentation - Firstfruits)

Lamech's kingdom. The ascension and
Sethite ministry. enthronement
Enoch is taken of Christ

Testing (Purification - Pentecost)

Violence and Kingdom comes.
intermarriage The harvest begins

Maturity (Transformation - Trumpets)

Noah's testimony. Apostolic testimony.
The ark is completed The Church is united

OATH/SANCTIONS
Conquest (Vindication - Atonement)

Noah's family is saved. The Church is delivered.
The Land is submerged Israel is conquered

SUCCESSION
Glorification (Representation - Booths)

Noah's rest and rule. The wedding supper.
A future guaranteed Heavenly government

The original world was corrupted by Adam's sin in the Sanctuary: *theft* from the Father and a curse on his children; Cain's sin against the Son: the *murder* of a brother; and *blasphemy* against the Spirit, the holy matchmaker. The "consumption" of true Priesthood and true Prophecy by a godless kingdom meant that the work of all persons of the Trinity had been rejected. This is what brought about the end of the first world.

Likewise, throughout the empire, both the righteous and the wicked were ready for harvest, as Jesus said. The sins against the Father (the Herodian *theft* of Kingdom and the massacre of the innocents) and the Son (the *murder* of Christ, as Abel) would be forgiven, but *blasphemy* against the Spirit who tries the hearts would result in the abandonment of the house, the desolation of the culture. When a nation stops it ears and rushes upon the saints, its end is nigh.

The rejection of the testimony of the Apostolic Church is what necessitated an epistle like the book of Hebrews. Since the Temple building continued (a false ark), this was a final warning for those who now doubted the words of Christ, who trust instead in the Temple to save them, and were considering apostasy.

Do not trust in these deceptive words: 'This is the temple of the Lord, the temple of the Lord, the temple of the Lord... From the day that your fathers came out of the land of Egypt to this day, I have persistently sent all my servants the prophets to them, day after day. Yet they did not listen to me or incline their ear, but stiffened their neck. They did worse than their fathers. (Jeremiah 7:4; 26)

Hebrews 6:4-6 must be read in this context. The Jews who had been "enlightened" were now crucifying the Son of God once again through the murder of His prophets, beginning with Stephen. Their sin against Christ had been revealed to them by the Spirit as it had been through the preaching of Peter, but they refused to repent. They saw their faces in a glass but turned away.

When God hardens people's hearts, He does not do it from the *inside*. Since they rejected the indwelling of the Spirit, He hardened them through a return to *external* law, the faithful witness of the prophets (1 Samuel 6:6; Romans 9:14-18).[2] Now deluded, they filled up their sins through the shedding of righteous blood and brought down vengeance.

In the minds of the godless, the Scriptures and the Church are always condemned as the source of all our problems. The preacher is the one who "troubles Israel."

Our culture is breaking free, as Israel did, that it might reach its full potential, a ripeness for judgment. As it was in the first century, infanticide is rife, Covenants are despised, and the words of men are hailed as the words of gods. As always, this is a blessing as well as a curse. The last sin is always the herald of a new beginning. By the Spirit of Christ, may our testimony be a pleasing savor.

2   Church discipline is the same process in microcosm, a legal witness which will either soften the heart or harden it.

TRANSFORMATION

21
ALWAYS TAKE THE WEATHER
THE AGE OF DANGEROUS IDEAS

"Things ain't cookin' in my kitchen
Strange affliction wash over me
Julius Caesar and the Roman Empire
Couldn't conquer the blue sky..."
(Crowded House, "Weather With You")

Climate change is currently a big worry for those who believe human life has no divine guidance or purpose. What worries me, however, is the consternation of many Christians who have swallowed the stories which have been sold to them as "history."

Scientific data is meaningless without metanarrative. As Christians, we know the beginning and the end. Bible history and Bible prophecy are the two bookends of a biblical worldview. Without the truth of our past we cannot interpret the present or predict our future. So perhaps the failures of climate science are due at least in part to a worldview which is a mere fiction.

INQUIÉTUDE

As Malcolm Muggeridge famously said, "It has been said that when human beings stop believing in God they believe in nothing. The truth is much worse: they believe in anything." Or, as Paul says in Romans 1:22, "Claiming to be wise, they became fools."

BAD SCIENCE

When it comes to climate science, we have more data than we know what to do with. As someone who loves to look for patterns in things, I can understand the desire of scientists not only to figure out what is going on, but also to predict future weather.

Looking for patterns begins with past records, and it is here that modern climate science is revealed as the victim of a modern philosophy, that is, Naturalism.

We are told that 97% of scientists believe in anthropogenic climate change. But 98% of paleontologists believe in evolution, and they are wrong. It seems that it does not matter if the science is illegitimate, as long as it is "consensual." But what must be noted here is that these two consensuses are related.

I do not deny the data used to support climate alarm, just as I do not deny the bones paleontologists dig out of the ground, or pretend that the devil put them there. What I deny is their story of how the evidence came to be, and this affects how the data is interpreted. The theories proposed by modern science are all based upon their deluded revision of the history of the planet. The account of history in Genesis is true, so if its historicity and reliability are denied, then much of our science will be wrong. Our models will be based upon a past that never actually happened.

Although the Creation event itself is foundational, the historic fact of a catastrophic global flood seems to have a direct bearing on the interpretation of climate data. Tas Walker writes:

> I just listened to a podcast by climate scientist Murry Salby to the Sydney Institute entitled "Global Emission of Carbon Dioxide: The Contribution from Natural Sources."
>
> During question time toward the end of the recording (55 min 15 sec) he says:

> Just a historical note: The guy who started this was a Swedish chemist in whose lab I used to work at Stockholm by the name of Arrhenius. He won the Nobel Prize for chemistry and for his understanding of the temperature dependence of chemical reactions he got the Nobel Prize.
>
> He got into this and he started the whole global warming thing because he was actually trying to explain ice ages and he saw CO_2 varied and temperature varied and he figured maybe CO_2 caused the Ice Age. Now I don't think anyone believes that any more...

In other words, the whole idea that global warming is caused by CO_2 came out of the need to explain what caused the Ice Age—a mystery that still eludes modern scientists.

INQUIÉTUDE

In the Wikipedia entry on Arrhenius it says:

> He was the first person to predict that emissions
> of carbon dioxide from the burning of fossil fuels
> and other combustion processes would cause
> global warming. Arrhenius clearly believed that a
> warmer world would be a positive change. From
> that, the hot-house theory gained more attention.
> Nevertheless, until about 1960, most scientists
> dismissed the hot-house / greenhouse effect as
> implausible for the cause of ice ages as Milutin
> Milankovitch had presented a mechanism using
> orbital changes of the earth (Milankovitch
> cycles). Nowadays, the accepted explanation is
> that orbital forcing sets the timing for ice ages
> with CO_2 acting as an essential amplifying
> feedback.

Note the term "amplifying feedback". This means
that Milankovitch cycles are not enough to explain
the Ice Ages, which is understandable considering
the relatively small variations in orbital parameters
for the earth. So, they added a positive feedback
mechanism from CO_2. A positive feedback means
the system is unstable, which explains why many
scientists today are concerned about global warming
and the earth reaching an unstable tipping point.

The problem is that these scientists have ignored
the huge climate catastrophe of Noah's Flood. By
ignoring the Flood they cannot explain the post-
Flood (Pleistocene) Ice Age. The Ice Age was the
earth's thermal response to the massive climate

shock caused by the biblical Flood. It was largely the volcanic activity during that year-long event that produced the necessary conditions—warm oceans and volcanic dust high in the atmosphere. But the earth returned to equilibrium in about 700 years, demonstrating that it is a stable system. The biblical Flood provides the only explanation for the Ice Age.

See how a wrong understanding of the true history of the earth leads to a misunderstanding of what is happening in the present. And a wrong understanding will lead to wrong decisions about what we need to do.[1]

Thus, the philosophy of naturalism and the failures of modern climate science are directly related. They both misinterpret the data because they base their interpretations on unproven uniformitarian assumptions.

Evolutionists constantly tell us that their science is constantly under review "because that's how science works," yet in practice they desperately protect their failing dogmas from real world scientific criticisms. Its most obvious failures are papered over with stories that are blatant fabrications.

However, bad science does not exist in a vacuum. It is a child of something, and it has to be nurtured to remain alive. Bad science is the product of bad philosophy, which is in reality a bad *religion,* a religion which goes way back.

---

1   Tas Walker, *Noah's Flood and Global Warming,* biblicalgeology.net

INQUIÉTUDE

BAD RELIGION

98% of paleontologists might be evolutionists, but 98% of westerners are now statists, and they, too, are wrong. Statism, practically-speaking, is a faith in human rule which is so strong that it ascribes divine powers.

> *Put not your trust in princes,*
> *in a son of man,*
> *in whom there is no salvation.*
> *When his breath departs,*
> *he returns to the earth;*
> *on that very day*
> *his plans perish.* (Psalm 146:3)

The state has the power to produce prosperity through mere cleverness, and now it seems these skills even extend to an ability to influence, if not control, the weather. But do these magic skills amount to anything more than a pagan rain dance? A recent climate action rally in Sydney was rained on, creating a sea of colorful umbrellas. These were most likely the height of any wisdom in this endeavor, since all other proposals amount to the climate equivalent of putting a paper bag over one's head in a nuclear attack.

Interestingly, a survey carried out by the Australian public broadcaster reported that Protestants are the least concerned about "Left wing" issues such as climate change. The reason for this might not actually be that Protestants do not care about them, but that

216

Protestants are far less likely to fall for statism and its pretenses. They know that government is rarely the solution, and usually the problem. Due to some *good* religion, Protestants generally have a better grip on not only the past and the future, but also the present.

There is a reason that the growing wisdom and prosperity of the nations of the world flowed initially from Christianity, and then from Protestantism. It is that God blesses faithful worship and obedience. The entire world was blessed through the principles of the British Empire, which brought good government when it arrived and left it as a blessing when it departed. But Protestant Christians understand that good government is an *extension* of Christianity, and not itself the spring of life.

Without Christ, Western culture cannot be "progressive." Progressive causes, including abortion and climate action, are nothing more than a reversion to paganism. James Jordan writes:

> The true religion of Israel said that fertility was obtained by submitting to the Creator, while Baalism said that fertility was obtained by stimulating Nature. Thus, in true religion, man is the servant/slave of God, in submission to Him; while in Baalism, man is the Lord of his god (Nature) who needs to be stimulated by him.
>
> Nature religion is a religion of stimulation. Man has to stimulate Nature in order to get results. Like the Baal priests of the ancient world, he may engage

in sexual orgies, or cut himself with knives (1 Kings 18:28), in order to arouse the sleeping god...

So, for the ancient Baalist to bow before his idol was not an act of submission, but an act of stimulation. What he believed was the same thing modern secular humanists believe: that man is the Lord of Nature, and that there is no Creator God to whom man is responsible.[2]

Technology promised to make Man into a god, but of course along with the cargo came the cult, which now commands blessings from the sky. Frustratingly, the weather is a vehicle which we have not yet learned to drive properly. The climate possesses an infinite number of complicated controls, and there always seems to be a new model. Like your average shopping cart on swiveling wheels, it appears to have a mind of its own. Well, it does have a mind of its own, but this mind is not mechanistic. The weather is the chariot of God, and He never takes His hands off the wheel.

COVENANT SCIENCE

Surprisingly, I do believe that Nature is Man's to manipulate. Man makes the miracles. However, this is not through oblations to the gods, infant sacrifice, or religious prostitution. The blessings of abundance, of "increase," are to be gained miraculously, but at the

---

2   James B. Jordan, *Judges: A Practical and Theological Commentary*, 36-37.

The Children of Israel Crossing the Jordan (1800)
Benjamin West

hand of God, not through manipulation but through *obedience*. We can see this in the life of Joseph, whose faithfulness resulted in abundance wherever he served. The increase *was* miraculous, since his masters recognized that the Spirit of God was with him.

Modern science was the direct result of men who submitted to God. The amazing discoveries and resulting advances were all gifts to the minds of men by His Spirit. Because we were made in the image of God, we can use these gifts as blessings or as curses. Nuclear fission and genetic modification of food are prime examples. This is because every gift, like the Tree of Knowledge in the Garden of Eden, is intended to bring greater judicial maturity.

Our leaders do esteem ethics, but not God's ethics. They intend to do what is right, but what is right in their *own* eyes, not the eyes of God, who can see much further and whose sight is far keener.

Watching commentators from the Right and the Left argue about how much taxation is appropriate, and where those dollars should be spent to solve our problems, is frustrating. Nobody ever mentions that sin is the primary cause of those problems. If anybody, even jokingly, suggested that it would be good if we all tried to keep the Ten Commandments, they would be ridiculed and shouted down. Religion is a private matter, they would say. And what goes on in the bedroom is nobody else's business. But it turns out these things are actually everybody's business, since they have outcomes which are public, even global.

Based upon the words of the One who rides a chariot of fire in a cloud of glory, anthropogenic climate change is indeed possible. In Deuteronomy 28, Moses gave Israel a great list of blessings for obedience and curses for disobedience. These cover the natural realm (the Land and the womb) as well as Israel's economic status in relation to other nations. Israel suffered many famines in her history, and it was always the result of the shedding of innocent blood.

But if the Covenant, through Jesus' death and resurrection, now includes *all* nations, is it beyond possibility that God would exalt a faithful, obedient nation or culture with rain in due season, with a decrease in mutating diseases or problems like diabetes, autism and cancer? Might our food allergies disappear if we revived the practice of giving thanks before our meals? Christian history has already demonstrated that righteousness exalts a nation, and sin is a reproach to *any* people (Proverbs 14:34).

I am a postmillennialist, and thus an optimist. This is not only because of the way in which I interpret Scripture but also my faith in the character of God. A population explosion, mass starvation, peak oil, or a climate tipping point, whether hot or cold, are out of character with Jesus' plan for the world. He kept fingers off red buttons during the Cold War and He will continue to restrain evil until His work is done and His words are vindicated before all nations.

INQUIÉTUDE

Things this side of the final judgment will never be perfect, but things are getting better, thanks to the many blessings brought about by the incarnation and resurrection, the Scriptures, and two millennia of Christianity. All improvement comes from the Spirit of Christ, whether it be in medicine, technology or even widespread literacy. If we do not wish to lose these blessings, we need to humble ourselves and repent before God as a culture. Stopping the murder of the unborn, the shedding of innocent blood, is the place to begin. Repenting of the "sexual freedom" sustained by the blood of these gruesome murders would be next.

Certainly, climate science is not a simple issue, and we must keep our wits about us, but we must not bow to a secular state which calls us to sacrifice our children for prosperity and give our wealth to the weather gods. They mistake blessings for curses and curses for blessings. Children, CO_2 and oil are blessings from God which require wisdom, but they are not curses.

The 20th Century brought blessings and curses which would have been unimaginable in the 19th. As history moves from Garden to City, who knows what our good God has in store for us next? Like Joseph, we simply need to trust and obey, let the Pharaohs be haunted and humbled by their bad dreams, and let God bring the increase to the nations through our Joseph, who is always one step ahead of the weather.

22

THE ETHICAL NUDE

EXPOSING NAKEDNESS

*I was at ease, and he broke me apart; he seized me
by the neck and dashed me to pieces.* (Job 16:12)

One only has to compare a portrait of Picasso's wife
to that of one his lovers to prove that his strange
perspective on reality worked from the inside out.

What we feel as we observe his works is what he
feels about his subjects as he paints them. The spirit
and desire which animate man and beast not only
move flesh but, in Picasso's world, distort reality. Time
and history without fail reveal the true character of
objects, people and ideologies. A Picasso is often the
exterior of a person or event refracted and distorted by
an impression of the spirit or emotion within. It is a
history in a single frame, an X-ray study that discovers
not the bones but the heart. Emotional reality is
revealed in shape and color. In these cases, Picasso's
subjects are "ethical nudes."

223

INQUIÉTUDE

None is more striking or famous than *Guernica*, a representation of the merciless destruction of a helpless Spanish town, a non-military target, in 1937. The painting itself has a striking history, culminating in the cover-up of a tapestry reproduction at the United Nations before a speech by Colin Powell. It was deemed unsuitable as a background for war mongering.

During his career, Picasso very suddenly turned his back on centuries of tradition. His new style was shocking to the critics of the day. It is *still* shocking. Reality is broken, cut into pieces and reconstructed— or perhaps arranged on the altar—by a madman. There is an order to it, but not an order we recognize. Or do we? As with the work of many other ground breakers, his work does resonate with us as *some* level. The gut level.

The book of Revelation is the Bible's *Guernica*. The Light of the World, come to show men the way, has suddenly become the harsh light bulb of the interroga-tor, the flash of bombs and machine gun fire from the sky. Yet men perceive it as darkness. They are helpless to escape the single electric eye in the sky, the heat ray of heaven.

> Then I saw another mighty angel coming down from heaven, wrapped in a cloud, with a rainbow over his head, and his face was like the sun, and his legs like pillars of fire. (Revelation 10:1)

Guernica (1937)
Picasso

225

INQUIÉTUDE

The Revelation is the last stage in a Covenant Lawsuit: the pronouncement of sentence. Central to this final act is the drinking of the Covenant cup by a harlot, representing those Jews who refused to drink with Christ. The rite originates in Numbers 5, where a woman suspected of adultery undergoes a "liturgy of inspection." The pattern of exposure in the liturgical "image" would be played out in her subsequent history.

Jesus turns this rite on its head in his exposure of the accusers of the woman caught in adultery, and He does the same in the Revelation. The Church-State institution ruled by those who accused and condemned the harlots and tax collectors is revealed as the *greatest* harlot and tax collector. She is made to drink the cup to the dregs. The Jews who refused to sup with their "Husband" drank instead the blood of His Body, the Church, and called down another Mosaic Pentecost as a holocaust (Exodus 32). Just as alcohol removes inhibitions and reveals the heart, so the true character of Jerusalem would be exposed in her final days. The whitewash of Temple worship would be ripped away in a brutal execution. This time, all the veils in Jerusalem would be torn (Hebrews 10:20).

Revelation uses color and shape—and a serrated literary structure—to reveal the thoughts and intents of the heart of a city abandoned by God. It is the entire Bible "gone all Picasso." The Apocalypse is the epic history of the Old Testament exposed in a thousand naphtha flashes on a single frame. All things came upon that generation. Even if we fail to understand it in detail, we comprehend it at a gut level. The eyes of God are looking for anything untoward about our entrails.

We *can*, however, understand it in detail. The modern practice of divorcing the Revelation from history and treating it as a general "picture book" of Christ's work in all ages, rather than as a prophecy of the destruction of Jerusalem and the investiture of a new human government in heaven, is a tragedy akin to removing *Guernica* from the historical context of the event which inspired it. The fact that the events depicted in the painting actually happened gives it not less but *more* power in application. The same goes for the Revelation. It is not "generic" men and women who call upon the rocks and hills to cover them. It was actual men and women in the first century. Those who stripped the righteous bare would be unveiled. Those who had hidden their faces from Him in the flesh would come face to face with Him in His glory.

> Your nakedness shall be uncovered,
> and your disgrace shall be seen.
> I will take vengeance, and I will spare no one.
> (Isaiah 47:3)

Like the Christians who first heard the seven letters, Jesus gives us in the Revelation an immunizing taste of death—the cup of Communion—that we might avoid condemnation. The Old Testament was given to us as examples, and post-Pentecostal Jerusalem would serve as the final example. If we read it with soft hearts, *we ourselves* drink the blood of the apostles and prophets, because we are murderers like Paul and adulterers like Mary. We feel it burn as it goes down, judging us from the inside out, revealing our own hatred of God, our own love of the darkness, our own fear of being laid bare. The exposure of the murderous whore is an ethical nude.

During the German occupation of France, Nazi soldiers inspected Picasso's Paris studio. An officer looked through some Picasso postcards and recognized a reproduction of *Guernica*. Picking up the card, he asked, "Did you do this?" Picasso replied, "No, you did." This was an ethical nude.

If someone is offended by the gruesome gang rape and dismemberment in Judges 19, or the ribald references to bestiality in Ezekiel 23, rather than feeling a deep sense of shame before God, it is likely they remain under the judgment of God. Such an "apocalypse" cuts us like a sword and arranges us in cubic pieces on the altar. Such a circumcised heart examines itself and insists on drinking with Christ. We expose ourselves to God that we might not be exposed. We judge ourselves that we might not be judged. We seek shelter in Christ that we might not be crushed by Him.

If we are not preaching to make lost people see their nakedness before God, like the nakedness of Adam, or the nakedness of the pastor of Laodicea, then we are not preaching. Like the biblical prophets, like Picasso, we must deconstruct reality and reassemble it inside out, displaying the *animus* of the animal. Sermons aimed only at the head, or only at the heart, create what C. S. Lewis called "men without chests." Head and heart must both be engaged in something which resonates at a gut level. It is not merely *enlightening*, nor merely *touching*, but the reassembly, the edification, of the whole man.

> When we as preachers drift into muttering like the scribes, or schmoozing like the therapists, we are trying to avoid what God has commanded us to face. Men are to meet with God when the Word of God is declared. When they do so, they must do so as men and not as partial men. They must not send their brains on ahead to see if it is safe. They must not offer up just their hearts to check out how it makes them feel. Rather they should unbutton the shirt and ask God to be merciful.[1]

Picasso did not paint for the eyes but for the gut. He painted for the gut that the eyes might be opened.

---

1   Douglas Wilson, *Preaching to the Chest*, CREDENDAagenda, Volume 15, Issue 2.

23
SEEING IN THE DARK

THE KNOWLEDGE
OF GOOD AND EVIL

"It often seems to me that the night is much more alive and richly colored than the day." — Vincent Van Gogh, in a letter to his brother Theo in 1888

A few years ago, I had the privilege of viewing seven Van Goghs, all in one room. This number included *Starry Night Over the Rhone,* the depth and texture of which has to be seen to be believed.

The Impressionists went out of their way *not* to paint what they saw. They stretched and strained the norms to communicate how the world made them *feel.* Their work was not a representation of reality but a *response* to it, not a recitation but an *exposition* of its visual text.

Our impressions, whether musical, literary or artistic, also portray how we *wish* to see the world. As with printed reproductions of the works of the Impressionists, pop-culture misrepresents human life, portraying it as unbearably dull. Our movies are filled with androgynous, transhuman perfections (the gods of heaven) and the gritty barbarism of wizards and warriors (the gods of earth), because being human is not enough.

A similar gnosticism now defines "Christianity," which exists in our *heads,* in our *hearts* or in *heaven and hell*—anywhere but *here.* Like spellbound medievals, we want angels and demons, not the subtle, underrated joys of a life of peace with God. The color gamut of modern vision, sacred and secular, is too narrow, and it creates a desire to escape this world for something, *anything,* different. Secularists abscond through surgery or narcotics, while the spiritual turn to *Tarot* or ecstasies.

The difference, however, is that medievals understood *this* world as mystical, a *foretaste* of future corruptions and glories, the *evidence* of things hoped for. We, instead, are hankering for something exorcised from the world in our quest for mastery of it. In place of demons and angels, we were given night and day, but the light casts shadows and the darkness reveals the stars. Both are reminders of Man's ethical obligation to God, a call to *judge.* Perhaps, like Adam, our desire for godlike extremes betrays an awareness of our own vulnerability, and our unwillingness to trust the God for whom the night is as bright as the day (Psalm 139:12). Henry Beston writes:

> Our fantastic civilization has fallen out of touch with many aspects of nature, and with none more completely than night. Primitive folk, gathered at a

Self Portrait (1887)
Vincent van Gogh

233

cave mouth round a fire, do not fear night; they fear, rather, the energies and creatures to whom night gives power; we of the age of the machines, having delivered ourselves of nocturnal enemies, now have a dislike of night itself. With lights and ever more lights, we drive the holiness and beauty of night back to the forests and the sea; the little villages, the cross-roads even, will have none of it. Are modern folk, perhaps, afraid of the night? Do they fear that vast serenity, the mystery of infinite space, the austerity of the stars? Having made themselves at home in a civilization obsessed with power, which explains its whole world in terms of energy, do they fear at night for their dull acquiescence and the pattern of their beliefs? Be the answer what it will, to-day's civilization is full of people who have not the slightest notion of the character or the poetry of night, who have never even seen night. Yet to live thus, to know only artificial night, is as absurd and evil as to know only artificial day.[1]

Solomon, the wisest king who ever lived, understood real life. He saw in both its lights and shades the glorious purpose of imperfections. In Ecclesiastes, the pictures he paints with words call us beyond the certainties of the *kingly* Proverbs to a subtler, more *prophetic* understanding of the world. Jeffrey Meyers writes:

---

[1]   Henry Beston, "Night on the Great Beach" in *The Outermost House: A Year of Life On The Great Beach of Cape Cod* (1928).

Christians must be realists about the world and life; the Bible is. The church celebrates Christmas season in the dead of winter for good reasons. Faith does not mean ignoring the "living death," as Augustine put it, of our cursed world; rather, it means trusting God while confessing our own bafflement and impotence to change our death-stamped existence in this world. This is where Solomon's Ecclesiastes can help us modern Christians... biblical wisdom does not give us the power to leverage the world to insure our own health or success. Death in its various forms is everyone's future. Nevertheless, we can genuinely enjoy life. Joy *and* curse, not one or the other. According to Solomon, the wise man will affirm them both...

The son of David is so honest about the difficulties in life that it scares many Christians, and he trusts God so much he has a bit too much fun—he drinks wine and actually enjoys sex with his wife! This is way too much "fresh detail" for some Christians.[2]

Meyers demonstrates that the observations of Solomon are not the desperate ramblings of a hopeless pagan soul, as many claim, but the wisdom of a faithful believer, and as such they must not be domesticated. Solomon calls us to maturity that we might handle the harsh realities of life.

Solomon's request for an understanding mind, able to discern between good and evil (1 Kings 3:9) and the

---

2 Jeffrey Meyers, *A Table in the Mist: Ecclesiastes Through New Eyes*, viii-x.

INQUIÉTUDE

Lord's subsequent gift of dominion was the exact opposite of Adam's failure in Eden, and this is something the reader is expected to notice.

The Knowledge of Good and Evil was not, and is not, something to be avoided at all costs. It was something to be *obtained* by faithful obedience. The serpent's lie threw the Law of God into rich relief. The blood of animals demonstrated the love of God. The loss of paradise created a hunger for a greater glory. The harshness of reality in Eden was not resolved through blame, litigation or legislation, and neither can it be today. The proliferation of these things in our culture is a sign of immaturity, not wisdom. The office of the king is not condemnation but redemption. This requires an ability to see into the darkness of human hearts as if it were high noon, as Solomon does in his first judgment (1 Kings 3:16-28). This can only come to us, after faithful obedience, as a gift from God.

> Learn to reverence night and to put away the vulgar fear of it, for, with the banishment of night from the experience of man, there vanishes as well a religious emotion, a poetic mood, which gives depth to the adventure of humanity. By day, space is one with the earth and with man—it is his sun that is shining, his clouds that are floating past; at night, space is his no more. When the great earth, abandoning day, rolls up the deeps of the heavens and the universe, a new door opens for the human spirit, and there are few so clownish that some awareness of the mystery of

236

being does not touch them as they gaze. For a moment of night we have a glimpse of ourselves and of our world islanded in its stream of stars—pilgrims of mortality, voyaging between horizons across eternal seas of space and time. Fugitive though the instant be, the spirit of man is, during it, ennobled by a genuine moment of emotional dignity, and poetry makes its own both the human spirit and experience.[3]

We thirst for the colors of both the light and the night; the glorious unknown, the world beyond the veil, a world where we are truly gods. But that world is hidden not only in the world around us, it is a world built deeply into us. We sculpt it, paint it, pointillize it, poem it and pixel it but it ever remains just out of reach.

Wisdom and maturity, like good wine and fine cigars, are well-rounded, bittersweet tastes to be acquired over time. But an experienced palate is easier to achieve than mastery of the tough moral dilemmas which it symbolizes. The Bible reveals God as a crafty king, and life as an angel to be wrestled with, that our eyes might be opened. Sanctification is not the improvement of the old nature but the ability to see it as it is. Just as the light shines in the darkness, an abundant life thrives in mortification (Philippians 2:14-15).

Jesus passed through the shadow of death and now there is nothing to fear (Hebrews 2:15). Now He beckons us to do the same, to be as deep and rich as He

3   Beston.

is in both the mundane and the crisis. The world of godhood is now well within our reach, but then it always was, as demonstrated for us in the ordinary life of Jesus.

The night now is more richly colored than the day because it is more blessed to give than to receive; because those who mourn are blessed; because the greatest love is demonstrated in death. Like Moses, we consider the reproach of Christ greater riches than the treasures of Egypt.

For the mature, dualism dies in the defeat of Death. The ascended Jesus holds the full reality of good and evil, *Yin and Yang*, in perfect balance, through perfect judgment. At Pentecost, He exalted us as sun, moon and stars, lights to rule both the Day *and* the Night. Darkness is once again, as it was for Adam, merely a field in which a seed can grow, or a heaven to be filled with sons (Genesis 37:1-11).

Postmillennialism is so agreeable because it is optimistic about the work of God *within* human lives and cultures. They are being and will be *redeemed* by the Gospel rather than *condemned*. Ultimately, nothing that is good will be wasted or lost. The world that is hungry and thirsty will be filled. Every new darkness heralds yet another wisdom-dawn.

And Jacob was left alone. And a man wrestled with him until the breaking of the day. (Genesis 32:24)

24
MAN AT THE CROSSROADS

BIBLICAL IMAGES IN 'INTERSTELLAR'

"Man was never meant to be a god, but he is forever trying to deify himself." — Martyn Lloyd-Jones

Few novels or movies manage to successfully capture the imagination of our entire culture. When they do, it is often because they not only present us with engaging characters and a gripping plot, but also a coherent worldview. And in most of these, if not all, to varying degrees that worldview is the biblical one. A culture founded upon the Bible is forever bound to tell the old story. Once we are exposed to the truth, there is no going back. Once we reject the truth, there is no going forwards, either.

Behind all the bluster and self-serving feigned offence, Western culture is still fixated upon the Bible. We are still telling its stories. Its worldview is either thinly veiled so that a people which has democratically rejected the Word of God can still consider themselves

INQUIÉTUDE

"intellectually satisfied," or else it is hijacked, perverted or defaced as a blatant expression of its rejection. The Bible is loved and hated, mimicked and oppressed, but it is never ignored. And even those who refuse to stand on its promises still have great expectations.

A NEW DRUG

What is unexpected is the fact that the shape of the biblical story is now less perverted in science fiction and fantasy than it is in the latest crop of "biblical epics," where the cinematic retellings of episodes from Genesis and Exodus are Trojan horses, that is, vehicles for agendas which are hostile to the Bible. Ironically, the cultural "children" bear the implanted image more faithfully than do the parents who are still mad at God. Perhaps this is because the children are now so unfamiliar with the Bible that they do not recognize how fundamental it is to the shape of our culture. What they assume is instinctive is in fact the result of millennia of enculturation.

The skeptic might claim that the Bible contains many truths which we still value, even though we now reject the supernatural, but that is quite another matter. Rejecting the supernatural entails rejecting any existential meaning other than that which we confer *upon* ourselves, and the novels and films we most enjoy betray our desire for a meaning sourced *beyond* ourselves. Surrendering completely to the meaning-lessness inherent in the materialistic worldview which permits us to lie and steal and sleep around is too big an ask. So, it turns out that naturalism, the belief that there is nothing beyond the physical, is unnatural to us. Deep down, we are simply not willing to embrace despair.

Since religion, the opiate of the people, is now a controlled substance, a new drug is required. Scientific endeavor has failed to provide us with the transcendence we crave, so we have settled for science fiction. Certainly there is much "cult" science fiction that is consistent with its worldview, and honest in its despair, but as a culture we cannot live without stories of hope and destiny. In this respect, the atheistic *cultus* has failed to become culture. No matter how gloomy the imagined Dystopia, post-Christendom will always view it as an arena for redemption, a garden that requires a better gardener, a dark night that brings an even brighter, and wiser, day. After a run of bleak, demoralizing films in the early seventies, the culture-wide popularity of the first *Star Wars* episode was due in part to its shameless proclamation of faith, hope and love. Given the choice between *A Clockwork Orange* and *A New Hope,* the average Joe will always choose the cowboys in space.

Now, there is nothing wrong with fiction *per se,* just as there is nothing wrong with food or sex or money *per se.* Fiction is a very effective means of understanding and commenting upon the world, and science fiction doubly so, but its misuse is plainly another form of idolatry. God gave us a book which explains the meaning of our existence, but we insist on "searching" elsewhere. Carl Sagan claimed that "If we ever reach the point where we think we thoroughly understand who we are and where we came from, we will have failed." But Sagan's claim is itself as dogmatic as the Bible. It was an attempt to obscure the truth, to veil the door, that he himself might not have to enter in (Matthew 23:13; Romans 1:18).

A FALSE HOPE

Despite the pretensions of interplanetary pioneering, even the science fiction with strong roots in scientific theory is more an exploration of the human heart. Alan Lightman writes:

> Science does not reveal the meaning of our existence, but it does draw back some of the veils ... Theoretical physics is the deepest and purest branch of science. It is the outpost of science closest to philosophy, and religion...
>
> I completely endorse the central doctrine of science. And I do not believe in the existence of a Being who lives beyond matter and energy, even if that Being refrains from entering the fray of the physical world. However, I certainly agree with [scientists who argue] that science is not the only avenue for arriving at knowledge, that there are interesting and vital questions beyond the reach of test tubes and equations. Obviously, vast territories of the

arts concern inner experiences that cannot be analyzed by science. The humanities, such as history and philosophy, raise questions that do not have definite or unanimously accepted answers...

There are things we take on faith, without physical proof and even sometimes without any methodology for proof. We cannot clearly show why the ending of a particular novel haunts us. We cannot prove under what conditions we would sacrifice our own life in order to save the life of our child. We cannot prove whether it is right or wrong to steal in order to feed our family, or even agree on a definition of "right" and "wrong." We cannot prove the meaning of our life, or whether life has any meaning at all. For these questions, we can gather evidence and debate, but in the end we cannot arrive at any system of analysis akin to the way in which a physicist decides how many seconds it will take a one-foot-long pendulum to make a complete swing. The previous questions are questions of aesthetics, morality, philosophy. These are questions for the arts and the humanities. These are also questions aligned with some of the intangible concerns of traditional religion...

Faith, in its broadest sense, is about far more than belief in the existence of God or the disregard of scientific evidence. Faith is the willingness to give ourselves over, at times, to things we do not fully understand. Faith is the belief in things larger than ourselves. Faith is the ability to honor stillness at some moments and at others to ride the passion and exuberance that is the artistic impulse, the flight of

INQUIÉTUDE

the imagination, the full engagement with this strange and shimmering world.[1]

This sounds like a rejection of scientism in the quest for greater purity and scope, but all it does is shift the focus of the analysis. Now unsatisfied with both God's revelation and the results of the search for meaning in the created order, the "thinking man" turns to his own existential angst, that is, from the stage backdrop to the actors. Instead of looking to the Author, our experience of the drama of life becomes the authority, which might explain why entertainment is now the primary means by which Western people learn how to live. Scriptwriters author our sermons, teaching us only the things we want to hear.

Of course, this includes to some degree the imaginations of popular science, which will even posit the existence of multiple universes before it will entertain the slightest thought of a supernatural God to whom we must submit in thought and deed. Science draws back *some* veils, but in the hands of man it is used to keep closed the one which really keeps us in the dark.

Turning from the darkness of space to the darkness of the human heart will be as limited in effectiveness and objectivity as any other internal investigation.

---

[1] Excerpts from Alan Lightman, *The Accidental Universe*.

EXISTENTIAL PORN

Science fiction not only gives us a godlike view of mother earth from the heavens, one which we ourselves can delineate, dominate and control, but promises all humanity an identity we can choose, and a destiny which we ourselves can decide.

Fiction becomes a way of imagining significance in a world which the fallen images of God have deemed to be meaningless. Estranged from God, it is an existential "feely," a virtual religion, a devotional without the constraints of actual devotion.[2] Our stories are no better than the stories invented by pagans throughout the centuries, with one exception. Our post-Christian explanations are all little tin versions of the true God-story we rejected. We wanted the freedom to party like animals (or aliens) but it turns out we are not willing to leave the home that gave us all the securities, both material and existential, that we enjoyed. At least, like Nietzsche, but unlike Dawkins, the biblical prodigal had the decency to move out. Intellectually-speaking, the modern atheist is an adolescent holed up in his bedroom living a virtual life behind an avatar of scientism, yelling at mother church while she dutifully continues to do his washing.

---

2   In Aldous Huxley's *Brave New World,* "Feelies" are a form of entertainment. The user rests his hands on metal knobs protruding from the arms of the chair, allowing him to feel the physical sensations of the actors on-screen, usually in sexually-themed films.

INQUIÉTUDE

This perspective sheds far more light on Christopher Nolan's *Interstellar* than any astrophysicist ever could. The film is an honest attempt to revive the spirit of the pioneer through story, but it is a desperate attempt to lessen the pain of the meaningless of our "accidental" origins through a fictional self-defined future. Its scientific wonders are the miracles of the Jannes and Jambres of today, performed to intimidate God's people and maintain the divine claim of the current human dynasty, rather than understanding all human technology as a wondrous gift from God.

The story compares those two dark spaces, the lonely human heart and the outer limits, to paint a hopeful picture. But the fusion is merely poetic, contrived, an overly clever paradox which fails to reinforce the arrogant notion that we ourselves are the ones we have been waiting for.

Despite this, the reason the story resonates with so many is because it is one which we already know. Even its diversions from biblical truth are merely inversions, placeholders for reality, and thus still easily recognizable. As much as the dusty old Bible makes moderns cough and choke, it is still the air we take with us to breathe between the stars. The story of *Interstellar* is simply an extension—or perhaps a hijacking—of the story of the Bible.

BIBLICAL IMAGES

Creation

The difference between *Interstellar* and most other science fiction stories is the upfront awareness of a benevolent intelligence. Although this "supernatural" element is defused later on, there is an underlying sense that all of human history has a purpose. Here of course it is more about survival than actual dominion, but the imminent end of the earth's fertility is a new beginning. The "new world" really is now a new world, and there is a sense that despite the hardships, betrayals and sacrifices, this was always meant to be.[3] These are all reflections of the dominion mandate, but the Nolans get around the required "divinity" by getting "timey-wimey" and playing kick the can.

Dust

The film begins with recordings of old people reminiscing about the "last days" and how they dealt with the dust storms ravaging the earth. It is at once foreboding and optimistic, a bittersweet taste of things to come, a testimony of death coming from beyond the grave in some unseen but rosy future.

Of course, dust is a prominent theme in the Bible,

---

3   See chapter 26, "Barren Worlds" for my thoughts on this from a biblical Covenant perspective.

and here it is linked with the removal of the "breath of life" as it destroys the lungs of those who live on the land. The slow extinction of crop after crop reminds us of the curse of barrenness bestowed upon Adam, Cain and Israel. But the film extends the death of plant life to the suffocation of the final generation, not through a flood but in an event similarly catastrophic. The entire world has become "the Land."

Writing in the Dust

It is interesting that the dust is combined with fingers and gravity to write the crucial coordinates on the floor. Rather than a moral code it is a bar code, which reminds us that the kind of knowledge Man values is not ethical but mere data. The goal of fallen Man will always be to achieve dominion over the earth without the blessing of God, through the stimulation of nature rather than submission to heaven. The code in the dust is an expression of Baalism, an inversion of the finger of God. The only possible alternative to Scripture is paganism, even for the modern mind.

Ascension

The trip to NASA is essentially a pilgrimage to the Tabernacle in the wilderness. It is heavily guarded, filled with "ministering angels" (both the humans and the "metallic" cherubim) and contains the only means of ascension to heaven. Coincidentally, *nasa* is the Hebrew word for "lifted up."

Twelve astronauts were sent as "apostles" to assess the twelve planets possibly suitable for colonization, but this final mission could visit only *three*. Any numbers could have been chosen here, but these are a nod not only to the tribes of Israel and Jesus' twelve disciples, but also to David's three "mighty men" and Jesus' core group of Peter, James and John.

The Door

Through the ministry of this tent, the mission ascends as "sacrificial head," with the promise that all humanity will later ascend as the body. This is repeated later on a smaller scale when Cooper sacrifices himself to the black hole.

Rather than being a source of terror (a dramatic tension saved for the black hole later in the movie), the wormhole is instead a source of wonder. Like the Laver and the Veil in the Tabernacle, it provides access to another place, the heavenly court which provided the blueprint for its earthly replicas.

Passing through this "crystal sea" allows the unseen benefactor to "draw near" to these ministers of salvation. The "handshake" is a sign that the entire mission is being watched by benevolent eyes, the one at the Right Hand. As mentioned above, while biblical epics are currently portraying the God of the Bible as hateful and capricious, other films are instinctively doing a better job of imaging the truth.

INQUIÉTUDE

Sacred Architecture

As the hero of the story, Cooper himself becomes "triune." As my friend Steven Opp observed, Cooper begins as the Father, goes on a mission of salvation as the delegated Son, then returns—as promised—as the Holy Ghost, to guide humanity into all truth. The blood goes up and the Spirit comes down. Finally, he is the eternal man, the Adam who will keep and govern the new earth prepared by the fertile Bride, the "mother of all living."

As in Scripture, this threefold architecture is measured out in geography. In the Bible, it is the Garden, the Land and the World, replicated in both the ark of Noah and in the Tabernacle. All of these are images of the relationship within the Trinity. In this case, the mission encompasses three planets:

Planet 1	Planet 2	Planet 3
The Father	*The Son*	*The Spirit*
The Deep, the Mountains	Cain and Abel	The Bride
Eternal Now	Conflict, Barrenness	Hope, Tents in the Wilderness

Steven observes that the gravity on the first planet was too heavy (the waters below), on the second it was too light (the frozen waters above) but that on the third it seems "just right." Perhaps here we find our "flood"

250

imagery also. While Cooper and Dr Mann fight it out in heaven, there are crops being burned on the earth, highlighting the nature of conflict in the corresponding *mediatory* roles/domains of the Son: the Land, and the Holy Place.

This leads to the "Day of Atonement" where Cooper sacrifices himself, leaving the "Bride" behind and passing through the Veil on her behalf.

Transcendence

Some Christians have criticized the fact that Cooper becomes godlike, but we must remember that as the ascended head, Christ is not only God in human flesh, but *a Man who is God*. The lifting up of Cooper as the means of communication, of mediation between "the heavens" and the earth within a holy cube encased in a circle is entirely consistent with the ministry of the Tabernacle, the cruciform Man within the four-cornered Land surrounded by a circular Sea.

There are many similarities between *Interstellar* and *2001: A Space Odyssey,* but the most significant is the positioning of the Man in "the odd room." Here, that room is like the ark of Noah and the house of the Father: a house of many rooms (Genesis 6:14; John 14:2). The *tesseract* is a four-dimensional "hypercube," and Cooper is placed in it as the High Priest in the cube-shaped Most Holy Place (1 Kings 6:20).

From this position, he can see the entire history of a room on earth. Just as the *tesseract* is a geometrical

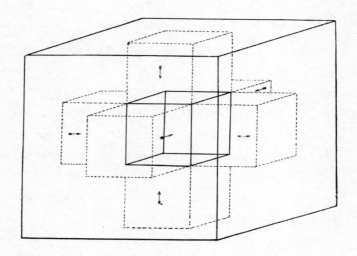

Tesseract (1924)
Theo van Doesburg

extrusion of a cube, so that single room is presented as many rooms, the mathematical "equation" from which all reality is derived. Since every story in the Bible follows the same matrix, the history is not only linear but also layered like tree rings, every layer a cruciform Tabernacle with the same architectural offices fulfilled by different people and events. Reading the Bible like this transforms it from dusty books on a shelf into an open house, one where every room is accessible to us.

It is interesting that the interface between life and death is presented here as a cross, just as it was in the Danny Boyle movie *Sunshine*. In that case, the Most Holy Place was a cube-shaped bomb borne on the back of a huge golden disc. In both films, a single man becomes the sacrificial doorway to a new earth.

One criticism of the film I had was something common to Nolan's movies, and that is that they feel like they have been constructed rather than composed. Although *Interstellar* focuses on human relationships as the "heart" of science, it seemed to me that the robots mimicked humanity better than the script did. However, the Bible faces similar criticisms because it is also literary architecture. Douglas Jordan has mapped the entire story of *Interstellar* as a three dimensional chiasm, at the center of which the two great lies are exposed. This might explain some of the film's pointy corners.[4]

4   See Appendix 4.

INQUIÉTUDE

The Ark

Finally, we have the ark of Noah, a microcosmic creation where the activities of human life can be carried on in a temporary safe space until the "waters recede" and the new Land is ready for population. This is also the New Jerusalem, waiting in heaven to descend upon a new, abundant earth. Just as Cooper ascended as head, now all humanity has been able to ascend through his ministry as the ghost. When he is rescued and "resurrected," he is the lamb and this ark is the city.

CONCLUSION

If we have eyes trained in the language of biblical symbolism, these highly imaginative and beautifully made films can be inspiring for Christians. But we must also remember that they are a two-edged sword. While these stories remind us of and illustrate for us the truths of the Bible, for most viewers they are a temporary anesthetic for the pain they feel because they have rejected it.

25
BIG LOVE
A HISTORY OF STOLEN FRUIT

"Blessed is the womb that bore you, and
the breasts at which you nursed." (Luke 11:27)

Arguing for Christian morality in a secular society is difficult. A culture which accepts evolutionary dogma has no intellectual place—or inherent desire—for absolute morality, since it believes morality is only helpful because it was shaped by an instinct to survive.

However, although the Scriptures give us hard and fast principles, even they do not give us a "timeless" list of commandments. Christians are rightly accused of arbitrarily picking laws from Leviticus that apply today from those that do not. As Peter Leithart writes,

> ...the common ordering of the Mosaic law into "moral, civil, ceremonial," while valid in a broad sense, does not give much assistance in dealing with specific passages. In the law, moral, civil, and ceremonial features are all mixed up together.[1]

---

1   For more discussion, see Appendix 5.

INQUIÉTUDE

But all the commandments *are* rooted in a single history, one which grows like a tree. The rules for children are not the same as the laws for grown men and women. The changes in the laws of God result from a growth in the maturity of the people of God.

Since the laws of God are always given as a means of *progress*, propositional truth is recorded for us as a *process*. Thus, to understand the commandments, we must study sacred history. The wisdom which results from such an understanding not only puts the critics of the Bible in their place, it enables us to proclaim with authority what the Lord demands of us today.

With that foundation, how is the Christian to answer the modern proponents of polygamy, since it is not condemned in the texts commonly used to support the case against other perversions of human sexuality?

The Old Testament often leaves the unrighteous acts of individuals to the reader to judge, based on the Law, that we might become wise. The practice of polygamy was clearly part of the culture of the patriarchs and many righteous men in later history, and it too must be judged in its Covenant context. Genesis is a book about fruit (seed, flesh, and skin), the promises given to Adam in Eden, and biblical polygamy must be understood in the light of the importance of offspring to dominion.[2]

---

2 For more discussion on this aspect of cultural survival, see "The Eternal People" in Michael Bull, *Sweet Counsel: Essays to Brighten the Eyes*.

Vision of Rachel and Leah (1855)
Dante Gabriel Rossetti

INQUIÉTUDE

THE FIRST WIFE

Adam's sin was the "Sanctuary" equivalent of seizing Kingdom before God's time. He was to submit as a servant that God might make him a "public" servant, a servant with authority, a shepherd-king. Moving from the Garden into the Land, his sin was repeated by Cain, but the stolen fruit was now that of the Land and the womb, those things which were cursed in Genesis 3. As firstborn, Cain was to be the heir, and thus required to demonstrate his servanthood. His submission to God was to be expressed not only in the firstfruits of his labors, but also in his willingness to accept the necessity for a blood sacrifice on his behalf, *in his place,* as the firstborn. Instead, Cain presented his "Land" offering *before* the "womb" offering, the blood of the unblemished animal. Servanthood was despised.

The stories of Cain and Lamech together form a "head" and "body," representing Church and State. Cain's sin is institutionalized in the first king (*Lamech* is possibly a play on *melech,* which means "king") who happens to be history's first polygamist. Cain's city was his remedy for his loss of the Land, and Lamech's polygamy is mentioned just before the birth of Seth.

THE FIRST WORLD

Just as Adam seized Kingdom in the Garden that he might possess the Land, Cain seized Kingdom of the Land that he might possess the World. Cities and abundant offspring are features of the World, not the Land. The sins in Genesis 4 are "bridal," that is, the promised "World" rewards for faithfulness were manufactured in the Land *before* God's time.

Biblical polygamy resulted from the enmity between the offspring of the Woman and that of the serpent. It enabled the acceleration of the "generations" and made possible an instant dynasty. Through intermarriage with the priestly Sethites, the Cainites again seized control, and the Lord wiped them out. When the "sons of God" took the "daughters of men," they compromised with idolatry and perhaps also with polygamy. The marriages of Noah and his sons stand in contrast.

After God wiped out the Cainite line, it seems that Ham's sin of "seeing Noah's nakedness" when he lay uncovered in his tent (Genesis 9:20-27) was an attempt to steal for his son Canaan the promises of fruitfuless given to Noah. The nature of the curses upon Ham's heir certainly suggest this. In each instance, the older brother attempts to seize the inheritance before God's time, and the inheritance is given to the younger.[3]

THE FIRSTBORN

This corruption of priestly Noahic *cultus* was once again expressed in "bridal" (city) terms in the culture. Since Canaan's inheritance rightly belonged to Shem,

---

3 Of course, in Jesus' parable of the prodigal (Luke 15:11-32), it is the *younger* son who squanders his inheritance, and the priestly character of the rightful heir is put to the test in this ironic way.

not only did the Canaanite kings, like Pharaoh, build their cities quickly through theft and slave labor, polygamy in the patriarchal era was a means of monopolizing a rule seized without submission to God.

Then, after the failure of Pharaoh to steal Sarai from Abram, polygamy became a means of hijacking the promised seed from *within* the Abrahamic people.

Abraham's impatience in taking Hagar the Egyptian as a concubine was his attempt to "manufacture" a *Succession* which God had promised, but which had not yet materialized. He eventually learned to trust God to the point where he was even willing to offer his miraculous "priestly firstborn" as an ascension. The Lord provided a substitute for Isaac as he did for Cain.

Hagar was cast out, and with her, the polygamy of Abraham. His dominion would come from God's hand, in God's time. Although not an explicit prohibition of polygamy, this might explain the Mosaic condemnation of taking a "rival" wife. Like the sin against "uncovered" Noah, Edenic "covering" enables Covenant *Succession*.

> And you shall not take a woman as a rival wife to her sister, uncovering her nakedness while her sister is still alive. (Leviticus 18:18)

Later polygamous rivalries were not so much about the affections of the shared husband as they were for the place of their sons in Covenant history.

There was rivalry enough between the sons of the *same* mother. Esau, the firstborn, was himself an entire world of sin. He despised his birthright (Garden), desired to murder his brother (Land), and took two Canaanite wives who embittered the lives of his godly parents (World). The Lord's answer to this was to give two wives to Jacob. Polygamy made Jacob like Esau, the kingly firstborn who acted like Cain. Yet Jacob's response was not theft or murder but *submission*. Laban acted like a Canaanite king, relying on Jacob's debt slavery to enlarge his own household. But Jacob outcrafted the serpent and left with great plunder.

What was the purpose of giving Jacob two wives? Just as God loved Jacob over Esau, so Jacob loved Rachel over Leah. Not only were there abundant sons, but the antagonism between Esau and Jacob was now "bridal."

The twelve tribes of Israel were eventually arranged as "social architecture" around the Tent of God, but there are earlier hints of this in the language of Genesis. These literary clues (such as Eve being "constructed" as a city) are often overlooked, and thus do not make it through translation. In Genesis 30:1-5, barren Rachel suggests that Jacob sleep with her handmaid Bilhah, "that she may give birth on my knees and I too shall be *built up* through her." Verse 5 in the Hebrew contains a pun. "I shall be built up" (*'ibbaneh*) plays on *banim*, sons, and so has the sense of "I shall be sonned."[4]

The continual failure of the firstborn to be a priestly king was now played out in the murderous intentions

4 See Robert Altar, *The Art of Biblical Narrative*, 186.

of the sons of Leah and the handmaids towards Joseph, the true priest-king who submitted to his father and was given authority over all of his brothers.

This gives us the context of, and requirement for, the Passover of Israel, where every firstborn belonged to either Hagar or Sarah, and every one of Sarah's sons was an Isaac spared through sacrifice of an "Abel."

The practice of polygamous surrogacy was *reversed* in the "firstborn" birth of Obed (whose name means "servant") to Ruth on the knees of Naomi. This surrogacy was not only generational, it was the product of a marriage between a faithful Jewish ruler and a single, faithful Gentile, a "daughter" of Lot's son, Moab.

Polygamy was a strategy for seizing the future. The target of the only *explicit* prohibition of polygamy (in Deuteronomy 17) is Israel's future kings. This is why God slew Bathsheba's "firstborn" to David and gave the kingdom to Solomon. It was why Absalom slept with his father's concubines. And it explains the fixation of John the Baptist with the adultery of King Herod.

Despite these "carnal" strategies, the Davidic dynasty survived through the mercy of God, a history of barren wombs culminating in a virgin birth (Garden), vengeance for the blood of Abel (Land) and the judgment of the harlot (World).

Jesus' response to the woman who called out in Luke 11 highlights the end of the significance of biblical polygamy: "Blessed rather are those who hear the word of God and keep it!"

VINDICATION

26
BARREN WORLDS

ALIENS AND SOJOURNERS

...and there was not a man to till the ground.
(Genesis 2:6)

The Bible does not simply record events. It presents them in sequences, as acts which have consequences, and in doing so it also shows us how God works. Unfortunately, most Christians are not taught to read the Scriptures with an eye on the processes going on in each narrative, let alone in the big picture. So when a question is asked such as, "Is there life on other planets?" even the best theologians can only reply, "The Bible doesn't tell us."

Well, in truth, the Bible does tell us, but only if we are paying attention. The Covenantal pattern inherent in every part of Scripture shows us precisely how God works, and identifying this structure not only enables us to interpret the Bible and history correctly, but also to predict the future.

INQUIÉTUDE

THE SEED

Biblical history is all about seed and fruit, barrenness and fruitfulness, gathering and scattering, in every domain—physical, social, and ethical—and this is achieved through the process of Covenant. God creates or calls a man, gives him a job to do, shows him the method for success, then leaves him alone until the time is right and the land is ripe. This is why Israel's harvest calendar is a picture of all Covenant history in microcosm.

The modern mind passes over this often repeated theme of sowing and reaping, limiting it to the historical concerns of subsistence farmers (Land) and their tribal life (womb), both cursed by unfaithful Adam in Genesis 3, and promised to faithful Abraham in Genesis 15. In once sense, through technology and its resulting prosperity, we moderns have indeed moved beyond an existence tied so closely to the ground, but God's Creation is a fractal. This means that although we move from a day of small things (such as "Do not eat from the tree of the knowledge of good and evil") to greater exploits, every advancement carries similar risk and similar promise. The process of growth in farming and families can also be perceived in investment banking, global demographics, software development, and even in spiritual warfare. "Increase" is always achieved through some kind of delayed gratification, an act of faith in a promise that the sacrifices made

Map of the New World (1540)

now will result in greater rewards down the track. We pray in secret that God might reward us openly. Paul chose personal suffering that he might receive a greater resurrection.[1] We fast privately that we might enjoy a greater feast in company with others. Indeed, Israel's final annual feast, a party for all nations, followed the culmination of her purification through fasting and self-examination prior to the Day of Atonement.

ONE WORLD

With such an understanding, is it possible to extrapolate an answer from ancient documents written for tribal farmers to the question of whether life exists on other planets? If the Bible is true, surely we must begin with the establishment of life on *this* planet.

The Spirit hovered only over *this* world, just as He overshadowed only Mary, and descended only upon Christ at His baptism. It is in our God's character to choose the one from the many, that the one might become many. Mary had other children, and Christ gave the Spirit to the saints at Pentecost.

Adam was given Eve that he might be fruitful. The "Land" is always feminine, given seed by Man but made fruitful only by obedience, with the increase coming directly from God (1 Corinthians 3:6). It seems to me that womb and the Land were only "opened" to

---

[1] Based on what we know of Paul, I suspect that he was not referring to a more glorious resurrection for himself, but a more numerous one from among the nations through the preaching of the Gospel.

Adam following the shedding of sacrificial blood, albeit with limiting curses intended to humble him.

All the famines in Israel were judgments according to the curses in the Law of Moses (Deuteronomy 28:15-24). Only the Land of Israel was subject to blessing and cursing under the Law. Yet God chose Israel from among the nations not only that Israel might be blessed by the nations but that all nations might eventually be blessed through one nation, Israel.

God is consistent in all His works, since they image Him. Out of all the worlds, God chose to bless only this one, and the sevenfold process of *Filling* in Genesis 1 is recapitulated in every Covenant which follows.[2]

So it is not entirely speculative to assert that while the other planets are currently barren, only this one has many children. Typologically speaking, life on other planets would be Creational "polygamy," something outside the character of God.

But neither is it a stretch to imagine that the separation, sanctification and fruitfulness of this world is intended to be a blessing to *all* worlds. Like the nations at Pentecost, they have already been *Formed* and are waiting to be *Filled*. But when might this be?

---

2   The sun, moon and stars (which include other worlds) were not created until Day 4, prefiguring a time of priestly training (the Land and its grain and fruit bearers) before kingly dominion. The Scriptures often use the heavenly lights as images to describe earthly rulers, including the saints. Deuteronomy 4:19 condemns the worship of the stars, but also suggests that they were, and perhaps also will be, a part of our inheritance.

INQUIÉTUDE

THE SOWER

God could certainly have put life on other planets, but the Bible shows us that He always works through mediators. The fruit of the Land and the womb depended on the fruits of the Spirit in Adam.

Some Christians believe the world existed long *before* the creation of Adam (if indeed Adam even existed!) but according to revelation and our own experience, the world is not self-sustaining. Like Israel, as a people set apart in Abraham and trained under the Law of Moses, nature itself requires guidance, or cultivation.

In social terms, circumcision was a kind of *pruning*, not a *cutting off* (or cutting down) but a cutting intended to lead to greater fruitfulness—a sacrifice now for a great blessing in the future. However, Abraham seized a firstborn via Hagar in the way Adam seized the fruit in the Garden. But Abraham matured until he was even willing to offer his firstborn to God, as a kind of first-fruits, and he was given many more children. The physical Creation by God, and the subsequent social Creation delegated to the charge of Adam, are inseparable. Fruitfulness in Land and womb depend not only on cultivation by the Man, but also cultivation *of* the Man. Where Adam failed, Noah succeeded. In a preliminary sense, Noah was the first "interplanetary" colonist.

Thus, it is not in the nature of God to make a self-sustaining "wilderness." Nature has its laws but that does not make nature *sovereign*. Nature itself requires "training." Since the world was created to be cultivated, the world cannot be fruitful *without* Man. Man can most certainly damage the world through exploitation, but a world without Man would not be the pristine utopia imagined by environmentalists. Gary North writes:

> The earth was never designed to be autonomous. Neither was the garden. Though the creation was able to function without man's immediate presence, it could not achieve its full flowering apart from man... Nature was allowed to operate briefly without man for five days. Man was allowed to operate briefly without woman for less than one day. Neither could be fully comfortable without its complement. Nature needed subordination under man. Man needed subordination under God... Like nature, he had been created good but incomplete. He knew from the very beginning that he was not self-sufficient.[3]

The care with which God had planted the Garden was to be noticed and replicated, *imaged,* by Adam in the Land. Tending and guarding the Garden as God's representative was training for dominion of the Land and then the entire World.

Although the Creation is still under the curse of death, we see the dominion of Christ working in the social realm, through the Gospel, expanding throughout history. "Covenant faithfulness" is now entirely

---

3   Gary North, *The Dominion Covenant: Genesis - An Economic Commentary on the Bible,* Volume 1, 84-85.

INQUIÉTUDE

wrapped up in one glorified Man, but working through all nations. If we do indeed colonize other planets, it will not so much be "by Covenant" but "in Christ," with technologies given to us by the Spirit of God, and through the sacrifice of individuals with the desire for new frontiers built into the Great Commission.

SHINING LIKE STARS

So, there is no life on other planets. Not *yet*. Based on how God has worked in the past, it is likely there may well be in the future. The Spirit will overshadow other worlds, but not as He did in Genesis 1. Since the Spirit now indwells the Sons of God, making us co-workers with the Son in the maturity, conquest and redemption of mankind, it seems that the glorified redeemed will be "governing lights" in the eventual conquest of Creation. Perhaps this task will be carried out by the saints in ways we cannot yet imagine, but we have already made a start, have we not? Despite the trials and tragedies that plague humanity, in many respects this world is a better place now than it has ever been.

One day, the phrase "the new world" could be used quite literally, with exploration motivated by more than mere exploitation, a desire for cultivation rather than plunder, a sustainable harvest established upon just measures. God's increase always begins with obedience and wisdom. The universe displays the glory of God, but like the earth, it is a gift which requires tending by Adam for it to reach the full potential of that glory.

27
WEIGHED AND FOUND WANTING
THE PERFECT LAW OF LIBERTY

And I looked, and behold, a black horse!
And its rider had a pair of scales in his hand.
(Revelation 6:5)

The book of Revelation is a mystery, yet like all good mysteries it is a book made entirely of clues. It is a glimpse through the torn Veil of the Temple, that is, the flesh of Jesus, into the heavenlies. The cloud into which He was taken up is opened to John's eyes that he might see the horses and chariots of God (2 Kings 6:17).

But like all the prophets, John is a man who *knows the Bible,* and like John *we* will only understand the symbols in Revelation if *we* know the Bible.

The conversation at God's table is for those who know their Master's mind, who hear His voice as children and thus quit themselves like men. To them, this is indeed a Revelation. To those outside His commission, it remains an enigma, terrible lightning and thunder and the sound of trumpets (Exodus 19:19; 20:18).

However, a familiarity with Old Testament facts and figures is not enough. There are plenty of commentators who pick up isolated allusions who still have no idea what the book is about. The sacred architecture of the Tabernacles and Temples is seen to be fulfilled in Jesus, and all the details in the Revelation are arranged in architectural patterns. Deeper meanings are conferred upon the symbols through their careful placement in textual forms first employed in the Torah.

NO LONGER NAKED

The Tabernacle was humaniform, indeed cruciform. It was a great metal man laid out upon the ground. Unlike Jesus at the crucifixion, this form was clothed in a "triune" robe of linen, ramskin and rainbow-colored beadwork, signifying the offices of Priest, King and Prophet. United in a single Spirit-filled Man, these coverings pictured the exaltation, glorification and ministry of Jesus *beyond* the cross (Hebrews 12:2).

The clothing of the Aaronic High Priest was a human replication of the Tabernacle, and Jesus is initially revealed to John as a High Priest who has completed His ministry. The rest of the book shows Jesus, now lifted up as a "tent," drawing all to Himself, that is, becoming a *household*. Replacing the earthly Temple of God, He is fulfilling the final two Mosaic commandments: *house* and *contents*.

TWO COVENANTS

In Revelation 1, this Jesus who "tabernacled among us" (John 1:14) is now Himself the Tabernacle, the "trysting tent," and every description of His appearance and His actions is designed to be understood in that light.

The seven stars in Jesus' right hand are the "angels" of seven churches, but these are *human* messengers, men commissioned with the evangel. They represent a new Lampstand, a New Covenant menora, like the one in Zechariah, but made out of flesh.

It seems likely, since this glorified Man took the scroll from the *right* hand of the enthroned One, that He did so with His *left* hand. Since John, like Ezekiel, is later given a portion of this scroll to eat, it would correspond to the Table of Showbread. The contents of the Table pictured the death of the Man who submitted fully to God's Law, who was *deformed* and *defilled*—a sacrificial lamb—that there might be a New Creation.

So, in Jesus' left hand is "external Law," the Law that comes to us from outside ourselves, from our fathers on earth, and then our Father in heaven. It is a tool that cuts us, and a scaffolding that shapes us.

In Jesus' right hand is "internal Law," the Spirit of God given as an intuitive principle, a moral compass, His peace as the arbiter in our hearts.

Seeing Jesus with these two kinds of Law, in a sense the Old and New Covenants, we can understand that as the now-qualified Judge of all men, He is the incarna-

Hair,
eyes,
voice,
mouth

Face

Stars

Golden Sash

Scroll

A robe to the feet

Feet like
fine bronze

tion of the scales of justice. He comes first to judge the churches, their *internal* devotion and their *external* service. In the cases where either is lacking, external law is the remedy: church discipline. Notice that His exhortations are not given to the congregations directly, but to representatives. Those in His right hand are priest-kings like Melchizedek, which means that the Aaronic priesthood has been superseded.

As the priests trimmed the wicks of the Lampstand, so Jesus tends these lamps. He is calling the churches to deal with sins which will destroy them if they are not judged. If allowed to grow, they will bring death. Once

Jesus takes the scroll, He opens it and turns His attention towards the worship of Jerusalem, where the same sins are indeed fully grown and ripe for judgment.

Opening the scroll releases four swift horsemen who measure out the Tabernacle of Jesus on earth.

The first announces the Gospel. He is like the Ark of the Covenant which scatters God's enemies. The sword of the second is the division among Jews caused by the Gospel (Matthew 10:34-35), a tearing of the Veil, the flesh of Jesus (Hebrews 10:20). The third weighs these sacrificial halves of a now-divided Abraham, judging between the priestly bread on one hand and the kingly oil and wine on the other. Those who rejected Christ remained under the Law of Moses, external Law, and they would be judged under it as Jesus was. Those who received Him received His Spirit, and the kingdom.

The Hebrew word for "glory" means *heavy*. In every case, the balance tips in favor of Jesus' right hand, the hand with the shining glory. The final horseman is the Levitical sword, the "right hand" which comes to execute the naked idolaters (Exodus 32:25-28).[1]

THE END OF BABYLON

The economic language of just weights and measures alludes not only to agriculture in the Promised Land, but also to the fall of history's previous Babylon.

---

[1] This interpretation of the four horsemen is from James B. Jordan's lectures on the Revelation, available from www.wordmp3.com

INQUIÉTUDE

In the light of a Lampstand plundered from Judah, Belshazzar and his court saw the fingers of a man's hand writing on the wall. The "fingers" allude to the Laws of God (Exodus 8:19; 31:18). The words were:

a mina;
a mina,
a shekel,
a half mina

Daniel interprets these nouns as verbs. As with the "Temple" body of Jesus, they are fulfilled in priestly, kingly and prophetic deeds. James Jordan writes:

> The first *mene'* is an introduction. It means "reckon." The whole oracle is a reckoning, broken into three parts. The initial phrase translates: "Reckoned. Reckoned, weighed, and assessed."
>
> These three words denote weights used in scales, particularly in counting gold or silver pieces. The word *teqel* is a variant Aramaic way of writing "shekel." A *mina* is either 60 or possibly 50 shekels. A *peres* is half a mina, 30 or possibly 25 shekels. We have seen above that the Lampstand can be said to weigh the bread of God's kingdom. Thus the weights listed on the wall are weights of bread. Belshazzar has sought to provide a "great bread" (v. 1), but his bread, displayed before God, weighs only a shekel, not a *mina* or even a half-*mina* (a *peres*)... Belshazzar has been weighed and found to weigh only one shekel. He is not fit to carry forward the 60-shekel *mina* of Babylon.[2]

---

2   James B. Jordan, *The Handwriting on the Wall*, 293-295.

The Statue of Liberty towers over Paris rooftops in 1884,
outside the workshop of sculptor Auguste Bartholdi.

INQUIÉTUDE

This is wonderful background for the role of Jesus in the Revelation. The metal man of Babylon, Persia, Greece and Rome cannot take dominion over Land *and* Sea. Its hybrid Jew-Gentile feet are crumbling. Jesus, the true metal man, walks on both Land and Sea in greater glory. His Jew-Gentile feet are united by the Spirit.

> So shall I keep thy law continually for ever and ever. And I will walk at liberty [in a wide place]: for I seek thy precepts. (Psalm 119:44-45 KJV)

Just as His glory, His weight, is now greater than that of the Herodian state, so also the glory of His New Covenant people is greater than that of the Old.

> For Jesus has been counted worthy of more glory than Moses—as much more glory as the builder of a house has more honor than the house itself. (Hebrews 3:3)

Thus, standing on Land and Sea, He delegates the final judgment, the final portion of the scroll, to John.

TRUE LIBERTY

The glory of Jesus is legal. Liberty flows from virtue. The obedience of Adam results in the freedom of Eve. The robe of Adam is a shelter for Eve. So the glory of the saints as the Bride of Christ is also ethical (Revelation 19:8).

Jesus "reckons. Reckons, weighs and assesses" the churches that they might be enthroned with Him as righteous judges, those who are able to discern good from evil (Hebrews 5:14), dividing light from darkness as human Lampstands, men "walking around in the fire," an incarnation of the seven spirits before the throne of God.[3]

Once the churches are purified, Jesus' glory is temporarily veiled. As He judges the Old Covenant people, His face is veiled like the face of Moses. He is described in Old Covenant terms. He is not Jesus the Christ but the Angel of the Lord. The voice which spoke on earth is the same voice which now speaks from heaven (Hebrews 12:25). Because they failed to discern in Him the glory of true Priesthood, and would not receive Him (John 1:9-14), He judges them as a faithful servant, not as the Son.

As in Daniel 5, where the prophet opens the mystery of the writing on the wall, the glory of the seven stars, the Lampstands whose wicks are now trimmed and shining brightly, provides the light by which Jesus judges the first century Babylon. With His fingers, He breaks the seals on the scroll. The first four seals are the four Gospels, sent out on a mission to

enlighten,
divide,
weigh
and slay.

---

3   As in Daniel 3, the burning of Christians as human torches at Nero's infamous garden parties in some sense brought the fire of Pentecost and the judgment of God to Rome.

28
LIGHTNING FROM EAST TO WEST

WHAT ON EARTH IS JESUS DOING?

And Herod and Pilate became friends with
each other that very day, for before this they had
been at enmity with each other. (Luke 23:12)

With same sex marriage now legalized in many Western countries, and militant Islam ravaging the East, Christians might be wondering what God is doing. With the repeated failure of predictions of an imminent second coming, is the Bible any help to us at all in predicting what will happen next? I believe it is.

The New Testament writers often quote the Old Testament in crazy ways because they understood that God's covenants are "harvest cycles." They could refer to events in previous covenants and say, "Look, it's happening again! See how God reunited Israel? Now He is reuniting Jew and Gentile!" (Hebrews 8:7-13)

INQUIÉTUDE

The moral degradation of Western culture and the rise of militant Islam make perfect sense when understood in the light of sacred architecture and the "harvest" process it represents. So we will take a brief look into the Holy Place of the Tabernacle, observe how this pattern shaped the events of the first century, and quickly trace it to the madness of our own day.

THE HOLY PLACE

As we have seen, in the Holy Place were three articles of furniture which represented three offices: Priest, King and Prophet. These three describe a process of maturity. The Priest *listens,* the King *acts,* and the Prophet *speaks.* This is what was required of Adam in the Garden of Eden, and it also gives us three clear stages in the history and literature of ancient Israel.

The **Table of Showbread** is the Priest (manna and grapes in the wilderness), the **Lampstand** is the King (the light of the law for wisdom in governing) and the **Incense Altar** is the elders who advise in the courts of heaven and guide history on earth. Of course, Christ is the first one who truly united these three offices.

Since the Tabernacle layout is cross-shaped, these three items are two hands, left and right, and the bosom or breastplate in the center. This is why Christ holds seven stars in His right hand in Revelation 1 (the church rulers). He is the Tabernacle fulfilled. As His body, Christians are a royal priesthood, a combination of priest and king with a voice from heaven.

Jesus Before Pilate: First Interview (1886-94)
James Tissot

INQUIÉTUDE

THE FIRST CENTURY

The conflict between Priesthood and Kingdom, Church and State, can be traced throughout Scripture, seen very clearly in the hatred of Abel by Cain, and Jacob by Esau, and in the Egyptians' regard of shepherds as detestable (Genesis 46:34). However, only a faithful combination of Priesthood and Kingdom results in a voice that is truly Prophetic. This is why the Ascension of Christ was followed by the Day of Pentecost and resulted in both the apostolic witness and the New Testament document.

However, Priesthood and Kingdom often collude against the true prophets. That is always the nature of Babel. The Jews hated the Romans, and yet Herod and Pilate became friends over the crucifixion of Christ. This was repeated "institutionally" a generation later, when Herodian worship (left hand) and Neronic rule (right hand) joined forces against the Christian church, the Body of Christ.

THE GLOBAL CHURCH

All of this helps us to understand the major tensions in the world today. On one hand, we have Islam, an insane parody of Priesthood, a religion which prohibits the wine, women and song of adulthood, everything Kingly and Prophetic. Holiness comes via coercion. One must listen and not question. It is a religion which puts everyone under the sword, a tyrannizing order like that of the Pharisees and Herods in first century Jerusalem. It expresses itself through bloodshed, circumcision for males *and* females, violence against girls and women, and *jihad*.

On the other hand, we have the Secular West, which no longer listens to God and has given itself to "kingly" sins, murder and adultery, the amassing of gold and war horses, and the infant sacrifice of abortion. Secular humanism is Kingdom taken to the extreme, the "guns, girls, and gold" prohibited by Moses (Deuteronomy 17:14-20) and amassed by Solomon, which began the downfall of Israel.

Islam and Secularism are vehemently opposed. Like the Roman Empire, secularism calls Muslims to assimilate. Like Jews under the Law of Moses, this is something Muslims under Sharia law are unable to do. In the wisdom of God, the two sides are forever set at enmity. One claims divine authority (Priesthood), the other claims infinite wisdom (Kingdom). Both invent history in order to claim the future (Prophecy).

In between these two perversions, one of Priesthood and the other of Kingdom, we have the Christian Church, a Body which unites true Priesthood and true Kingdom, a royal priesthood given the task of divine testimony to the world. Like Herod and Pilate, the only thing Islam and Secularism have in common is a hatred for Christianity, the fragrant bride in the bosom of Adam, the supernatural institution which, by the

Spirit of the ascended Christ, is truly Prophetic.

It is easy to blame the Church for the degeneration of Western culture, but the prophetic witness in our culture has in reality been reasonably consistent. Based on Covenant history, the fact that God's words now enrage His enemies is not a sign of our failure. It is a sign of their imminent doom.

Romans 1 tells us that cultural homosexuality is a sign of the end of a culture, the final proof that it has gone insane. But subsequent chapters also describe the hypocrisy and futility of a carnal priesthood. Paganism and Judaism were castrated forever, their "ministries" replaced by the enthronement of the fragrant firstborn from the dead.

This explains the natures of Islam and Secularism. In this age, everything is Christian. With paganism and Judaism disempowered, to have any real longevity, any idolatry must now be a distorted form of Christianity. Islam is Christianity without sacrament, without grace. Secularism is Christianity without discipline, without self-government. Islam and Secularism are thus the bipolar moods of Christless Christianity, schizoid faces of a global perversion of the prophetic Gospel. Christians in the East testify like Elijah against false Priesthood. Christians in the West, like the angels sent to Sodom, testify against false Kingdom. Sacrament and Government can only be united under the Word by the Spirit.

But both extremes are not only the enemies of the Gospel, they are the *results* of the Gospel. Islam and Secularism are rebellion against Christ taken to its logical conclusion in opposite directions: legalism or licentiousness. With no spiritual weapons, both "hands" are reduced to bearing the sword in their respective ways. They can be united only in death, and their current victories are suicides in disguise. As it was in the first century, the only solution to the enmity is faith in Christ.

THE WHOLE WORLD IN HIS HANDS

When God's people persevere, God confuses their enemies and sets them against each other. Rome devoured Jerusalem, and then the New Jerusalem devoured Rome. The prophetic voice of Christ and His martyrs was vindicated. Released from the trappings of the old order, and possessing both the divine authority of the Jew and the earthly abundance of the Gentile, the Gospel began its transformation of the empire.

What does the future hold? If the events of the first century are repeated, the false kings will destroy the false priests, but the false kings will be entirely shaken up in the process, being humbled that they might bow the knee to Christ. Many saints will die but through their testimony they will eventually conquer the false kingdom from the inside. The Future belongs to the Bride.

When Sodom was destroyed, Sarah conceived. When Israel committed similar sins, Ruth and Hannah conceived. In God's kingdom, the last days are only ever the last days of the old order. A bipolarity of Priesthood and Kingdom expressed in global culture means some kind of Prophetic resurrection across the world is at hand, a Christendom more faithful, wiser, and bigger than even the saints could imagine, the next "growth ring" of the kingdom of God.

The inheritance of Jesus includes both East and West, just as it included Jew and Gentile, set in opposition by the Law: divide and conquer, circumcise and baptize.

> For he himself is our peace, who has made us both one and has broken down in his flesh the dividing wall of hostility by abolishing the law of commandments expressed in ordinances, that he might create in himself one new man in place of the two, so making peace, and might reconcile us both to God in one body through the cross, thereby killing the hostility. (Ephesians 2:14-16)

With the Spirit of God in us, and the lessons of the millennia, God's thoughts are not so high above ours any more. And that was always the plan: that all His people might be Prophets, wise as serpents and harmless as doves.

The original version of this chapter was written for
Theopolis Institute, published at www.theopolisinstitute.com

29

CRUEL AND UNUSUAL

SECULARISM AND INQUISITION

*"If I were in charge, they would know that waterboarding
is how we baptize terrorists."* — Sarah Palin

Despite its Messianic pretensions, the secular state has no authority over the spiritual realm, and militant Islam exposes this incompetence to us again and again. The "War on Terror" banner illustrates perfectly the failure of statists to comprehend, or perhaps to admit publicly, the true nature of this nemesis of Western culture.

The grisly facts revealed in the recent CIA "torture report" have brought a torrent of moral outrage from the political Left, and to a lesser degree from the political Right. This is not because the Left has a more tender conscience or has, in practice, a more compassionate take on things. It is simply because those on the Left are unable to think beyond the short term, or beyond the experiences and "rights" of the individual.

INQUIÉTUDE

This is also the case with many Christians who believe that they are fighting for "social justice," and will not take into account the long term consequences of weakness in government policy.

The Right, whose thinkers are generally more willing to look at the bigger picture, and possess a better understanding of the dire long term consequences if we fail to take strict measures (economically and politically) in the short term, will not deny that the techniques described in the report are barbarous. But the truth is that when it comes to the bloodthirstiness of the "religion of peace" in wartime, let alone the violence of Islam's backward practices in peacetime, we really are dealing with barbarians.

One can argue, as many have, that we must not sink to the level of these organized hooligans, but the fact remains that other than resorting to selective bombing or the use of "enhanced interrogation techniques" (either to extract information or to promote terror as a countermeasure), the secular West's big bag of tricks is disturbingly empty when it comes to fighting militant Islam. The use of "cruel and unusual"[1] punishments behind closed doors in a nation which ostensibly promotes peace, tolerance and understanding, is a sign of desperation.

---

1 Punishment prohibited by the Eighth Amendment to the Constitution. Cruel and unusual punishment includes torture, deliberately degrading punishment, or punishment that is too severe for the crime committed.

TERRORIST CELLS

While traditional warfare is state against state, body against body, terrorism achieves its goals in the realm of cells and viruses. A single civilian, with an excellent plan and a lot of luck, can murder tens, hundreds, or even thousands. The secular West is faced with an entity which has mimicked the strengths of historic Christianity: it is not a body of flesh but a "virus," an invisible *animus* able to infiltrate any part of society as "sleepers" which are able to suddenly betray that society when called upon. The more its members are punished, the more other members are emboldened. There is no centrally-located authority on earth, only a book which must not be questioned.

Resorting to the "cruel and unusual" indicates that the "just" and "usual" methods of warfare have failed. Technological advancements changed the nature of warfare in the early 20th century. Consequently, those who lacked such technology were forced to resort to terrorism. As in Vietnam and Northern Ireland, the bad guys do not wear uniforms. They look just like us. Their primary weapons are disguise and stealth, a form of betrayal from the inside. Anyone—man, woman, child—could be carrying a weapon. The only way to deal with such operatives is to create antibodies, "spooks" who also operate in disguise and outside the usual constraints of the law. Since the expertly defined rules, codes of honor and identifying uniforms were rendered meaningless by terrorism, one cannot expect the spies employed to counter the terrorists to be bound by them.

When the number of terrorist attacks prevented by the various Western "spook" networks is taken into account, no one complains that their actions are outside or "above the law." Certainly, all operatives must be held accountable for their actions, but the question is, how bad is the *means* allowed to get before it can no longer be justified by its *end*?

> Consequentialism is not a biblical ethical system. There are times when it seems to turn up a no-brainer answer to your question—if we could prevent a nuclear bomb from going off in Baltimore by slapping Khalid Sheikh Muhammed a couple of times, why wouldn't you do that? That seems reasonable. But without an ultimate anchor, the little dingy of secular smart people can drift a long way out to sea. Now suppose you can prevent the Baltimore nuke by having a dark ops team rape KSM's mother, sisters, and daughters. Suppose the threat of that prospect would break him sooner than waterboarding would? At some point, pretty soon in the process, you will need more ethical light than horrendous consequences of not doing "something" can ever give you.[2]

The unwillingness of many on the Right to completely condemn the use of torture is likely due to the fact that

---

2   Douglas Wilson, *A Grab Bag of Observations About Torture*, www.dougwils.com

The Water Torture
in Joos de Damhouder's
"Praxis Rerum Criminalium" (1556)

for the state there are no other avenues to explore. Faced with an opponent which is primarily religious and only *secondarily* political, neither coddling by the Left nor the counter-terror of the Right is going to be effective in the long term. How do you kill death without becoming a *dealer* in death?

DEMOS VS. THEOS

The vacuum left after the exorcism of Divine authority is now flooded by the perverted remnants of the once Christian state.[3] Faced with the tactics and strategies of Islamic terrorists, the "just and usual" institutions upon which the West was founded and has prospered will always fail. This is because Islam targets the secular West at the point at which it is most vulnerable: its empty religious heart, the seat once inhabited by Christ.

Assuming that religion is a private matter, a mere accessory or "supplement" to life, over which national allegiance takes precedence, statists assume that Islam can be "privatized" within a secular state in the same way in which they have attempted to "privatize" Christianity. But Islam is a religion whose battle is "against flesh and blood," making it a counter-culture at both the religious *and* state levels. This is why, compared to Christianity, the attempt to privatize it is a far more obvious failure.

---

3   For more discussion, see "The Exorcism of Christ" in Michael Bull, *Sweet Counsel: Essays To Brighten The Eyes.*

Unwilling to identify this conflict as one of religion, the media and the legal system downplay the Islamic identity of offenders and focus instead on their actual crimes, while pandering to the officials of the "religion of peace" as though the offenders had betrayed their religion. This certainly puts a damper on unthinking retaliation against innocent Muslims in Western countries, but since the true culprit, Islam, is not called to repent, it will offend again and again.

This practice of overlooking the religious nature of the crimes also assumes that our legal system, based on the Law of Moses but now corrupted, can deal effectively with Islamists as Western citizens. Punishment (including corporal and capital) and restitution are fine ideals, but what we are dealing with here is *another law* and *another spirit*. Being primarily theocratic, Islam submits only to its own "divine" legal system, one which *also* claims the Law of Moses as a foundation, thus any convictions are logically considered to be illegal, mere acts of persecution by lawless infidels. For the Muslim, as for the Christian, the conflict will forever be a primarily religious one.

The establishment of a regimen of systematic torture is always a symptom of the secularist's inability to deal with the heart of a man. McCarthyism was just the beginning. If incarceration and beatings will not conquer the defiant "kingdom" within you, *we ourselves* will get inside you. You say we can only kill the body, but we will take away your soul. Given the right circumstances, it will be no surprise if these exact measures are eventually used by these secular inquisitors upon Western Christians, who similarly claim an allegiance to a Law beyond the laws of men.

MORAL AUTHORITY

When it comes to moral authority, the secular state does not have much of a case against the Islamic one. Nick Gillespie writes:

> The torture report is simply the latest and most graphic incarnation of an existential leadership crisis that has eaten through Washington's moral authority and ability to govern, in the way road salt and rust eat through car mufflers in a Buffalo winter. "America is great because she is good," wrote Tocqueville back in the day. "If America ceases to be good, America will cease to be great." We've got a lot of explaining to do, not just to the rest of the world but to ourselves. How much longer will we countenance the post-9/11 national security state, which Edward Snowden's ongoing revelations remind us are constantly mutating into new forms and outrages?[4]

There is some truth in this, but it is not the use of torture which has brought about the loss of moral authority in the West. Torture, along with military intervention, is actually a form of life support, an artificial

---

4   Nick Gillespie, *After Torture Report, Our Moral Authority As A Nation Is Gone*, www.thedailybeast.com, December 11, 2014.

means of maintaining the appearance of life in a culture which is dying.

Those complaining the loudest about the tactics of the "pigs" running the state are usually the ones sucking the hardest on its nipples. They are anti-establishment and antinomian when it comes to moral authority, and yet they expect the state, the law, the establishment, to clean up the messes that result from their immorality. Because the administration relies on popularity with the media and the voters, it is forced to do some brutal scapegoating to deliver its "adolescent" populace from the consequences of their behavior. Because these are the same delinquents who generally approve of the execution of inconvenient infants and aged people, their outrage at the use of torture as yet another means of maintaining the lifestyle to which they have become accustomed lacks credibility.

If the consensus in our secular *Fifty Shades of Grey* public square is that "Dehumanization through ass play is fine as long as it's consensual," no real discussion concerning dehumanization through the use of such tortures as "rectal feeding" is possible. If "whatever turns you on" is the guiding principle behind our own closed doors, its social and medical consequences "contained" through abortion and "alleviated" through taxation and welfare, how is pragmatism not a viable guide behind the closed doors of the CIA? Why should our freedom on the streets not also rely on the mistreatment of others?

INQUIÉTUDE

SOLDIERS OF CHRIST

With the laws of God being stripped from courthouses, and His words banished from schools, the only way for statists to maintain morality is legislation, coercion. It is exactly the same under Allah, the difference being that subjection to Allah promises an afterlife. Secularists are rarely willing to die for their cause. Not only do Muslims obey another law (outwardly at least), their physical crimes are ruled and fueled by an eschatology of hope.

Reality is "religious," and the only religious options are to fight against flesh and blood or to preach the Gospel in the Spirit of God. Sadly, the apostate West has chosen the flesh and blood route. Even worse, its idiotic worldview has seen American soldiers forbidden to distribute Bibles in Islamic countries for fear of claimed "offence" while its government agencies hypocritically spread a homosexual agenda which is highly offensive in such cultures. Instead of soldiers of Christ carrying the Gospel on the back of the nation's global influence, the message is now the antithesis. Is it any wonder that the glory is departing?

The promise given to Israel by God now applies to any nation which will honor Him. If we obey God, He will give us rest from our enemies. If we disobey, our house will be left desolate, unprotected from the invading hordes. The history of modern America recapitulates that of the kingdom of Solomon, whose descendants relied on compromising treaties and military power as a substitute for the protection of God. The torture report is simply exposing one more means in which the secular state does the dirty work of protecting the people from the judgment of God.

The work of missionaries testifying and dying in Muslim countries is doing more to conquer Islam than sending troops abroad and extracting testimonies from terrorists at home will ever accomplish.

However, where the worst elements of Islam have organized themselves into a "state," the results will be different. In that case, it is finally flesh and blood versus flesh and blood. In the Islamic State, the serpent has grown legs and raised itself as a dragon, but that military strength means a loss of what has made militant Islam so terrifyingly effective. Dragons are easier to see. They are not merely spirit but spirit *and* flesh. One cannot easily hide a dragon. Torture has been an attempt to deal with the unseen by a culture that *denies* the unseen.

WELCOME TO THE KINGDOM OF GOD

When Sarah Palin made her maligned comments about water boarding as "baptism," she was attacked by both secularists and Christians alike. When taken in context, however, she is right on the money. This is a religious conflict. Those who will not submit to Christ and be baptized face a future like "the days of Noah."

INQUIÉTUDE

I do have to apologize for that. Not all intolerant, anti-freedom, leftist liberals are hypocrites. I'm kidding. Yes they are. And they are not right. Policies that poke our allies in the eye and coddle adversaries, instead of putting the fear of God in our enemies. Come on. Enemies who would utterly annihilate America. Those who would obviously have information on plots to carry out jihad. Oh, but you can't offend them. You can't make them feel uncomfortable. Not even a smidgeon. Well, if I were in charge, they would know that water boarding is how we baptize terrorists.[5]

Palin is wrong in her assumption that vengeance is in our own hands rather than in God's. Her statement is another "over-realized eschatology." Outside of the "just" and "usual" processes of law, anything else is compensation for our spiritual failure. We are torturing because we have failed to evangelize, water boarding instead of baptizing, spending millions on military interventions when we should be funding missions. "To torture or not to torture" is not the question at all. The best confession is a voluntary profession of faith.

5   From Sarah Palin's speech at a rally of the
    National Rifle Association, April 2014.

30
THE END OF HUSBANDRY

DEATH BY UNNATURAL CAUSES

"I am the true vine, and My Father is the vinedresser."
(John 15:1)

One result of giving Enlightenment thinking any or all authority over the Scriptures is a theology disconnected from the real world. One is left to wade through and deal with the sometimes stimulating but mostly irrelevant tomes of philosophers who jettisoned our only source of light.

The main reason modern Christians need to be up-to-speed in philosophical language is so that they are able to answer and rebuke godless philosophers in terms these moderns can actually understand.

To any Christian with a biblical worldview, many if not most of the questions philosophers believe to be profound are merely the shadows which remain once Jesus is locked out. Thankfully, the average man has more pressing matters to contend with than questioning whether or not he truly exists. For instance, we could spend hours swatting up on the works of every available philosopher and lawyer on the existence or nature of natural law, and interact with all of them, or we could simply ask the man on the land.

THE MYSTERY OF LAWLESSNESS

Thomas Aquinas (1225-1274) was a natural law legal theorist. He perceived that any law of human invention which did not conform to the laws of nature was actually a perversion of law.[1] For the Christian, in the light of the Scriptures, this is self-evident. Yet the Bible's history recounts the many tyrants who used and abused law to murder and steal, beginning with the serpent in Eden.

Made in God's image, man is given room to become a lawmaker, for good or ill, blessing or cursing. In a perfect world (and indeed in the lives of the Bible's prophets and great kings) these manmade laws result from careful meditation upon the Law of God. It seems Adam himself had wisely instructed Eve not even to *touch* the forbidden fruit, since God Himself made no such prohibition. But then Adam joined the serpent's conspiracy and became the channel of tyranny.

We live in an age when our lawmakers have torn the Laws of Moses from the walls of our courthouses and now not only seek to prohibit the promotion of such

---

1   Thomas Aquinas, *Summa Theologica*, I-II, Q.95, A.II.

Noah's ark on the Mount Ararat (1570)
Simon de Myle

standards, but even label such constraints as "danger-ous." Since the Bible has been removed from intellec-tual currency, an argument from "natural" law is the only acceptable "truth" which remains available to the Christian apologist.

However, even any understanding of natural law is incomplete without the Bible. The early chapters of Genesis show us that, in a very real sense, natural law does not exist. It is merely the first part of a *process,* the part which can be seen *without faith.*

Since most Bible academies have shafted the very chapters of the Bible which lay the foundations for our understanding of the natural world, their arguments "from nature" must be made on the turf of the godless, those who believe that nature is not only self-creating but also self-sustaining.

With their bag-full-of-myths, these ill-equipped saints either take a valiant but one-legged stand against the perverse wisdom of the age or they give up altogether. The "battle" has been one retreat after another, mostly because the "nature" in natural law has been defined by the opposition.

Enlightenment thinking allowed men to fashion themselves as gods, able to manipulate nature (which includes themselves and other people) according to their whims. But as Adam discovered, although human lawmaking is required, there are firm boundaries estab-lished by heaven. We do not break God's laws so much as they break us. Douglas Wilson writes:

Nature was intended to be tended. Adam was placed in an untended garden that was entirely natural, and he was commanded to make it more like itself. A garden is more like nature than a weed patch. Nature was created to be cared for. Now when it is cared for, that care shows. It is manifested...

When Adam was tending the garden, it was perfectly fine for him to figure out how to prune a tree, and how to oversee a process like grafting. But if Adam started trying to plant trees with their roots in the air, so that fish could build their nests up there, we would all start to worry that a serious problem had developed. We would begin to suspect that Adam had been taking some graduate classes. In other words, there is a line. Nature wants to be messed with, up to a point, and nature must not be messed with past that point. What is that point exactly? Well, we have to pay close attention to nature to let her tell us.[2]

An argument from "natural law" can be effective, since it relies upon common sense. But such common sense, as is given and reinforced to those on the Land (men of the soil, Genesis 9:20) through their vocations, is easier to ignore in the City. Here the dependence upon the natural order becomes uncommon, being deliberately and successfully exorcised by the self-styled demigods in education and government. This freedom from nature began with our lawmakers but we are no longer

2   Douglas Wilson, *Why Nature Is Necessary*, www.dougwils.com

merely dealing with vain thinking by academics. Years of twisted teaching at the top has filtered down to the man on the street. And if it has not, he is labeled ignorant, condemned as a bigot and finally convicted as a criminal. The promise of godhood to the godless always ends in bondage for the godly.

NATURE IS NOT NATURAL

Since stating the obvious (natural law) is now hate speech, the best witness is an argument from natural law which reinstates what has been torn down, that is, the true nature of the world, the true nature of man, and the true nature of man's office. Right from the beginning, the *process* of Creation involved a *super* nature. The seen simply cannot be divorced from the unseen. In Genesis 1, the unseen is God. In Genesis 2, heavenly authority is delegated to Adam. This brings us to my main point. Any discussion of natural law is missing the mark if it neglects to discuss the *telos* of nature, which is fruit. Fruit is the *end* of husbandry. The rejection of the Law of the supernatural *source* of nature is what threatened the supposedly "natural" fruit of the Land and the womb.

God brought the animals to Adam, in pairs, that he might name them. This process of familiarization was the beginning of "husbandry." Although modern English translations use words such as vinedresser, the King James reminds us that all fruitfulness on the earth relies upon a marriage made in heaven, a grafting together of two natural things in a supernatural way.

Adam was made responsible for the fruitfulness of the world. Yet Adam's own fruitfulness, as the one on earth who would answer to heaven, required a supernatural act. According to the flesh, Adam was natural, but he was cut open that he might bear physical fruit. Adam himself was *cultivated* by God. This involved teaching him to discern between light and darkness in the moral realm. The *telos* of the *Testing* of Adam was the fruit of righteousness. If he obeyed, the fruit of the Land and the fruit of the womb would be given to him. This fruit was, and is, always conditional upon the obedience of the Man (Colossians 1:17).

Likewise, circumcision was a deliberate boundary for the cultivation of one nation, Israel as God's "firstborn," and the curses of the Law were a regular pruning. As with Adam, thanks to the mercy of God, Israel was not cut off like Sodom. The miraculous promises concerning Land and womb were not aborted by the curses but purified, magnified, revealed as blessings that were not inherent in the earth but gifts from the hand of God. Gentile believers were grafted in to restore Israel's fruitfulness, and the final grafting was the miraculous reunion of Jew and Gentile in "one new man."

The crucial element missing from our natural law arguments is the fact that, like circumcision and the Law, mere cultivation cannot bring forth fruit *per se*. Since everything is upheld by the power of God's Son (Hebrews 1:3), without the continual work of the Spirit in the world there would be no fruit. All fruitfulness comes from the hand of God, who sends rain on both the righteous and the wicked. "Natural law" is discerned by what makes things fruitful. That is the role of Man, but it is only the first part of the process, the work of the Man. In truth, there is no such thing as natural law, because *every* increase is from God.

> So neither he who plants nor he who waters is anything, but only God who gives the growth.
> (1 Corinthians 3:7)

The man who believes the fruits of his labors on earth are not gifts from heaven will be condemned.

> "But God said to him, 'Fool! This night your soul is required of you, and the things you have prepared, whose will they be?' So is the one who lays up treasure for himself and is not rich toward God." (Luke 12:20-21)

Fruitfulness in any endeavor is Covenantal, the result of a labor carried out in faith in the promises of God. In the case of a culture which does not believe the Bible's account of origins, the promise of God to Noah that "While the earth remains, seedtime and harvest, cold and heat, summer and winter, day and night, shall not cease" (Genesis 8:22) is taken for granted as a natural state rather than being received as a supernatural gift.

The modern ecological movement takes things one step further. It assumes that the world is capable of being fruitful even without the labors of man, that is, without a husbandman. But any gardener knows better. Just as a man (such as the carpenter Joseph, in the training of Jesus) would cut down a tree and turn *nature* into *culture,* all the natural world requires some kind of cultivation. Indeed, Man himself was created to be cut down and lifted up—in that order.

We live in a culture that has come to its end. Due to continued rebellion, God has given it a reprobate mind, but it is helpful for Christians to look beyond the deluded claims of sexual freedom, or the demonization of patriarchy. These are all elements of the one project, an insane attempt to end every sort of husbandry, to eradicate not only the image of God but every godly office of Man and Woman. The Land and the womb must be rendered barren, and eventually the gathered Bride of Christ must be denied her heavenly mate. All of this is being undertaken because of an understanding of nature divorced from the Scriptures.

Romans 1 reveals that natural barrenness, a famine of righteousness, offspring or crops, is a supernatural act of judgment. As in Eden it is not the *intervention* of God so much as the *withdrawal* of God. He cuts off the wicked that the righteous might become more fruitful in the process. Despite their attempt to break every tie with heaven, even the vessels of destruction have an "office." What is judgment for sinners is merely discipline for the saints, and all the treasures heaped up by the wicked become the inheritance of the meek.

INQUIÉTUDE

For the moment all discipline seems painful rather than pleasant, but later it yields the peaceful fruit of righteousness to those who have been trained by it. (Hebrews 12:11)

THE BRIDE

A false confidence in natural law divorces earth from heaven, but the worship of nature divorces earth from Man. Extreme environmentalism is against forestry, farming and family, that is, all forms of *husbandry*, but this philosophy unwittingly condemns its beloved goddess *Gaia* to spinsterhood. Her unnatural "purity" is a cover for the whoredoms of her protectors.

This stripe of sin is also found in those who glory in the Church rather than in Christ. This is why the Revelation pictures first century Jerusalem as a woman who, like David's wife Michal, has rejected the Man who is the image and glory of God, and is no longer the glory of the Man, but a glory unto herself, and thus condemned to barrenness (1 Corinthians 11:7; 2 Samuel 6:16-23).

> As she glorified herself and lived in luxury,
> so give her a like measure
> of torment and mourning,
> since in her heart she says,
> 'I sit as a queen,
> I am no widow,
> and mourning I shall never see.'
> (Revelation 18:7)

REPRESENTATION

31

THE LANGUAGE OF RAINBOWS

QUANTUM FIELD THEOLOGY

"Show me your tomes and I will draw you a napkin."

The usual way to approach a theological problem is to read just about everything written on the subject by just about everybody else, and quote just about every one of them in a book that almost nobody is going to read. And the result most often looks like the same landscape just slightly rearranged. There is little or no progress.[1]

Although the value of such work should never be underestimated, true innovation in any field seems to be achieved by someone willing to attack its problems from an entirely fresh angle.

---

[1] And some people even get paid to do this.

INQUIÉTUDE

VISUAL LANGUAGE

Mathematician and Nobel Prize winner John Nash (the subject of the movie *A Beautiful Mind*) was one such individual. Another, also a Nobel Prize winner, was physicist Dr Richard Feynman. His approach to science is very much like the approach of the school of biblical theology to which I subscribe. The scientist observing the laws of nature is like someone who does not know the rules of chess watching the game being played and attempting to make sense of it. Feynman said:

> A fun analogy to get some idea of what we're doing to try to understand nature is to imagine that the gods are playing some great game, like chess. You don't know the rules of the game but you're allowed to look at the board, at least from time to time, and in a little corner, perhaps. And from these observations you try to figure out the rules of the game and the movement of the pieces. You might observe, for example, that if there's only one bishop moving around on the board that the bishop maintains its color. Later on, you might discover that the law for the bishop is that it moves on a diagonal, which would explain the law that you understood before, that the bishop maintains its color. That would be analogous to finding one law and later gaining a deeper understanding of it. You've got all the laws, and your understanding of chess is going well.
>
> Then, all of a sudden, some strange phenomenon

Dr. Richard Feynman giving a Special Lecture:
The Motion of Planets Around the Sun (1964)

occurs in some corner, so you begin to watch out for it so you can investigate it. This phenomenon is "castling," something you didn't expect. By the way, in fundamental physics we are always trying to investigate areas in which we don't understand the conclusions. The thing that doesn't fit is the thing that's the most interesting—the part that doesn't go according to what you expected. We can have revolutions in physics after you've been noticing that the bishops maintain their color and go along the diagonals and so on for such a long time, and everybody knows that that's true, but then you suddenly discover one day in some chess game that the bishop doesn't maintain its color, it changes its color. Only later do you discover a new possibility: that the bishop is captured and a pawn went all the way down to the queen's end to produce a new bishop. That can happen, but you didn't know it. So it's very analogous to the way our laws are. Things look positive. They keep on working. Then all of a sudden some little gimmick shows that they're wrong and then we have to investigate the conditions under which this bishop changed color, and gradually learn the new rule that explains it more deeply.

In the case of the chess game, however, the rules become more complicated as you go along. But in physics, when you discover new things, it looks more simple. It appears on the whole to be more complicated because we learn about a greater experience, about more particles and new things. And so, the laws look complicated again. But what's kind of wonderful is that as we expand our experience into wilder and wilder regions, every now and then we have one of the "integrations" where everything is pulled together, unified in a way which turns out to be simpler than it looked before.[2]

This explanation by Feynman struck a chord with me, because it is exactly what I am proposing is the case when it comes to the literature of the Bible. Theological libraries are filled with forests cut down and flattened to record centuries of isolated observations about the Bible, gathered and labeled under terminologies designed to describe similarity of appearance. One thing missing from theology is a "unified theory" which makes the entire book simpler rather than more complicated. Systematics are some help but overall they are just collections of data, not a window into the internal logic of the "game" of biblical literature.

What is also missing is a way to *express* this "unified theory," and Feynman is a help here as well.

Known for his assistance in the development of the atomic bomb, and honored for his work in quantum electrodynamics, Feynman is also famous for introducing a new "visual language" to express quantum field theory processes in terms of particle paths: the "Feynman diagrams." This "simplification" required a mind not only familiar with the intricacies of physics, but also at ease with the logic behind them.

2   Richard Feynman interviewed in "The Pleasure of Finding Things Out," a documentary filmed in 1981. (Edited for clarity.)

INQUIÉTUDE

This was Richard Feynman nearing the crest of his powers. At twenty-three ... there was no physicist on earth who could match his exuberant command over the native materials of theoretical science. It was not just a facility at mathematics... Feynman seemed to possess a frightening ease with the substance behind the equations, like Albert Einstein at the same age, like the Soviet physicist Lev Landau—but few others.[3]

So, what are the Feynman diagrams?

In theoretical physics, Feynman diagrams are pictorial representations of the mathematical expressions governing the behavior of subatomic particles. The scheme is named for its inventor, Nobel Prize-winning American physicist Richard Feynman, and was first introduced in 1948. The interaction of subatomic particles can be complex and difficult to understand intuitively, and the Feynman diagrams allow for a simple visualization of what would otherwise be a rather arcane and abstract formula. As David Kaiser writes, "since the middle of the 20th century, theoretical physicists have increasingly turned to this tool to help them undertake critical calculations," and as such "Feynman diagrams have revolutionized nearly every aspect of theoretical physics." (Wikipedia)

Though Feynman was not the originator of this visual language, he was the first to develop it fully and to teach other physicists to use it. What am I saying here?

3   James Gleick, *Genius: The Life and Science of Richard Feynman.*

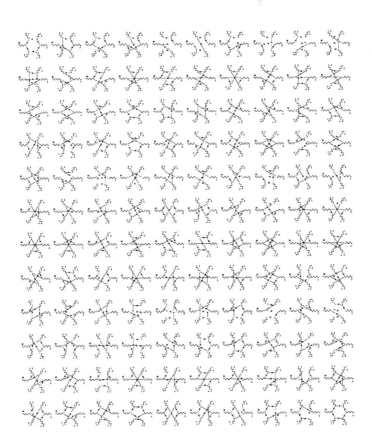

Feynman diagrams: A small multiple of the 120 possible
event-sequences for 6-photon scattering.

Image source: www.findingpatterns.info

INQUIÉTUDE

Well, of course, that I believe that what I refer to as the "Bible matrix" is such a language. It not only allows us to understand the complexities of the Bible's history, architecture and theology in a simpler, more integrated way, but also to express them more efficiently.

Predictably, my "workings" need to be explained in long-winded prose for those unversed in this theological shorthand, but the visual solution itself is simple.

OLD SCHOOL RESISTANCE

For Feynman, persuading the physics establishment to give up pages and pages of complicated calculations for simple diagrams was not so simple.

> Feynman had to lobby hard for the diagrams which confused the establishment physicists trained in equations and graphs.[4]

While many adults' eyes either glaze over or else look daggers at me for teaching something "new," children and teenagers most often "get it" straight away. The young not only pick it up but with little training are able to "speak it" quite fluently. It not only gives them an understanding of Scripture beyond their years, it explains the patterns of human life. As a friend commented to me, "Once you've seen it, you see it everywhere." If the Bible is the Word of God, we should not expect anything less.

---

4   Leonard Mlodinow, *Feynman's Rainbow: A Search for Beauty in Physics and in Life.*

Thus, my dream is to see this "quantum field theology" with its simple diagrams become the language of Bible teachers everywhere.

LAWS OF ATTRACTION

Though quite a few have dismissed this approach, I have been working on it for a number of years now and am more convinced than ever. The primary reason for continuing with it is, quite simply, *it works*. As Feynman describes, when the study seems to have hit a wall, or there is something which appears to confound the theory, further study reveals even greater unity and simplicity. There are now elegant—and extremely consistent—solutions to a growing number of supposedly complex theological debates which have occupied scholars for centuries. For every problem, I could sketch the resolution in a diagram on a napkin.

This method almost always provides a fresh angle in approaching a problem, a "third way," but this means I cannot fit into any particular denomination or theological framework, and explains why my take on many controversial Bible texts is unfamiliar. I can hear the heartbeat of the text, and it is often a different drum.

But this "unified theory" also means that the logic behind every one of my positions, on every topic, is identical. What is more, they all gel together perfectly, just as they should. Readers often do not like my conclusions, but I defy anyone to fault my logic. Show me your tomes and I will draw you a napkin.

INQUIÉTUDE

The second reason is that further study not only reveals greater unity but also more profound beauty.

I am no Feynman. Like Warhol, I take other people's ideas, fit them together and repeat them endlessly to the annoyance of the establishment. But in doing this, Warhol changed our culture forever. Like Feynman, and like me, Warhol's ease with the "mechanics" of his field was the result of his fascination with its beauty.

'Do you know who first explained the true origin of the rainbow?' I asked.

'It was Descartes,' [Feynman] said. After a moment he looked me in the eye.

'And what do you think was the salient feature of the rainbow that inspired Descartes' mathematical analysis?' he asked.

'Well, the rainbow is actually a section of a cone that appears as an arc of the colors of the spectrum when drops of water are illuminated by sunlight behind the observer.'

'And?'

'I suppose his inspiration was the realization that the problem could be analyzed by considering a single drop, and the geometry of the situation.'

'You're overlooking a key feature of the phenomenon,' he said.

'Okay, I give up. What would you say inspired his theory?'

'I would say his inspiration was that he thought rainbows were beautiful.'[5]

5   Mlodinow.

32
THE FACES OF JESUS CHRIST
A SON AS EVIDENCE OF A FATHER

For God, who said, "Let light shine out of darkness," has shone in our hearts to give the light of the knowledge of the glory of God in the face of Jesus Christ. (2 Corinthians 4:6)

Modern art is a world where faces are obscured, distorted, or missing altogether, a portrayal of a loss of identity. Perhaps this is a reaction to God's unwillingness to reveal Himself in any way other than the frustratingly obscure life of Christ, for which we have little evidence beyond some personal testimonies and correspondences. Douglas Wilson writes:

> We honestly have very little idea what Jesus Christ looked like. We worship Him as the visible image of the invisible Father, and yet we do not know what that visible image *looks* like. What kind of visible image is that? We know what the *paintings* of Him look like, and they generally all have something in common with one another, but the fact remains that

325

if you ever passed Jesus Christ on a crowded city street, you would have no idea that you had done so.

Nevertheless, we all still think of Him as a recognizable figure. But He is *only* "recognizable" because of the various forms of shorthand shifts we have come up with that prevent us from recognizing Him properly. And so what do I mean by "properly?"

I mean the way God intended for us to recognize Him—in and through the proclamation of the gospel. We are supposed to see the face of Jesus Christ in and through the declaration of what Scripture describes as good news—gospel truth. This is where we are supposed to find the only authorized portrait of Jesus.[1]

This is a profound truth, and Wilson illustrates it with a long list of other profound truths (in over 5000 words). For me, however, he has failed to tie it all together. What is the significance of the *face* of Jesus Christ? Could the reason we have no description of his looks be the fact that He has more than one face?

The "face" theme runs throughout the Bible, although it is often masked in English translations where some translators saw the word "face" as too awkward to make sense in English. A quick word search reveals how common "face" is in the book of Genesis, beginning with the face of the deep, the face of the ground, the face of the earth, and the face of Cain.[2]

---

1   Douglas Wilson, *The Face of Jesus Christ,* www.dougwils.com, January 4, 2014.
2   Adam's "face" in Genesis 3:19 is actually "nose" in the Hebrew.

TWO FACES

What is the significance of the face? In the Bible it is shorthand for a relationship where there is no guilt, and no shame. This can be a fellowship between equals, or between a master and his servant. Yahweh said he would hide his face from Israel if they turned to other gods (Deuteronomy 31:18).

When the master hides his face, his true intentions are hidden. This might be because fellowship has been broken. Joseph hid his face from his brothers, that they might be tested to see if their hearts were now pure. But sometimes it is because fellowship has not yet been established. The Lord also withdrew from the sight of Adam so that he might be tested and qualified. The intentions behind the single Law were hidden. Adam was supposed to deduct the meaning of the Law based upon faith in God's character.

The "face" of the servant expresses a response to the word of the master. Cain's face fell when his offering was rejected. The blood offering was required first, so this was an act of Kingdom usurping Priesthood, a denial of sin through a presumption of fellowship.

> Behold, you have driven me today away from the ground, and from your face I shall be hidden. I shall be a fugitive and a wanderer on the earth, and whoever finds me will kill me. (Genesis 4:14)

INQUIÉTUDE

BREAD OF THE FACE

This notion of servanthood and firstfruits became architectural in the "showbread," the twelve loaves placed on the Golden Table in the Tabernacle. This is also rendered as the "bread of the presence" but it is literally the "bread of the face."

Bethlehem means "house of bread," and it was the birthplace of kings who submitted to God. One of the rare descriptions of physical beauty in the Bible is the face of David. His good looks were a type, a physical sign, of *ethical* beauty. David's face is described as "ruddy" or "blood-filled" in the Goliath narrative (1 Samuel 17:42). Better than Adam, he is the young man who can face God because he crushes the head of the accuser. He renders the scaled giant *face down* before beheading him.

On the run from King Saul, who later became just like the spear-throwing Goliath, David and his men *ate* the forbidden bread of the face without judgment from God, an event which remained unexplained until Jesus used it to reveal the good intentions of God towards man in the institution of the Sabbath.

Jesus' face was bloodied first in the Garden of Gethsemane, then in the house of the High Priest, and finally by Roman soldiers. His looks are not described because the blood willingly shed revealed the holiness of the heart. At this point in history, no physical type for ethical beauty was necessary. God sees the heart.

He had no form or majesty
that we should look at him,
and no beauty that we should desire him.
He was despised and rejected by men;
a man of sorrows, and acquainted with grief;
and as one from whom men hide their faces
he was despised, and we esteemed him not.
(Isaiah 53:2-3)

SEEING GOD'S FACE

Christ is now enthroned in heaven, the human "angel" of the Lord who always sees the face of the Father (Matthew 18:10). But the face of the Father remains hidden to us. Or does it?

An obedient son is not one who trusts in the *commands* of his father, but in the *good character* of his father behind the "dark sayings," or to use Paul's phrase, he perceives "the *spirit* of the law" (Romans 2:25-29), that is, the invisible but loving *intentions* of the Lawgiver. Thus, Adam's failure was inherently relational, as was that of the Jews.

The sons of Adam continually failed to trust God's intentions, so God gave them a human father, Abraham. Of course, the Jews turned this blessing into an idol. The only cure for this was to bring an end to Abraham by revealing the true Father in the sacrifice of the Son.

When Philip asked Jesus to show them the Father, He instead revealed the true character of the Father indirectly, through a reflected image. They would

329

perceive the goodness of the Father through the perfect trust of the faithful Son (John 14:7-14).[3]

So, the bread faithfully displayed upon the Table was a response to the *intentions* of the One hidden behind the Veil. If the Son obeyed the Father without question, as Isaac obeyed Abraham on Moriah, then it was clear that the Father only intended "peace on earth, and good will toward men" (Luke 2:14). The incarnation was the first peek through the Veil, which could only be opened through the total tearing of the flesh of Jesus Christ.

> Therefore, brothers, since we have confidence to enter the holy places by the blood of Jesus, by a new and living way which He consecrated for us, through the veil, that is, His flesh... (Hebrews 10:19-20)

This good will was revealed in Jesus' birth, obedience and ministry, and vindicated in His resurrection. The good will of the Father towards us, as revealed in Christ, is the foundation of our confidence. The new birth transforms us into blessed sons.

Moses spoke with God "face to face." The same light which blessed Moses was a terror to Israel. Moses became a mediator whose face was veiled, just like the face of the Father. The tablets of Moses were hidden in a box and placed behind the Veil.

3   Michael Bull, *The Shape of Galatians: A Covenant-literary Analysis*, 112.

As mentioned in chapter 7, at the Altar, God's face is *against* Man, until blood is shed *(Priesthood/ Firstfruits)*. Once blood is shed, God's face *shines upon* Man *(Kingdom/Pentecost)*. Once Man is of one mind with God, Man *becomes* God's face, his eyes and mouth, vision and prophecy *(Prophethood/Trumpets)*.

This explains the sequence of events at the first Christian martyrdom. The Sanhedrin condemned Stephen for blaspheming the Law of Moses, yet all who sat in judgment saw Stephen's face as that of an angel. The Lord was shining upon him as He shone upon Moses. The face of the Father in heaven was being revealed to them *in reflection* (Acts 6:15). Stephen was a son of God. Though he was accused by those who had "received the law as delivered by angels," it was in fact Stephen who was now sitting in judgment.

Before his martyrdom, Stephen saw the heavens opened and Jesus *standing* at the right hand of God (Acts 7:55). The one who "ascends" as the Firstfruits (the Table) is the Lamb who is able to *stand* before God because He has been faithful even to death (Revelation 5:6). *Standing* at God's *right hand* is thus a union of **Priesthood** (the servants who waits at Table but never sit) and **Kingdom** (the position of the Lampstand), a combination fulfilled in the **Prophetic** witness of Stephen, against which the council stops their ears.

So, Jesus has *three* faces, the Table, the Lampstand and the Incense Altar, which, when combined, reveal our unseen Father's intentions for us: *Glorification*. The

331

suffering, ruling, witnessing Church is the threefold face of Jesus Christ in a million faces. As with Jesus, our affliction is a witness to the good intentions of the Father toward mankind.

> For I consider that the sufferings of this present time are not worth comparing with the glory that is to be revealed [into] us. (Romans 8:18)

Since we are His Triune face in the world, the faces of men are not to be feared (Jeremiah 1:8).

THE FACELESS MEN

The face of Christ is ubiquitous in the world of art, yet the Rothko Chapel Houston, Texas, is a space hung with black paintings. Here, the contemplative modern may pretend that the Veil has not been torn, that the spiritual darkness, formlessness and emptiness of mankind is profound and has not been lifted, and that the face of God has not been revealed in Jesus Christ.

Mark Rothko (1903-1970) was a Jewish atheist who committed suicide, a microcosm of first century Israel, the first nation to reject Jesus. Rothko painted only one self-portrait, in which his eyes are hidden by dark glasses.

Those who deny Christ love darkness and will be given what they love, a place of outer darkness, hidden from the face of God.

"The Rothko Chapel, founded by Houston philanthropists John and Dominique de Menil, was dedicated in 1971 as an intimate sanctuary available to people of every belief. A tranquil meditative environment inspired by the mural canvases of Russian born American painter Mark Rothko (1903-1970), the Chapel welcomes over 80,000 visitors each year, people of every faith and from all parts of the world."

www.rothkochapel.org

INQUIÉTUDE

Then the kings of the earth and the great ones and the generals and the rich and the powerful, and everyone, slave and free, hid themselves in the caves and among the rocks of the mountains, calling to the mountains and rocks, "Fall on us and hide us from the face of him who is seated on the throne, and from the wrath of the Lamb, for the great day of their wrath has come, and who can stand?"
(Revelation 6:15-17)

33
PUSHING THE LANGUAGE FORWARD

ART MADE FOR REPRODUCTION

"The human heart requires more than 'products and services.'"

Andy Warhol's "soup can" series of paintings brought him fame via infamy. The works initially received little response. Then they attracted the scorn of the art world. However, Irving Blum, the art dealer who took a risk to promote Warhol, observed that day after day the soup can paintings in his LA gallery had an increasingly profound effect upon him.

Blum could not put it into words, but he realized that, together as a unit, and *only* as a unit, the paintings silently but persistently asked a deep question.

Blum eventually bought the paintings from Warhol for $1000, on the condition that he would never sell them separately. In 1996 they fetched him 15 million. But the paintings are only valuable because they are famous, and only famous because they posed a question. They divided the art world by questioning the art world, its dichotomy between the "commercial" and the "fine," a wall which had kept Warhol himself, a commercial artist, *out* of the art world.

For better or worse, pop art was a marriage between the mundane and the sublime, an ironic glorification of the ordinary. It presented soap boxes as articles to admire for their outward design *per se* rather than as glorified expressions of what they contained. Similarly, it immortalized the fading surface beauty of passing Hollywood stars as gilded icons to adore.

Warhol is fascinating because he was not condemning consumerism but *rejoicing* in it. For a boy raised in poverty, mass production and overnight celebrity meant that everyone, regardless of status, could potentially live like kings and queens. The nobody Andrew Warhola from Pittsburg could drink the same Coca-Cola enjoyed by the President of the United States.

Initially *hindered* by their backgrounds in commercial art, Warhol and others succeeded precisely *because* of them. With the savvy of professional visual communicators, they redefined fine art. The mass-produced popular culture despised by the art industry was copied, minimally reworked and its mass-produced "originals" of mass-produced products were exhibited in galleries as fine art—and thus as a *question*. Like Nathan before David, the prophet is the divine mirror who exposes what we cannot see for ourselves.

Campbell's Soup Cans (1962)
Andy Warhol

INQUIÉTUDE

Chief Curator of the Whitney Museum, Donna De Salvo, said about Warhol's controversial career,

> [Warhol] had to deal with art directors who constantly needed to perfect an image, who had to get an image that would communicate not to just one person or ten people, but tens and hundreds and thousands of people. So he saw something perhaps more than his other illustrator contemporaries did about what makes an image communicate.
>
> Throughout his career, Warhol understands scale, he understands texture, he understands movement of the eye. He understands how to make a composition, but he also understands something that I think makes him probably one of the most extraordinary figures since Matisse and that's how to use color. His sense of color is just unbelievable. And then on an aesthetic level, Warhol had a great capacity for finding permutations within the same... to find a single image, a single theme and to endlessly, endlessly change it, to mine a territory that was very narrow to some extent and then push it as far as he could. This is something that print making made absolutely possible... The capacity of his mind seems without boundary in that kind of way... He pushed the language forward. That's the thing we want from great artists.[1]

---

1   Donna De Salvo, interviewed in "Andy Warhol – A Documentary Film," PBS, 2006.

TRASH OR TREASURES?

Important works of art are rarely understood or appreciated in their day. But with the passing of time their value becomes apparent. The political essays of famous novelists, written to meet immediate needs, are almost entirely ignored, while the universal appeal of their fictions continually wins new audiences.

Time not only threshes art and music for us so that only the best endures, it is often the case that the arts remain the best window upon any period of history. This goes doubly for Warhol, whose early artwork is like an album of family photographs, a recording of the mundanities, idols and terrors of the early sixties.

The enduring influence of pop is as upside-down as its revolution of art. Pop art was never intended to last, which was another attack on institutional dogma. In this respect, the pop artists failed precisely because they succeeded in capturing the public imagination. Their work was commercial but its popularity meant that it was not, after all, disposable. We murder our prophets, but once their greatness is recognized, we insist on adorning their tombs.

ART IS PROPHETIC

Art which truly moves things forward always involves a risk, or some kind of sacrifice. This is why whenever art is greatly subsidized, the lowering of the risk to the artist also reduces the quality and the value. The art and music and architecture that really matters is that which simply *must* be made at any cost. Risk is a qualifier of great culture as it is of great men.

Since the most objective observer is generally an outsider, the prophets of culture are fringe dwellers. Great innovators are often those who struggle with basic life skills, or ignore them as secondary concerns. They exist on a different plane and often endure rejection and loss because they are gripped by a vision which totally consumes them. Calling for change also makes one the enemy of one's own. In whatever arena they choose, the prophets in any field are far more effective outside of the establishment which they target because they are not subject to its constraints—or on its payroll. As art critic Dave Hickey has said:

> You can't lead in America. You can't get up in front with a flag and make people go anywhere. What you do is you move to the edge, declare that the center and let everybody reorganize the world around you.

This is precisely what Warhol did. He is almost invisible to us today because we live in a culture which communicates in the visual language he established. Practically illiterate, Warhol always relied on ghost writers, including his mother, who even signed his paintings for him. From early childhood he understood the language of images, and this was sometimes the only way he would communicate.

Art speaks to us when words fail. It is the offspring of the union of the flesh and the Spirit which employs colors, sounds, images and allusions to communicate the unspeakable (Romans 8:26). Physical life is *priestly*. It is mere survival. It is putting food on the table, or the wearing of socks, the needs of the hour. Political essays are *kingly*. They concern the economic and social needs of the day, but that day passes. Art is *prophetic*. It is the future, the glory, and somehow a ravishing "she." It completes life and adorns it, as women complete what men begin. Inspired art is cultural *Succession*. It lasts.

WHEN WORDS FAIL

The Spirit, through the Church, is the only true muse, moving the world from mere survival to scientific marvels. New technology, like cultural beauty, comes from the hand of God, and brings with it prosperity. We now rule the world as kings, and every new discovery is a Tree of Good and Evil, a source of great blessing or great cursing depending upon the hearts of men.

Modern science began as an endeavor of faith, but faithless science has led us down a blind alley. Despite the insistence of its "priestly" submission to data, it dictates like a king, limiting us to the needs of today. With little regard for eternity it obfuscates the big questions. However, it is dawning upon moderns that the truth which really concerns us lies not in science but in the prophetic, in art. Imagination has always preceded invention. John Maeda writes:

INQUIÉTUDE

...what people want today goes well beyond technology and design. They don't just want four wheels and a means to steer, or to be surrounded by music and information wherever their eyes and ears may roam. What people are looking for now is a way to reconnect with their *values:* to ground how they can, will, and should live in the world.

The innovation now needs to occur elsewhere. Outside the design. Into, quite frankly, the world of art... Designers create *solutions*—the products and services that propel us forward. But artists create *questions*—the deep probing of purpose and meaning that sometimes takes us backward and sideways to reveal which way "forward" actually is. The questions that artists make are often enigmatic, answering a why with another why. Because of this, understanding art is difficult: I like to say that if you're having difficulty "getting" art, then it's doing its job.

In the business world, Steve Jobs was the iconic CEO-as-artist. One way to learn from that example, as revealed by Isaacson's biography, is to see the artist as a mercurial asshole in bloodthirsty pursuit of an ideal others cannot yet envision. For better or worse, though, most people don't see themselves in this definition. But when we manage to shed our stereotypes of artists as psychologically unstable, we get to see what an artist really is: someone who often exchanges his own welfare and even his life for a cause that may have no meaning to anyone else, but means everything to him or her.

In other words, an artist is truly in it for themselves—

not just for reasons of wanting to get rich, or get famous, or find a path to comfort. The artist needs to understand the truth that lies at the bottom of an enigma.[2]

The Bible is literary art, but under the influence of modernism, its study has been perverted into a science, a realm where the analysis of images and rhythm are all but forbidden. The text is dismembered with clinical instruments instead of being recited with musical ones, and much of its message—and power—is lost.

PROPHECY IS ART

The methodology of modern Bible teachers is entirely out of step with the Spirit of God, and thus out of step with the people the Bible was intended to reach. Our preaching from the Scriptures is uninspiring because it is uninspired by the Scriptures. Pastors and teachers scratch around for something to share from a book which after two thousand years is nowhere near short of ideas. God gives us images which should shock and awe and make us swoon yet we limit our study to the origin and grade of the canvas.

The Bible was designed to be difficult, to be thought-provoking and profound. If we have trouble "getting it," then it is doing its job. The human heart requires more than "products and services" (Matthew 4:4). It desires

---

2   John Maeda, *If Design's No Longer the Killer Differentiator, What Is?*, wired.com, September 21, 2012.

not merely to hear or perceive but also to be transformed, to *resonate* in a manner beyond its control. This is why many artists refer to their work as "spiritual." Art is communication which requires participation—*touch*.

Sadly, the Bible has ceased to resonate with us because, like fine art, it has become the domain of the elite. The Scriptures are *objets d'art* to be analyzed, authenticated and traded instead of movies to thrill to and songs to sing. The academy starves the people of God, so we look elsewhere for sustenance. Ironically, while lowly saints who are biblically illiterate go for Christian schlock (pop art and music that reflects commerce and culture back to the world without asking any questions), the art and music of two millennia of the Christian Church are studied and celebrated more than ever before by cultured unbelievers. But the greatest work of art, the Bible itself, is largely ignored. This is because the Bible can never be the establishment. To our frustration, it ever remains *outside* the institutions of men, dwelling on the fringes that it might speak to the heart. Like artists, the biblical prophets dare to question those in power. And, like artists, they employ a language of spirit which cannot be understood or received by those who resist transformation.

MASS SOCIETY

The future will be the presentation of the Bible to both the godly and the godless as literary art. But the Bible is more like the kind of art found in the works of Andy

Warhol. It takes the disposable, the ordinary, even the trashy, and somehow makes it immortal.

The Scriptures will never be a commodity, and they will never be ordinary, yet they deal with both. The Bible is everyday life reimagined as liturgy: food and sex and commerce, the mundane and disposable borrowed, broken, multiplied and given back to us as spiritual vehicles and sacred signs.

The deepest questions are asked in innovation, so it should be no surprise that the prophets, like artists, also take familiar items, things we see and do every day, reimagine them and present them to the world in a startling, and often controversial, new way: dominion of the world is wrapped up in a single piece of fruit; the annual harvests become a festal calendar; a nomadic tent becomes a dwelling for the God of the universe; a Moabitess makes Israel fruitful; an overturned cauldron foreshadows invasion; the death of a gourd pictures Israel's failure to shelter the nations; and of course, bread and wine are the body and blood of Christ.

The Bible is high art that we can understand, mass-produced that it might be possessed by everyone down to the most common. Even to the simple, it reveals the glory of the ordinary, captures the imagination, exposes our pretenses but never insults our intelligence. It invades us, consumes us, inspires us, opens our eyes and carries us into the future, as works of art are intended to do.

Moreover, it asks the profound questions through

subtle changes in a framework of repetition. The daily occupations of preparing food, of washing ourselves, of family and work and travel, all the priestly and kingly duties of life are transubstantiated in the mirror of the prophets, those mercurial assholes who continue to arrest us, enlighten us and spur us on.

As a lover of art and music, I am passionate about biblical typology. An understanding of its profound process of gradual growth and change through repetition will break through the artificial constraints of an ossified establishment and "push the language forward." Teaching the Bible as art will build on the existing foundations but take us somewhere unexplored in previous ages, altering the culture so much that it will once again become indistinguishable from it. A deeper appreciation of its beauty will renew the vision of believers and captivate the minds of unbelievers.

The Bible is God's mind, yet the Bible is the history of us, and the Bible changes the world. It is, as we are, "art made for reproduction."

34

THE CRYSTALLINE VISION

BAUHAUS AND THE BIBLE

"What is in the nature of these materials?"

The Bauhaus, founded by architect Walter Gropius in Germany in 1919, had a profound influence in every area of design, from graphics and typography to clothing, furniture and architecture. The institution was not so much a style as a method, its philosophy based on the idea that if something is well-designed it will be beautiful of its own accord.

The means to this end involved the founding of an art school where every student was also a tradesman, and every tradesman was also an artist. The Bauhaus manifesto expressed Gropius' desire to unite the trades and the arts that their works might possess the grace of an inseparable marriage, a union of function and form.

Let us therefore create a new guild of craftsmen without the class-distinctions that raise an arrogant

347

barrier between craftsmen and artists! Let us desire, conceive, and create the new building of the future together. It will combine architecture, sculpture, and painting in a single form, and will one day rise towards the heavens from the hands of a million workers as the crystalline symbol of a new and coming faith.

The original publication of the manifesto includes a crude impression of this "crystalline symbol," a woodcut which has the appearance of a cathedral of glass filled with beams of light.

The name Bauhaus was derived from "hausbau," which means construction, although inherent in Bauhaus thinking was not only the encouragement of new methods of design and construction but also the task of reconstruction. The Bauhaus process thus begins with a cleaning of the slate, paring things back to the basics and starting from scratch. Reconstruction necessitated a degree of deconstruction, and the rejection of the ornamental clutter of the 19th Century resulted not only in greater efficiency in design and production, but also in the subsequent affordability of mass produced items for the common man.

Raw materials became scarce during the Great Depression, so scavenging for scrap and redeeming it in the production of art was initially part of Bauhaus training. The student was to look afresh at objects which had outlived their usefulness and ask, "What is in the nature of these materials?" A stress was laid on

The Bauhaus's incantatory 'Manifesto' formed part of the prospectus in which Walter Gropius presented the programme of the newly founded college of design in 1919, using Lyonel Feininger's 'Cathedral' woodcut as the title image. The Bauhaus Director's proclamation focuses on the need for the fine arts to be unified under the primacy of architecture and for a return to craftsmanship in order to reveal the 'craft quality' as the 'ultimate source of creative design'. <u>bauhaus-online.de</u>

texture, even in drawing, with the utilization and imitation of wood, glass, wool and even hair.

The training was likewise "holistic," designed to deconstruct and reconstruct the entire craftsman. The compulsory foundation course included breathing exercises and introspection, with an emphasis on the nature of the individual student as a raw material to be understood that it might be employed and appreciated.

A new beginning flows from a new *logos,* so new languages of construction were also required. "Color theory" and "design grammar" were formulated, codes with which we are familiar today, even if only subconsciously. The new vision was simplified without being folksy, functional without being industrial. Frequently relying on basic shapes—circles and squares—and on primary colors, its outcomes are both childlike and sophisticated. Ornament was eradicated. An austere geometrical "nakedness" was the new beautiful.

We know today that the simpler a tool appears to be, whether hardware or software, and the easier it is to use, the more thought and effort has gone into its design. Gropius' shoe factory, with its walls of glass instead of brick, was designed to remove not only the mystique of manufacturing but also to communicate the hope of a new transparency, a world where the removal of compartmentalization and complication from life might also remove the disenfranchisement and limitations of class from society.

Paring things back to the basics was also an expression of the removal of history, cleaning the cultural house of its demons. For Bauhaus, the past was complicated and dirty and the future was found in clear lines of steel and glass. The Dessau Bauhaus, restored since the reunification of Germany, still stands as a testimony to his clear, though not always entirely practical, vision. The building lets in too much sunlight.

This philosophy, with its practice of submitting people, materials, form and color to scientific laws, was a child of the scientism of the times, but as with any form of self-discipline, voluntary constraints led to prolific innovation. However, the freedom of expression encouraged by the Bauhaus was a shock to the working class people in its industrial locations, and its cultural openness was a concern for the Nazis, whose new world was in reality a deification of the old country.

The Second World War meant that the benefits of the foundations laid in the brief fourteen year history of the Bauhaus were not initially reaped by Germany but by the nations into which many of its creatives fled. The steel and glass skyscrapers which grew first in America and now beautify every major city owe their existence to the "crystalline vision" of Walter Gropius.

The German "higher criticism" of the Holy Scriptures was born of the same desire to deconstruct and reconstruct, though with less honorable motives. Moses was considered a part of the history which needed to be cast off that there might be a brighter future. The immediate consequences of the abolition

351

of Adam were eugenics, tyrannies and genocides.

Although these bitter fruits are now condemned, their doctrinal foundations still underpin modern secularism. Much like the Bauhaus, the rejection (or clever revision) of the past is considered to be a clean slate for the future. Postmodernism is an unwitting acknowledgement that the "crystalline vision," though effective in architecture, is ineffective when it comes to people with a corrupt nature. Modernism deconstructed the *cultus* and attempted to reengineer the culture. But true culture flows only from *cultus*. Deep breathing and introspection are helpful, but they fail to deal with corruption of heart, the true nature of the raw materials. Deconstruction through conviction of the Spirit, expressed in repentance and faith, is the only truly clean slate. The Law of Moses cuts us to our hearts that God might then bring us to Christ. The knife of God is indeed unpleasant, and often brutal, but it is only ever a temporary measure, that the waters of the crystal sea might stand up as the walls and gates of righteous judgment, a crystal city for the people of God.

The attempt by higher critics to deconstruct Moses is thus an ironic reversal. Seeking to discern the means by which the Scriptures were assembled, as though they were recycled parts of other documents haphazardly cobbled together, they failed to recognize the careful "Covenant-literary" architecture of the Words of God. The text of the Bible does indeed appear to be a shambles to varying degrees to the modern mind, but the Bible is constructed organically. These "scientists" of literature mistook the design for ornament. The Bible has many parts yet its apparent randomness is not evidence of tampering. Like the best of the Bauhaus, its varied facets are one in function and form, and I believe Walter Gropius would likely have appreciated it very much if it were explained to him.

The structure of the Bible is fractalline, and it is so because it is crystalline, a *haus* capable of infinite growth whose every part is a miniature of the whole. This crystal city, established on a foundation of circles and squares, is constructed of Spirit-filled artisans like Aholiab and Bezalel, and the carpenter-Christ. These men understood not only that every material could be redeemed to glorify God, but also that the leaven of a soiled history could only be cut off through the shedding of sacrificial blood. The world can only be reconstructed with guidance from a holy man with a vision from God. The eternal city is a city with a soul, and its heart is the purity of the lamb.

The crystalline vision of St John is the only true way forward. A culture of clean lines must begin with a clean heart, the "nakedness" of transparency, the knife of God rather than the swords and scalpels of men. The present might be postmodern but the future is postmillennial, a city where function and form are united in the beauty of holiness.

> The wall was built of jasper, while the city was pure gold, clear as glass. (Revelation 21:18)

353

35
MAD MAXINE
REDEMPTION OF THE FEMALE EUNUCH

"WE ARE NOT THINGS."

George Miller's *Mad Max: Fury Road* is a two hour chase movie. It is also, unwittingly, a bold portrait of biblical feminism.

BALLS TO THE WALL[1]

Miller delivered the expected testosterone-fest but not a few men felt like they had been had. The central character is not Max, the ex-cop of the previous films, but a woman called Imperator Furiosa. Even worse, Max spends most of the movie surrounded by women. The film has been called triumphantly feminist by some critics. In some ways it is, but I would argue that Miller's gender politics, understood in a biblical light,

---

[1]   A term used by pilots. When accelerating quickly, the throttle is pushed all the way to the panel and the throttle lever (ball) actually touches the panel (wall).

bring feminism full circle. Womanhood ends up back where it began, but it will never be the same again.

BLOOD BAG

There are only two ways to achieve prosperity. The first is the promised abundance from the hand of God given after faithful obedience. The second is through slavery and robbery, which turn Eden into Egypt. Miller's post-apocalyptic story begins in an Eden-gone-wrong, a tree-covered mountain in a desert which withholds its life giving springs as a means of control, releasing only occasional streams of water pumped up from the depths of the earth as a reminder of its power over life and death. An enormous carving above its ruler's balcony tells us that this is the place of the skull.

The longevity of this city depends upon raids against other gangs of survivors by "war boys," a brood of Cains, male children rendered sick by radiation but raised to murder and pillage. This is a world filled with violence, the bloodshed given divine sanction through a false religion welded together of relics from the old world, a fusion of scraps of men and machines, ferocious, glorious and hilarious, much like the cars and trucks which serve as extensions of the characters.

The ruler of the citadel is Immortan Joe, the Adamic everyman who has ascended to power—and extended his natural life—through unnatural means. Indeed, everything natural is farmed, exploited and hoarded, from human blood to breast milk. Max, who has told us that his only goal is survival, is himself strapped to a cross on the front of a war vehicle, silent as a lamb beneath a metal muzzle.[2] He is attached to its dying driver with an IV line, supplying the blood required to sustain the warrior while he takes part in the chase. Despite his claims, right from the beginning, where Max crushes under heel and devours a two-headed desert dragon, he is the truly *great* one, the Christ.

HELL HATH NO FURY

The driver of the plot—and of the largest tanker, the War Rig—is Imperator Furiosa, a one-armed woman with a crew cut who is one of Joe's best raiders. Furiosa was kidnapped as a small child and thrown into the breeding program, but now she is barren, unable to bare children or produce milk. Without her cunning as a raider, she would have remained a throwaway in the eyes of Joe. But now, she uses a convoy supply journey to rescue the young women of Joe's harem, girls kept for the purpose of breeding healthy sons, so it is apt that the body of the stolen War Rig tanker is filled with human milk.

Here is a female action hero who is actually a woman. Sexuality after the apocalypse is back to the needs and wants of men—sex and offspring. This angry empress is a used-up supermodel, now devoid of

2   The two "war boys," Nux and Slit, represent the two thieves at the cross. Both curse Max but Nux eventually comes to bless him, reaching paradise through a spectacular act of self-sacrifice.

everything that made her desirable, including her hair. She is what feminism has become: a womanhood which escaped exploitation by becoming the exploiter. Germaine Greer's "female eunuch," repressed sexually by the constraints of culture, sought to be free of the chains of nature but became something unnatural, something sexless. These things were stolen from Furiosa, but the barren has cause to rejoice. She is not a hero because she can kick and punch but because she has the motivation of a bereaved mother, the fury of a she-bear. Without children of her own she risks her life to rescue the daughters of men.

MAD WORLD

Some view Max as Furiosa's sidekick, but in reality he is her enabler. Indeed, he and one of the war boys come to be the only men whom the numerous women in the film learn to trust. It is the women who blame the men not only for their continued exploitation, but also for bringing about the end of the world. Land and womb are both made barren by Adam's desire for godhood. The planet is poisoned, and even the promised land, the "green place of many mothers" is now a bog filled with scavenging crows, both human and animal.

The refreshing thing about all of Miller's women is that they are real. Even the stolen supermodels are real people. When Joe discovers that his prized possessions are missing, he sees "We are not things" scrawled in large letters on the wall of the empty harem. Even better are the old women of the desert, grannies on motorbikes who live under the stars, with leathery faces but soft hearts. They are the biggest surprise of the film. They have become suspicious of all men since men view even the *end* of the world as an opportunity for gain and control. But they still maintain hope even though their own days are numbered. In Max and Furiosa, they see a reconciliation of man and woman and a new beginning, a world where Adam will not rule over Eve, and all her desires will be met by him. The two begin in fisticuffs but instead of romance there develops a deep, reciprocal sense of honor.

In the film's one heartrending scene, after Furiosa's hopes of reaching the green place are dashed, she falls to her knees, alone in the sand, and lets out a cry of despair. The only way this crew can survive is to return to Joe's citadel. The movie is a there-and-back-again, which on one level makes the rescue and the chase seem pointless. But as in the Bible, the trip to Egypt and back to Canaan changed Israel forever. Feminism's green pastures are not "out there." They are back where women began, but in a home transformed. For Eve to be truly free, she must be empowered by Adam.

WORSHIP THE VEHICLES

Joe loses his heir, his "mobile throne" (called the Gigahorse) and finally he loses his face, all important biblical symbols, in gasoline fuelled chariot battles that take the spectacle of live action to a new level. With sparse dialogue, the film is like the loudest silent movie ever made. As one reviewer noted:

> Imagine if *Cirque du Soleil* reenacted a Hieronymus Bosch painting and someone set the theatre on fire. This is more or less what Miller has come up with.[3]

Joe has gained the whole world but loses his own life. Max and Furiosa have lost everything and yet choose to serve. Max donates his blood once again, but this time voluntarily—to save his counterpart.

The final scene is a revelation of the ascension of the bride. Like the Church of Christ, she is beaten and bloodied, her face marred more than any woman. But she has her prize.

Max watches as Furiosa is lifted to glory while he humbly disappears into the adoring crowd, a new kind of everyman, a real hero, a Christlike one. And the living waters are released as streams in the desert.

BIBLICAL FEMINISM

"We're seeing in the world in many places that women are emerging as a unifying or healing force..." says George Miller. "I think that's in the zeitgeist."

Like the women in the wilderness, biblical womanhood is not a state. It is a process of redemption by

---

3   Robbie Collin, *Mad Max: Fury Road review: 'a Krakatoan eruption of craziness,'* The Telegraph UK, May 20, 2015.

Esther Denouncing Haman (1888)
Ernest Norman

Covenant. Eve was given to Adam as a gift but he treated her like a "thing" (Genesis 3:12). To protect himself, he depersonalized her. If he had been faithful and protected her, she would have been glorified at his side as a co-regent. We see the same process in the two givings of the Ten Commandments. In Exodus, the women are included with all the other chattels, but in Deuteronomy, they are now listed with their men. The book of Esther tells the same story. Esther, although married to the emperor, is merely a possession until the serpent is crushed and she is enthroned, judging beside her husband. Women must be empowered, but women can only be empowered by faithful men.

APPENDIXES

APPENDIX 1

BREATHING WISDOM:
EDUCATING JESUS, EDUCATING US

Victor Chininin Buele

Have this mind among yourselves, which is yours
in Christ Jesus, who, though he was in the form of
God, did not count equality with God a thing to be
grasped, *but emptied himself, by taking the form of a
servant*, being born in the likeness of men.
(Philippians 2:5-7)

Chapter 3 takes us to a head-on collision with a concept that often sends Christians running for cover.

- How did the man Christ Jesus turn water into wine and know that it would actually happen?
- Well, He is God!

- How did the man Christ Jesus know that Lazarus died and that He was to go and effectively awaken him?
- The answer hasn't changed! He is God!

We run to the divinity of Jesus when we do not know how to answer similar questions. It is easy to sound pious and flee apparent trouble, but every time we do this, one of our most valuable weapons in the fight of faith loses power.

The reason that discussions like the one in chapter 3 hit a nerve is because we are uncomfortable when we deal with the humanity of Jesus. The kind of thinking that chapter 3 requires is essential to a proper understanding of the Spirit's role in the humanity of Jesus and a greater faith in His work in our very own lives.

Paul is crystal clear in showing us that Jesus emptied Himself *by taking*. Gerald Hawthorne expands on this,

"I affirm that Jesus was *truly* God, *fully* God, God undiminished by emptying himself of even a single attribute! [...] One should not think that the phrase means that Christ discarded divine substances, essences, or attributes [...] Christ's self-giving was accomplished by taking, that his self-emptying was achieved by becoming what he was not before, that his *kenosis* came about not by subtraction but by addition, that his *kenosis* (an emptying) was in reality a *plerosis* (a filling)."[1]

And what, precisely, filled the man Christ Jesus? The answer is the Holy Spirit. So, when we discuss the full obedience of the Son; His unwavering faith in the process of growing in maturity, wisdom, and knowledge; and His faithful obedience, we must delight and grow in understanding that the *credo ut intelligam* from chapter 3 is available to all of us who profess the name of Jesus and are indwelt by His Holy Spirit. The Spirit is the reason why the sons of Adam can look at the life of Jesus and rejoice in the fact that the same Spirit empowers our sanctification, our growth in maturity, wisdom, and knowledge.

Let's use our minds, then, and consider this. Every time Jesus read the Scriptures, the Spirit breathed upon the Word. When Jesus, the man, flesh and bone, like you and I, read the scroll of Isaiah, the Spirit breathed wisdom saying, "This is you." When Jesus sang Psalm 22 or the servant

---

1   Gerald F. Hawthorne, *The Presence and the Power: The Significance of the Holy Spirit in the Life and Ministry of Jesus*, 207. See also, Bruce A. Ware, *The Man Christ Jesus: Theological Reflections on the Humanity of Christ*. The line of reasoning presented here reflects insights obtained from these works.

songs of Isaiah, the Spirit grew Him in wisdom to comprehend that these texts spoke of Him. When Jesus obeyed His carpenter dad, the Spirit empowered this obedience. When Jesus offered up prayers and supplications, with loud cries and tears in the days of his flesh (Hebrews 5:7), it was the Spirit guiding His heart, His words, and strengthening His faith. When Jesus agonized at the cross, it was the Spirit who brought back the words of truth to His lips. And why does this matter to me? Because it is the same Spirit who awakens you from spiritual despondency and calls you to read the Word, who puts the song of praise in your heart, who ministers to you in your suffering, who brings the Word to remembrance in the heat of battle, who is perfecting you from one degree of glory to the next, and who empowers your faithful obedience.

Jesus did not cheat. He did not just recall divine, superhero-like powers, when adversity came. In the days of His flesh, His obedience was true, His faith was tried and confirmed, and His love for the Father was indestructible. And He made sure before He went back to the Father's side to leave us the same Spirit—

The Spirit breathes upon the Word,
And brings the truth to sight;
Precepts and promises afford
A sanctifying light.

A glory gilds the sacred page,
Majestic, like the sun:
It gives a light to every age;
It gives, but borrows none.

– William Cowper

JESUS KNEW

JARED LEONARD

It can be established, with a fair degree of certainty, that there is indeed an eternal to-and-fro between Father and Son (and Spirit), but let's focus a minute on that pesky adjective: eternal. Here the perennial theological/philosophical question of God's relationship to time must be asked. Is he beyond it? Is it part of his nature? Did he somehow bind himself to it in the act of creation? Allow me to briefly cut through some academic ballyhoo: since relationships require time in order to function, and God exists minimally as an interrelated tri-personal unity, we must conclude that time is a fundamental component of God's nature, like holiness or omnipotence.

There are some key doctrines that, I believe, also hinge on the eternality of God *not* implying whatever is meant or communicated by the concept of timelessness. Pre-destination, for instance, requires that God have prior-to-creation knowledge of his people. Obviously this is not possible if we equate eternity with timelessness since there is no "prior-to" if there is no time. Another example is the incarnation of the Son/Word in the person of Jesus. This is an event that is impossible without time already being fundamental to the nature of God. And perhaps most clearly, the doctrine of creation teaches us that time is a part of who and what God is. Paul informs us that God's invisible attributes, eternal power, and divine nature, have been clearly seen since the creation of the world. How? Well, they are understood through what God has made. And what has God made? He made heaven and earth and set off the to-and-fro of human history, a to-and-fro patterned on the eternal intra-Trinitarian relationship. What makes this to-and-fro possible? Time.

Now, you may be wondering what any of this has to do with the "Educating Jesus" essay in the book proper. The author of the book proposes what I believe to be a problematic proposition; namely, he supposes that the to-and-fro of human history is a necessary correlate of the to-and-fro between the Father and the Son. This is what I take "crucial" in the text of page 30 to imply. The consequent is that the Son cannot be fully realized, in some sense or another, without this crucial step (the to-and-fro of human history) initiated by the Father prior creation.[1] What we end up with, or what we start out with, perhaps, is a God that isn't perfect. We have a God that is dependent on his creation rather than sublimely transcendent. We have a God that didn't willingly set aside his pre-creation glory for the sake of "the plan", but rather was divested of it out of necessity for the eventual wholeness of the Trinity. The story of humanity's redemption is reduced to a tertiary benefit of divine self-actualization.

For this self-actualization to occur, it is further proposed that the Son's obedience to the Father must have been blind.[2] This is tied to his trust, his faith, in the Father's plan; in other words, Jesus's faith, as a man, is supposedly blind in relationship to what the Father's true intentions were in the Son's activities[3] on Earth. This seems highly implausible, especially when we factor in the sheer amount of Messianic prophecy that Jesus intimately knew.[4] Now also factor in his deep knowledge and understanding of the sacrificial system, of the types and symbols we moderns are only just beginning to uncover through the covenant/creation sequence, and who knows what else! How, then, can we suppose that the Father's intentions were hidden? That the Son, pre or post incarnation, didn't know the plan or his Father's will? It is claimed that "faith assumes an absence of sight"[5] but in actuality faith is simply a different kind of sight. Faith, as James Jordan might say, gives us new eyes and brings a spiritual clarity that otherwise cannot be had. Surely the faith of Jesus counts for something in this regard! We believe so that we can understand, *credo ut intelligam*. But Jesus believed because he understood, *credo quia cum intelligam*.

I would, here, like to conclude by noting that none of this undermines the humanity of Jesus. Jesus as the God-man, the Word made flesh, experienced the fallen creation the same as you and me. He was born, he wept, he hungered, he thirsted, he ate, he drank, he laughed, he aged, he bled, and he died. The real education of Jesus was in the acts of the transcendent Creator to experience his creation *as a created being*. This was for *our* benefit, not his. There is no need to concoct some lacking in the relationship between Father and Son, an emptiness that could only be filled by the to-and-fro of human history, in order to justify the story of redemption. Sometimes we don't get to ask why and at those times we need to humbly acknowledge that God is true and all mere mortals are liars.

1   Page 30.
2   Page 32.
3   This is on account of the proposed "firmament/veil."
4   Just do a quick word search for "fulfill" in the New Testament.
5   Page 35.

THE RIGHT TO KNOW

CHRISTOPHER OSWALD

That the divine Christ willingly surrendered his "right to know" is beyond dispute. Chapter 3 merely asks when that surrender occurred. The humanity of Jesus doesn't get enough "play" and that neglect is leading to all sorts of institutional dust bowls.

As Christ pressed his way through the thick crowd, he asked, "who touched me" because he really wanted to know who touched him (Luke 8). When the gospels say that Jesus was astonished they mean that Jesus was astonished. We are not, therefore, left to wonder if Jesus can be God without knowing the day and the hour of the eschaton (Mark 13:32) or the seating arrangement at his own wedding supper (Mark 10:40). God's attributes belong to him and not the other way around.

However limited the Son's foreknowledge was, his knowledge of the Father was, is, and always will be, perfect. That, my friends, is a distinction of glorious consequence. The elevation of Father-knowledge over foreknowledge means that Jesus found obedience empowering satisfaction in the Father and not merely in the full possession and exercising of divine attributes. The Father is pleased with the Son (Matthew 3:17, 17:5), and we know that without faith it is impossible to please God (Hebrews 11:6). God-pleasing faith fills the gaps of limited foreknowledge with Father-love. Jesus is the author and perfector of that kind of faith. It is this Father-loving faith that moves mountains.

Speaking of terraforming, the larger point is that devotion (and devotion alone) fuels dominion. Perhaps those initiated into the Bible gardens of Jordan, Leithart, and Bull know where I am headed. Our natural father Adam was tripped up on precisely this issue. God made man to rule and subdue the world by fruitful multiplication. Fruitful multiplication happens via love. Love comes from the Father.

When the dragon came peddling promises of divine attributes, the first man took the bait. Adam decided it was better to grip godlike knowledge than the Father's hand. Or, in keeping with the theme of the chapter, we might simply say that Adam mistook the tool of forming with the tool of filling, and, as Lewis suggested, he lost both.

This is where the discussion of Jesus' self-imposed limitations start bearing cosmic fruit. By entering the world naked, covered only with Father-love, Jesus was tempted in every way, yet without sin. Not only does this total and victorious reliance upon Father-faith make Jesus a sympathetic priest (He knows what it feels like to feed on faith alone), it also makes Jesus an efficacious king. The land is always won or lost through the acceptance or rejection of father-love.

As he cried out *Eloi, Eloi, Lama Sabachthani,* Jesus entered Adam's curse (Father-loss) and through that suffering brought many sons to the glory of dominion via the glory of devotion (Revelation 5:9-10). Christ, the perfect Adam pressed through death, the ultimate veil. He rose to rule and subdue with the bride born from his wounded side. He is filling the earth with verdant praise.

One day of knowing and loving God is better than a thousand days worth of foresight—on earth and in heaven?

APPENDIX 1

LITERARY STRUCTURE OF HEBREWS 2:10-12

Michael Bull

The following chart was cut from chapter 3, but since Chris mentioned this text, I include it here.

Creation: For it was fitting that he, *(Initiation)*

> **Division:** for whom and by whom all things exist, *(Delegation)*

>> **Ascension:** in bringing many sons to glory, *(Presentation)*

>>> **Testing:** should make the founder of their salvation *(Purification)*

>> **Maturity:** perfect through sufferings. *(Transformation)*

> **Conquest:** For he who sanctifies and those who are sanctified *(Vindication)*

Glorification: are all of one. *(Representation)*

Creation: For which reason *(Initiation)*

> **Division:** he is not ashamed *(Delegation)*

>> **Ascension:** to call them brothers, *(Presentation)*

>>> **Testing:** saying, "I will tell of your name to my brothers; *(Purification)*

>> **Maturity:** in the midst of the congregation I will sing your praise." *(Transformation)*

> **Conquest:** And again, "I will put my trust in him." *(Vindication)*

Glorification: And again, "Behold, I and the children God has given me." *(Representation)*[1]

---

1   The ESV rendering has been edited to reflect more clearly the "matrix" significance of certain Greek words.

Bible Matrix	Feast	Sacrifice	Abraham	Moses	Israel 1	Israel 2
Creation DAY 1	*Sabbath*	INITIATION (*Choosing*)	Call of Abram & birth of Isaac	Call of Moses	Ministry of Moses	Ministry of Moses
Division DAY 2	*Passover*	DELEGATION (*Cutting*)	Jacob separates from Esau	Circumcision of Gershom	Passover & Red Sea	Passover & Red Sea
Ascension DAY 3	*Firstfruits*	PRESENTATION (*Offering*)	The rule of Joseph	Pharaoh's oppression	Meal on the Mount	Sinai & the Law
Testing DAY 4	*Pentecost*	PURIFICATION (*Fire*)	Sons of Egypt vs. sons of Israel	Signs before the king	Sinai & the Law	Death of old Israel
Maturity DAY 5	*Trumpets*	TRANSFORMATION (*Witness*)	Ministry of Moses & Aaron	The ten plagues	Israel sins ten times	The Law repeated
Conquest DAY 6	*Atonement*	VINDICATION (*Blessing*)	Conquest under Joshua	Passover & Red Sea	Death in wilderness	Conquest under Joshua
Glorification DAY 7	*Booths*	REPRESENTATION (*Rest & Rule*)	Promises fulfilled	Israel at Sinai		Promises fulfilled

MINISTRY AND DECONSECRATION
IN THE LEVITICAL OFFERINGS

The five books of Moses correspond to the offerings in Leviticus 1-5, of which the last concerned the deconsecration of the priest. Since his ministry was complete, he could once again become a commoner.

This pictures the purpose of circumcision in history. Israel was bound as a sacrifice that the nations might be loosed. It was a temporary ministry. Abraham could be deconsecrated because through the ministry of Christ, everything was made sacred once for all. Since His ministry is "after the order of Melchizedek," that is, a priesthood of all nations, the Aaronic Priesthood was loosed from its vow once for all in AD70.

Creation - **Genesis:**
Ascension Offering: an Isaac for all nations

Division - **Exodus:**
Tribute Offering: no leaven or honey

Ascension - **Leviticus:**
Peace Offering: dining with God

Testing - **Numbers:**
Purification Offering: blood on the
horns of both altars cleans the house

Maturity - **Deuteronomy:**
Guilt Offering: the Levite is loosed

'INTERSTELLAR' CHIASM BY DOUGLAS JORDAN

A. Videos describing old home; Coop dreaming of aborted flight (due to computer error caused by a gravitational anomaly -- probably 10 years earlier).

  B. Murph at Cooper's bedside. "I thought you were the ghost."

    C. Grandpa tells Cooper to repopulate Earth.

      D. Cooper *dismantles* an Indian Air Force drone primarily to *take* the solar cells, which "could power an entire farm."

        E. Cooper attends parent teacher conference, where teachers tell him about the brilliant propaganda of pouring resources into "rockets and other useless machines."

          F. Coop: "I still don't think your bookshelf is trying to talk to you." Also, "It's like we've forgotten who we are, Donald. Explorers, pioneers – not caretakers." Brand outlines the plan for human survival. Brand promises to have the gravity problem solved.

            G. Cooper leaves Murph.

              H. Docking with the space station, then initiating spin. Peace.

                I. Miller's Planet and return to the station:

                1. A lie is revealed: those are not mountains, they're waves.

                2. Nature tries to kill them.

                3. Amelia disobeys a direct order.

                4. Amelia almost dies.

                5. Doyle dies.

                6. Cooper tells Amelia that being a parent rules out telling a child the world's ending.

                7. Team receives messages from home, including news of death.

                8. When asked, Amelia declares Mann to be the best and bravest of us.

                  J. AMELIA'S SPEECH ABOUT LOVE BEING THE MOST POWERFUL FORCE IN EXISTENCE.

                I' Mann's planet:

                1. Lies are revealed: Mann faked the records, Plan A was never feasible.

                2. A person tries to kill them.

                3. Amelia obeys Cooper instantly when he calls for help.

                4. Cooper almost dies.

                5. Romilly dies.

                6. Mann tells them there never was any hope for Plan A.

                7. Team receives a message from home, including news of death.

                8. Cooper calls Mann a coward. (Only use of the f-bomb in the entire film.)

              H' Space station spinning, then initiating docking. Chaos.

            G' Cooper leaves Amelia.

          F' The Tesseract. Murph's bookcase IS talking to her, and Coop realizes that there's a future for mankind that has remembered who they are. Coop outlines the plan for human survival. Murph solves the gravity problem.

        E' Cooper visits the recreation of his house, indicates he thinks it's a useless waste of resources.

      D' Cooper is *given* a power cell that he uses to *restore* TARS to operations.

    C' Murph's large family visits her bedside.

  B' Cooper at Murph's bedside. "It was me, Murph! I was your ghost!"

A' Murph describing new home; Coop flying away (with help of TARS).

APPENDIX 5

THE JUDICIAL LAW OF MOSES

The common claim that some of the Levitical laws apply today while others do not is based on the assumption that the Laws of Moses can be divided into moral, civil and ceremonial categories. This is not the case. James Jordan writes:

> It has been contended that the Older Testament does not actually set forth a series of judicial or civil laws. With this criticism we may agree. A simple reading of Exodus or Deuteronomy will show that there is no place where a set of laws constituting a legal civil code is to be found. Rather, social, personal, civil, familial, and "ceremonial" laws are found all mixed up together. This shows that the law of God all stands or falls together. It would be improper to maintain, as some of the Fifth Monarchy Men did, that we find in the Bible a full-blown legal system. Rather, what we find is the *basis* for a Christian legal system. The laws of the Bible are case laws, and it is the duty of the Christian ruler to extend the equity of these cases to cover the details he finds in his own society.[1]

Peter Leithart writes:

> The Mosaic law establishes the death penalty for a number of crimes. Not every violation of the 10 commandments was a capital crime (theft, for instance, required restitution), but the death penalty is given for some form of nearly all the 10 commandments... Several preliminary points must be made about this.

---

[1] James B. Jordan, "Calvinism and 'The Judicial Law of Moses,'" *The Journal of Christian Reconstruction*, Symposium on Puritanism and Law Vol. V., Winter, 1978-79, No 2. 17-48. Note that while Jordan still sees the overall historical argument for Biblical theocracy as valid, he holds a somewhat different view of "theonomy" today.

First, we have to remember that this is the Word of God. Christians cannot pretend that these passages do not exist, or simply ignore them, nor can we let modern sentimentality determine our evaluation of these texts. If they seem harsh to us, the problem may well be ours. Second, this is specifically the Word of our Creator and Redeemer, the same God who sent His Son to take the capital crime in our place, the same God who sends rain on the just and the unjust, the same God who says "turn the other cheek." We cannot say that these laws are "unreasonably harsh" without saying God is unreasonably harsh, which is a lie.

Third, the basic purpose and meaning of the Mosaic law is not to provide blueprints for a civil order, but to provide foreshadowings of Jesus Christ. Our main framework for understanding the Mosaic system and applying it in our day is typological. The Mosaic system provides both types and shadows of Jesus (He is the Priest, the Sacrifice, the Tabernacle, etc.) and typological patterns for the life of the church, the totus Christus (cf. 1 Cor 9:9, 13). Fourth, the common ordering of the Mosaic law into "moral, civil, ceremonial," while valid in a broad sense, does not give much assistance in dealing with specific passages. In the law, moral, civil, and ceremonial features are all mixed up together.[2]

Instead, we find that the time-bound laws of God are expressions of the wisdom of God in various circumstances, as Jesus highlights in His apparent "violations" of the Sabbath. James Jordan again:

Since God's law is a transcript of His personal character it cannot change, any more than God can change. Jesus

2   Peter J. Leithart, *The Death Penalty in the Mosaic Law*, www.theopolisinstitute.com, July 3, 2015.

makes this point in Matthew 5:17-19: "Do not think that I came to abolish the law or the prophets; I did not come to abolish, but to fulfill (or, put into force). For truly I say to you, until heaven and earth pass away, not the smallest letter or stroke shall pass away from the law, until all is accomplished. Whoever then annuls one of the least of these commandments, and so teaches men, shall be called least in the kingdom of heaven; but whoever does and teaches them, he shall be called great in the kingdom of heaven."

Yet we know that there has been some change. We no longer sacrifice bulls and sheep, as the epistle to the Hebrews makes clear. If the law has not changed, then what has? It is the *circumstances* which have changed...

When Scripture sometimes refers to a change in law, as in Hebrews 7:12, the reference is to particular laws or to the system of the law, which system undergoes a death and resurrection in Christ, becoming the New Covenant. Our point here is rather simple and non-technical: The unchanging essence of the law is a reflex of its source in God's own character; the changing manifestations of the law are a reflex of changes in circumstances relative to the creature.[3]

The greatest difference between Old Covenant Israel and the Church is that between the first Pentecost, the giving of the Law at Sinai, and the last Pentecost, in which the fire on the mountain now inhabited believers. External law and internal law are not the same thing, and yet they are. Together they are a process of judicial maturity.[4]

---

3   James B. Jordan, *The Law of the Covenant*, 11.
4   For more discussion, see "Internal Law" in Michael Bull, *Sweet Counsel: Essays to Brighten the Eyes.*

COVENANT-LITERARY TEMPLATES

INQUIÉTUDE

Following are the most common and helpful instances of the "matrix" structure of the Bible. It is this which underlies all my thinking concerning the Scriptures.

I believe we must identify the structure (forming) if we are to understand the glory (filling).

If you would like a detailed introduction to the use of this method of interpretation and the philosophy behind it, please refer to my books *Reading the Bible in 3D,* and then *Bible Matrix: An Introduction to the DNA of the Scriptures.*

Creation

Division

Ascension

Testing

Maturity

Conquest

Glorification

CREATION

Creation - **Day 1:**
Light - Night and Day

Division - **Day 2:**
Waters - Above and Below

Ascension - **Day 3:**
Dry Land, Grain and Fruit

Testing - **Day 4:**
Ruling Lights

Maturity - **Day 5:**
Birds and Fish

Conquest - **Day 6:**
Animals and Man

Glorification - **Day 7:**
Rest and Rule

FORMING

FILLING

FUTURE

TABERNACLE

Creation - **Ark of the Covenant:**
The Law written on stone

Division - **Veil:**
The face of God veiled

Ascension -
Bronze Altar:
The Adamic body formed
and Golden Table:
The face of Adam presented

Testing - **Lampstand:**
The eyes of God opened

Maturity - **Incense Altar:**
The Evian body formed

Conquest - **Sacrifices & High Priest:**
The face of God unveiled

Glorification - **Shekinah:**
The Law written on flesh

SACRIFICE

DE-FORMING

Creation - **Called:**
Animal chosen

Division - **Sanctified:**
Animal separated / sacrifice cut

Ascension - **Presented:**
Sacrifice lifted onto Altar
Sacrifice awaits

DE-FILLING

Testing - **Purified:**
Holy fire descends

Maturity - **Transformed:**
Clouds of fragrant Smoke

Conquest - **Vindicated:**
The savor accepted by God

FUTURE

Glorification - **Sent:**
Reconciliation and reunion

FEASTS

Creation - **Sabbath:**
Weekly rest - House of Israel

Division - **Passover:**
Sin removed (external Law)

Ascension - **Firstfruits:**
Israel as Priest

Testing - **Pentecost:**
Israel as King

Maturity - **Trumpets:**
Israel as Prophet

Conquest - **Atonement:**
Sin removed (internal Law)

Glorification - **Booths (Ingathering):**
Annual rest - House of all nations

DOMINION

Creation - **Genesis:**
Israel called from the nations

Division - **Exodus:**
Israel cut from the nations

Ascension - **Leviticus:**
Israel presented to God (Man)

Testing - **Numbers:**
Israel threshed (People)

Maturity - **Deuteronomy:**
Israel reassembled (Army)

Conquest - **Joshua:**
The nations cut from the Land

Glorification - **Judges:**
Israel among the nations

COVENANT-LITERARY TEMPLATES

CREATION	DOMINION	FEASTS
Day 1 Light - Night & Day *(Ark of the Covenant)*	**Genesis** *Creation*	**Sabbath** (promise of rest) *God's rest*
Day 2 Waters divided *(Veil)*	**Exodus** *Division*	**Passover** (sin covered) *Adam's sin removed*
Day 3 Dry Land, Grain & Fruit *(Altar & Table)*	**Leviticus** *Ascension*	**Firstfruits** (priesthood) *Adam brought to God*
Day 4 Ruling Lights *(Lampstand)*	**Numbers** *Testing*	**Pentecost** (harvest) *Law revealed*
Day 5 Birds & Fish *(Incense Altar)*	**Deuteronomy** *Maturity*	**Trumpets** (armies) *Eve brought to God*
Day 6 Animals & Man *(Mediators: High) Priest & Sacrifices)*	**Joshua** *Conquest*	**Atonement** (sin expelled) *Eve removed from sin*
Day 7 Rest & Ruling *(Shekinah Glory)*	**Judges** *Glorification*	**Booths** (ingathering) *Adam's rest*

387

COVENANT

<u>TRANSCENDENCE</u> - "Who's the boss?"

 Creation - **Initiation:**
God begins a new era in history

<u>HIERARCHY</u> - "Whom has he put in charge?"

 Division - **Delegation:**
He sets apart His representatives

<u>ETHICS (LAW)</u> - "What are the rules?"

 Ascension - **Presentation:**
Law is given to them

 Testing - **Purification:**
Law is opened to them

 Maturity - **Transformation:**
Law is received by them

<u>OATH/SANCTIONS</u> - "What are the
rewards?"

 Conquest - **Vindication:**
His representatives submit to
God's blessing or cursing

<u>SUCCESSION</u> - "What's next?"

 Glorification - **Representation:**
The faithful are commissioned as rulers
and given an inheritance in history

FORMING

FILLING

FUTURE

TEN WORDS

FORMING
(Head - Adam - Priest)

FILLING
(Body - Eve - People)

TRANSCENDENCE

I
Word from God
False Gods

2
Word to God
False Oath

HIERARCHY

3
Work
Sabbath

4
Land
Father and Mother

ABOVE

BESIDE

KNIFE   ETHICS   *FIRE*

5
Murder
Sons of God

6
Adultery
Daughters of Men

SANCTIONS

7
Stealing
False Blessings

8
False Witness
False Curses

SUCCESSION

BELOW

9
Coveting Shelter
Formed House

10
Coveting the Sheltered
Filled House

---

1   See *Bible Matrix II: The Covenant Key*, Chapter 4, for an explanation of why I have arranged the Ten Words in this fashion.

FOOD LAWS

ADAM'S PROHIBITION

Creation - **Initiation:**
Springs water the Land,
but there is no Man.

Division - **Delegation:**
Adam is formed out of the dust,

Ascension - **Presentation:**
given a single, temporary
PROHIBITION, then broken
and opened to construct Eve.

Testing - **Purification:**
The serpent seduces Eve.
Adam and Eve eat, and their
eyes are opened.

Maturity - **Transformation:**
The PROHIBITION is now
obsolete. They attempt to hide
their nakedness.

Conquest - **Vindication:**
and are judged by the Lord. Innocent
substitutes are de-formed.

Glorification - **Representation:**
Instead of ingathering, there is scattering.

EVE'S PROHIBITIONS

Creation - **Initiation:**
Rivers of blood (genealogy and sacrifice) flow from Eden but there is no mediatorial Man.

Division - **Delegation:**
Israel is formed out of a barren womb *(Circumcision),*

Ascension - **Presentation:**
raised up and put into the Land. They are given many temporary PROHIBITIONS, then broken in two, opened to build a new Body.

Testing - **Purification:**
Christ defeats the serpent and opens the Church's eyes.

Maturity - **Transformation:**
The PROHIBITIONS become obsolete. The Firstfruits Church is robed in white, witnesses boldly,

Conquest - **Vindication:**
and Herodian worship is judged by the Lord. Old Covenant Israel is de-formed. *(un-Circumcision)*

Glorification - **Representation:**
Under the Married Mediatorial Man, rivers of living water flow out into all the nations.

ISRAEL

DAY 1 - LIGHT

Creation - **Patriarchs, Abraham:**
Light dawns upon the "waters" of the 70 nations

DAY 2 - WATERS DIVIDED

Division - **Exodus Moses:**
Israel is separated to mediate for the nations

DAY 3 - DRY LAND

Ascension - **Promised Land, Joshua:**
Israel possesses the Land

DAY 4 - RULING LIGHTS

Testing - **David & Solomon:**
Mighty men rule under God

DAY 5 - SWARMS

Maturity - **Captivity to Gentiles:**
The prophets witness to the kings.
Gentile armies plague Land and Sea

DAY 6 - MEDIATORS

Conquest - **Joshua the High Priest, to Jesus:**
Israel ministers within the *oikoumene*.

DAY 7 - REST & RULE

Glorification - **Jesus and the Church:**
The saints receive the kingdom and judge the Land.

THE LAST DAYS

TRANSCENDENCE

Creation - **Perfect Life of Christ**
Peace on earth *(Sabbath)*

HIERARCHY

Division - **Perfect Death of Christ**
Nakedness, flesh torn *(Passover)*

ETHICS (LAW)

Ascension - **Rule of Christ (AD30)**
Jesus rules at the Father's right hand
(Firstfruits)

Testing - **Sending of the Spirit**
The harvest begins *(Pentecost)*

Maturity - **Witness of the Apostles**
A Jew-Gentile Body mustered
(Trumpets)

OATH/SANCTIONS

Conquest - **Temple Destroyed (AD70)**
All righteous blood avenged *(Atonement)*

SUCCESSION

Glorification - **Priestly Rule of the Church**
Gospel carried to all nations *(Booths)*

GARDEN

LAND

WORLD

INQUIÉTUDE

HISTORY

<u>TRANSCENDENCE</u>

Creation - **Adam to Noah:**
World united as one blood

<u>HIERARCHY</u>

Division - **Abraham to Joseph:**
World divided by blood *(Circumcision)*

<u>ETHICS (LAW)</u>

Ascension - **Moses to AD30:**[2]
Centralized priesthood
EARTHLY MEDIATORS

Testing - **Christ:**
The harvest begins

Maturity - **Christ to AD70:**[3]
Centralized priesthood
HEAVENLY MEDIATORS

<u>OATH/SANCTIONS</u>

Conquest - **AD70 to final judgment:**
World divided by water *(Baptism)*

<u>SUCCESSION</u>

Glorification - **final judgment:**
World united by one Spirit

---

2   The death of Christ.
3   The destruction of the Jewish Temple and the city of Jerusalem.

RECOMMENDED READING

James B. Jordan
Through New Eyes:
Developing a Biblical View of the World

Peter J. Leithart
Deep Exegesis: The Mystery of Reading Scripture

Robert Alter
The Art of Biblical Narrative

"When things were going badly for her husband,
Madame Monet felt the urge to cover up the Cézannes."
— Alex Danchev

51435140R00244

Made in the USA
Charleston, SC
21 January 2016